Classic Egyptian Movies

101 MUST-SEE FILMS

Sameh Fathy

Translated by Sarah Enany

First published in 2018 by
The American University in Cairo Press
113 Sharia Kasr el Aini, Cairo, Egypt
200 Park Avenue, Suite 1700, New York, NY 10166
www.aucpress.com

First published in Arabic in 2017 as *Ahamm mi'at film wa-film fi-l-sinima al-misri*

Exclusive distribution outside Egypt and North America by I.B. Tauris & Co Ltd., 6 Salem Road, London, W2 4BU

Dar el Kutub No. 19673/17
ISBN 978 977 416 868 0

Dar el Kutub Cataloging-in-Publication Data

Fathy, Sameh
Classic Egyptian Movies / Sameh Fathy.—Cairo: The American University in Cairo Press, 2018.
p.cm.
ISBN 978 977 416 868 0
1. Motion Pictures—Egypt
791.430962

1 2 3 4 5 22 21 20 19 18

Cover Poster for *Maw'id 'ala al-'asha' (Dinner Date)*. Courtesy of Sameh Fathy.

Designed by Gadi Farfour

Printed in China

To my late father, without whose unwavering support and wise advice this work would not have been possible. May he rest in peace.

Contents

عمارة يعقوبيان
Yacoubian Building

Introduction

ABOVE Cinema Miami on Talaat Harb, Cairo. Photograph by Van Leo.

IT HAS BEEN OVER a century since the first short, silent movies were made in Egypt, with the first full-length feature, *Layla*, appearing exactly ninety years ago as I write, in 1927. Since then, Egyptian cinema has been at the forefront of culture, civilization, and enlightenment in the Arab world.

My main aim in writing this book has been to direct attention toward some of the finest achievements of those nine decades of Egyptian filmmaking. In doing so, my hope is that I might illuminate some of the great artistry involved in directing and screenwriting, cinematography and lighting, editing and scoring, and, of course, not forgetting the acting. Along the way, I have looked beyond what we see on the screen to ponder questions such as why certain stories were chosen; the points they sought to make; how well they reflected the era in which they were made; and whether the messages they sent out can be taken at face value or whether they were sometimes more manipulative.

In my personal opinion, the movies in this book represent the best of a truly Egyptian cinema. The only foreign influences here are seen in a handful of movies which represent historic Arab cultures that have had a significant impact on Egyptian society. I have also sought a balance between different generations of filmmakers and directors of different styles, encompassing movies that are direct, sometimes even didactic, and those which are more symbolic.

Every movie is illustrated with a poster and publicity still. Depending on how old you are, you may remember seeing some of these posters when the movies were shown at the cinema for the first time. If your memory does not stretch back that far, hopefully you may still find the posters a source of enjoyment, as they evoke the days when such things were painted by hand, as finely crafted as the performances they were designed to promote.

While researching and writing this book I made a few observations that are worth sharing, of which the most important is that Egypt's preeminent novelist, Naguib Mahfouz—and this is a little-known fact—was, in addition, a prolific screenwriter. He also tops the list of authors whose stories have been most often adapted for film. However, when it comes to writing screenplays even Mahfouz is left behind by Ali al-Zurqani, who has more credits among the 101 movies in this book than anyone else. (Sayyid Bedeir is the chief supplier of dialogue.) In the same vein, Salah Abu Seif tops the list as the individual who directed most movies, while Abd al-Halim Nasr appears most times as director of photography. Farid Shawqi is the actor who appears most in this book and Su'ad Husni is the actress with the most starring roles. Mahmud al-Miligi appears in the most supporting roles. Fu'ad al-Zahiri is the most represented composer of musical scores, while Maher Abd al-Nour is first among set designers. The production house responsible for the most movies is the Egyptian Cinema Foundation, while Dollar Film crops up the most as distributor.

Special thanks go to Mr. Abbudi Abu Gouda for permitting me to borrow and reproduce a number of posters from his personal collection (those for *Safir ghuhannam, Shabab imra'a, Shari' al-hubb, Djamilah Bu-Hreid, 'Ashat li-l-hubb, al-Zawja al-thaniya, Kilmit sharaf, and Ghurub wa shuruq*). ★

ستوديو مصر
يقدم
نجيب الريحاني
في
سلامة في خير
راقيه ابراهيم
روحيه خالد
حسين رياض
انتاج شركة مصر للتمثيل والسينما
IMP. "EL RAGHAIEB"

Salama fi khayr

Salama Is Doing Fine | 1937

A humble company employee trades places with the crown prince of a fictional eastern kingdom

Director Niazi Mustafa

Screenplay Badi' Khairy, Nagib al-Rihani

Produced by Studio Misr

Music Mohamed Hassan al-Shuga'i

Director of photography Mohamed Abd al-Azim

Editor Galal Mustafa

Set design Waliyy al-Din Samih

Starring Nagib al-Rihani, Raqya Ibrahim, Rawhiya Khalid, Hussein Riyad, Stephan Rosti, Fu'ad Shafiq, Fardus Mohamed, Mohamed Kamal al-Masri, Hassan Fayiq, Mansi Fahmi

Running time 98 minutes

First screening 29 November 1937

Black and white

THIS FILM WAS a watershed in the history of Egyptian comedies. With it, the team of Niazi Mustafa and Nagib al-Rihani finally broke the mold of al-Rihani's previous fare of loosely linked sketches and comic scenes to fashion a tale in which the comedic element worked completely in the service of the storyline. This has a humble department-store dogsbody, the Salama of the title (al-Rihani), sent to deposit a large sum of company money in the bank. Finding the bank closed and the streets seemingly swarming with thieves, Salama decides to place the money in a safe at the luxurious Nefertiti Palace Hotel. Things start to go hilariously awry when the hotel manager mistakes him for an eagerly awaited guest, the wealthy Prince Kandahar of Bloudestan.

Although the film's credits do not list Mustafa as a scriptwriter, his memoirs, as well as the texture of the work, confirm that he was a co-author and probably responsible for making the dialogue fit so perfectly

LEFT Salama (Nagib al-Rihani, *center*), Rustum's daughter (Raqya Ibrahim, *right*), Rustum (Stephan Rosti, *left*)

with the images. This was Mustafa's first feature and the film on which he established his credentials. Al-Rihani had initially been skeptical of the young director but the veteran artist soon realized the value of Mustafa's work, and admitted that he had underestimated his talent.

The pair were joined by Badi' Khairy, who brought more diverse gags and comic dialogue to the mix. One of the biggest laugh-out-loud scenes is when we see the street sign for the alley where Salama lives, which reads, "Aristocrats' Alley." There is a double joke as the camera pans down and directly under the sign is where the local beggar sits. The film is well cast, the camera motion and editing are finely crafted, and, as a bonus, we see front and center the religious tolerance that was the hallmark of Cairo at this time. Salama is a Muslim and we see him get along well with a wide range of characters of different religions, including the Christian owner of the store where he works and the store's Coptic accountant, Armanios. Closer to home, Salama's wife, Sattuuta, gets along well with their Armenian neighbor, Nicola, and Nicola's wife, Helen, accompanies Sattuuta to the police station when Salama goes missing.

Al-Rihani remains the undisputed champion of Egyptian comedy, and a continuing inspiration to many of the greats in Egypt and the Arab world. It is worth noting that this is one of the first Egyptian films to be completely executed by local talent, from the director and cinematographer right down to the sound recordists and gaffers. ★

KEY SCENE

The point of the film is that fortune favors the humble and honest. Witness the schoolroom showdown between Salama and his neighbor and arch-nemesis, Bayyumi Effendi. Salama has been mistaken for the crown prince and rather than reveal the error, he has instead decided to bluff his way through. As part of the royal itinerary the "prince" pays a visit to the school. As luck would have it, this is the school at which Bayyumi teaches and the prince is taken into his classroom. Bayyumi leads the students in a song in honor of their royal visitor but as they sing he stares at the prince, convinced he knows him from somewhere. Exploiting the situation, Salama as the prince starts to poke fun at Bayyumi: he gets his name wrong, calling him Aubergine, he cuts him off when he tries to speak, and finally he commands him imperiously to go on with his lesson. Bayyumi begins with mathematics, giving the students examples of prices from a fabric store. The prince halts him and tells him he is talking nonsense—the prices he is quoting do not reflect reality at all and the prince reels off the correct prices for all different types of fabric. This just confirms what Bayyumi Effendi suspected all along—this is no prince, it is his hated neighbor Salama.

Al-'Azima

Determination | 1939

A pioneering slice of new realism in which a commoner from the alley battles prejudice to get ahead in business

THE KEY ELEMENT in *al-'Azima* is realism, a style of filmmaking of which director Kamal Selim was a leading exponent. (His assistant director on the film was Salah Abu Seif, who would also go on to become a prominent director and pioneer of movie realism.) But this is not just a great slice of realism; it is also one of the finest Egyptian films, period. In this movie, Selim tackled unemployment and its effects on society—still fertile ground for films today—in a way that has never been handled as well on celluloid before or since. It is the story of a young couple, Mohamed (Hussein Sidqi) and Fatma (Fatma Rushdi), who fall in love and marry. When Mohamed loses

Director Kamal Selim

Story and screenplay Kamal Selim

Dialogue Badi' Khairy

Produced by Sharikat Misr li-l-Tamthil wa-l-Sinima (Misr Company for Acting and Cinema)

Music Abd al-Hamid Abd al-Rahman

Director of photography Ferri Farakash

Editors Kamal Selim and Salah Abu Seif

Set design Waliyy al-Din Samih

Starring Fatma Rushdi, Hussein Sidqi, Anwar Wagdi, Zaki Rostom, Abbas Fares, Abd al-Aziz Khalil, Mukhtar Uthman, Mary Munib, Hassan Kamil, Thuraya Fakhri, Sayyid Bedeir, Mohamed al-Kahlawi

Running time 111 minutes

First screening 6 November 1939

Black and white

LEFT Fatma (Fatma Rushdi, *right*), Mohamed (Hussein Sidqi, *left*)

شركة مصر للتمثيل والسينما
تقدم
العزيمة
فاطمة رشدى
حسين صدقى عبد العزيز خليل زكى رستم
مختار عثمان عباس فارس انور وجدى
عمر وصفى مختار حسين حسن كامل
مارى منيب حكمت فهمى ثريا فخرى
اخراج كمال سليم
انتاج ستوديو مصر
IMP MISR S.A.E. Le Caire
مطبعة مصر شركة مساهمة مصرية

his job and is forced to work as a fabric salesman he hides it from his wife, and looks to go into business for himself with an old friend, encountering numerous obstacles along the way.

For the film, Selim recreated the setting of a working-class alley so convincingly that the viewer is completely immersed in its world, despite the whole thing being entirely fabricated in the studio. The main characters are rendered in similarly convincing detail—they are all real people, just like those anyone might encounter in their day-to-day life.

Further realistic touches come in the depiction of religious and folk traditions, such as Ramadan, a wedding, and the celebration of the *mulid*, with all the sideshows, rides, and street performances that go with it. The café in the alley is particularly authentic and Selim uses it for some of the most dramatic scenes between Hussein Sidqi and Fatma Rushdi. Both these stars were veterans of the theater, but Selim was careful to direct them in a manner that encouraged them to jettison the affectations of that era's stage style and act naturalistically for the camera. They clicked as a duo and helped ensure that *al-'Azima* was way ahead of its time cinematically. Sidqi, in particular, excelled as the embodiment of an ambitious, hardworking young Egyptian whose progress is thwarted by a lack of financial resources. This is a film in which the message stays with viewers long after they leave the cinema, a recipe for success that is not often replicated. ★

KEY SCENE

Mohamed goes to visit his colleague Adli (Anwar Wagdi) at his mansion, where he finds him in the company of some rich friends. Mohamed is there to discuss their proposed joint business venture; he tells Adli that he has taken care of all the paperwork and all that remains is for Adli to accompany him to the bank to deposit the guarantee needed to open the business account. Adli stalls; meanwhile his friends start to ask Mohamed pointed questions that are filled with derision. When they begin to openly mock him, Mohamed gives them a lecture on respect for others' feelings and demands that Adli come with him to the bank. Adli demurs—the truth is, he has lost half the money his father gave him for the business venture at the gaming tables and he plans to use the other half for his own further gratification. Mohamed punches him in the face and storms out.

Safir ghuhannam

Ambassador of Hell | 1945

Egypt's first horror film is a Faustian tale involving a devil of an escape from poverty

Director Yusuf Wahbi

Screenplay Yusuf Wahbi

Produced by Nahhas Film

Music Ibrahim Haggag

Director of photography Sami Brille

Editor Albert Naguib

Set design Robert Scharfnerberg and Ga'far Wali

Starring Yusuf Wahbi, Layla Fawzi, Fardus Mohamed, Fu'ad Shafiq, Abd al-Ghani al-Sayyid, Amina Sharif, Fakhir Fakhir, Mahmud al-Miligi, Hagar Hamdi, Lutfi al-Hakim

Running time 120 minutes

First screening 19 February 1945

Black and white

THE OBVIOUS INSPIRATION for Yusuf Wahbi's story of a man whose desperation drives him to a pact with the Devil is the sixteenth-century legend of Faust. But in bringing this oft-told tale to the screen the director employed an array of the most advanced cinematic techniques of the time. Wahbi portrayed the Devil as a towering giant walking the Earth—in reality, small model houses, crafted with great realism. He employed fast cuts and superimposed photographs over film with a special camera to make it appear as though a palace was being built piece by piece. This was revolutionary filmmaking and cinema audiences were suitably wowed.

RIGHT Baher (Yusuf Wahbi, *right*), Farid Ramadan (Fakhir Fakhir, *left*)

نحاس فيلم
يقدم
سفير جهنم
تمثيل وإخراج
يوسف بك وهبي
بالاشتراك مع
ليلى فوزي . فؤاد شفيق
فردوس محمد . عبد الغني السيد
هاجر حمدي
تصوير
سامي بريل (S.C.F.)
انتاج
نحاس فيلم
Marcel
Imp. L'ART GRAPHIQUE

As Ramadan, the unfortunate teacher suffering through life in a needy household, whose every member is constantly asking him for cash, Fu'ad Shafiq is masterful. A scene in which he makes fun of the rich but ancient suitor who has come to ask for his daughter's hand is particularly well done (*see* the Key Scene box). When unrelenting financial hardship takes Ramadan to the end of his tether and he turns to the Devil for money, it is the culmination of an emotional arc that has carried the audience and allows them to believe in his fall from grace. Fardus Mohamed, as his wife, has fun playing a stereotypical hypochondriac, who does nothing but complain of her various ailments and her husband's neglect, for which she mocks and derides him. When the deal with the Devil is struck and their fortune is secured, the couple excel in their vices and dissolute behavior.

Yusuf Wahbi was so convincing in his expressionistic portrayal of the netherworldly, bombastic, and ultimately repulsive Devil that the movie received the first "horror" classification in the history of Egyptian cinema. Wahbi's screenplay included lots of doggerel and rhyme, which suits the fable-like nature of the story. Accosted by a beggar, the schoolteacher says, "My wife, she lies abed; my boy is easily led, boozing away his bread; my girl can't get ahead." The beggar responds, "Why, man, you look half-dead!" ★

KEY SCENE

Poor underpaid teacher Ramadan is at home, correcting copybooks, while his wife lies on the couch complaining loudly about her various ailments. He is annoyed and snarkily comments on the improbability of all these different ailments coming together in the body of one person. When she insists that he bring a doctor, he tells her, "No doctor could cure everything that's wrong with you." His young daughter arrives home accompanied by an elderly man, who wants to talk to Ramadan. He has come to ask for the girl's hand in marriage. Ramadan mocks him and then throws him out. Next, his son enters, saying he has been studying; Ramadan calls him a dissolute boy and locks him in his room. At this point, Sheikh Gad al-Mawla appears and is subjected to a rant from Ramadan about his children's behavior. The sheikh counsels him to be patient. Ramadan says that it is enough to make a man lose his religion. He announces his intention to turn to the Devil.

Fatma

Fatma | 1947

A working-class girl falls for a wealthy pasha's son who is reluctant to abandon his decadent ways

AFTER UMM KULTHUM had finished filming *Sallama*, she asked her friend, the writer Mustafa Amin, to come up with a new vehicle for her. He obliged with a story written one evening at the songstress's home. It drew upon a case that had not long ago been before the courts—a paternity suit filed by Fatma Sirry against Mohamed Sha'rawi, son of the feminist Huda Sha'rawi, to prove her daughter's parentage. Sha'rawi (and his mother) had denied the parentage of the child, born out of an *urfi* marriage. The court ruled in favor of the plaintiff, whereupon Huda Sha'rawi took the child away from its mother to raise in her own aristocratic home.

The resulting film was a musical in which director Ahmad Badrakhan fully indulged his signature idiosyncratic style, focusing

Director Ahmad Badrakhan

Screenplay Ahmad Badrakhan

Story Mustafa Amin

Dialogue Badi' Khairy

Produced by Studio Misr

Music Abd al-Hamid Abd al-Rahman

Director of photography Abd al-Halim Nasr

Editor Kamal El-Cheikh

Set design Anton Polysius

Starring Umm Kulthum, Anwar Wagdi, Suleiman Nagib, Zuzu Shekib, Fardus Mohamed, Hassan Fayiq, Mohamed Kamal al-Masri, Abd al-Fattah al-Qusari, Mohamed al-Dib

Running time 132 minutes

First screening 15 December 1947

Black and white

LEFT Fatma (Umm Kulthum, *right*), Fathi (Anwar Wagdi, *left*)

ستوديو مصر يقدم
أم كلثوم
فاطمة
تأليف
مصطفى أمين بك
★ انور وجدي
★ سليمان بك نجيب
★ زوزو شكيب ★ فردوس محمد
★ حسن فايق ★ محمد كمال المصري
★ عبد الفتاح القصري ★ محمد الديب
إخراج أحمد بدرخان
تصوير عبد الحليم نصر
انتاج وتوزيع شركة مصر للتمثيل والسينما س.ت ٢٩٧٣
مطبعة الرغائب بمصر

on spectacular scenes and aesthetics, fast camera movements, and new ways of filming songs that focused on their orchestration. In his hands, songs were no longer an interlude that held up the action, they advanced it. *Fatma* contains nine songs, including the classic "Ya sabah al-kheir" ("Good Morning"), which begins the film as the Fatma character opens her window, and we see the Citadel from her point of view and the opening credits roll. This song introduces the alley where our heroine lives. Umm Kulthum, in her final cinematic role, is exceptional as Fatma: her natural demeanor was well suited to the character of a proud and dignified woman who holds tight to her self-respect in the face of stiff opposition. Anwar Wagdi brings conviction to his role as the wealthy young Lothario, Fathi, who falls for Fatma and resorts to legitimizing their relationship through an *urfi* marriage. Unable to bear the constraints of life in the conservative alley that is Fatma's home, he flees back to his old lifestyle and former girlfriend. The necessary moral of the film is served up when he discovers that this girlfriend has betrayed him and he returns to the alley and its steadfast values.

A little-known fact is that the editor of this movie was Kamal El-Cheikh. He deserves particular credit for the manner in which scenes flow seamlessly, avoiding rush or tedium, achieving a slice-of-life rhythm that contributes unobtrusively to the success of the film. ★

KEY SCENE

The film portrays the traditional alley as an unsullied bastion of authenticity, purity, and morality, contrasting it unfavorably with the debauchery of the rich. In the key scene, wealthy Fathi takes working-class Fatma to see the apartment he has furnished for their marriage. In a ruse familiar to moviegoers of the era, he shows her a closet filled with fabulous clothes, then presents her with a nightdress which he says he would like her to model for him. Fatma demurs, telling him she is not yet his wife. "I thought we were as good as married," says Fathi. "Traditional marriage is nothing but ink on paper, but our love is a union of souls that needs no paper!" Fatma responds, "Every marriage needs its birth certificate," and goes on to point out that without "ink on paper" he would have no proof of his relationship to his own father and so no social standing. He gives her a necklace, the latest in a long line of expensive presents, and asks her again to put on the nightdress. She tells him to leave the room so she can change but when he goes, ashamed at the situation he has put her in, she takes off all the jewelry he has given her and quietly slips out of the back door.

Ghazal al-banat

A Girl's Flirtation | 1949

A landmark in Egyptian comedy as multiple suitors fall for the charms of Layla Murad

Director Anwar Wagdi

Screenplay Anwar Wagdi

Story Anwar Wagdi

Dialogue Badi' Khairy with Nagib al-Rihani

Produced by Anwar Wagdi, Sharikat al-Aflam al-Muttahida (United Film Company)

Music Mohamed Abd al-Wahab

Director of photography Abd al-Halim Nasr

Editor Kamal El-Cheikh

Set design Anton Polysius

Starring Nagib al-Rihani, Layla Murad, Yusuf Wahbi, Anwar Wagdi, Mohamed Abd al-Wahab, Mahmud al-Miligi, Farid Shawqi, Stephan Rosti, Suleiman Nagib, Abd al-Warith Assar, Said Abu Bakr, Fardus Mohamed, Zinnat Sidqi

Running time 115 minutes

First screening 26 September 1949

Black and white

GHAZAL AL-BANAT HAS a comic energy that in its most shining moments remains unparalleled in any other Egyptian film, bar none. Along with *Salama fi khayr*, it remains the movie par excellence for the viewer wishing to make acquaintance with the father of Egyptian cinematic comedy, Nagib al-Rihani. Until today, there is scarcely a comedian who has not benefited from his legacy. Although *Ghazal al-banat* was made in 1949, it remains as fresh as the day it was premiered. Seven decades later, many of the predicaments al-Rihani portrays on the screen remain familiar to audiences today.

The archetypal al-Rihani character is essentially an Everyman who radiates goodwill to all, despite frequently being beset by bad luck.

RIGHT Ustaz Hamam (Nagib al-Rihani, *right*), al-Pasha (Suleiman Nagib, *left*)

شركة الأفلام المتحدة
تقدم
غزل البنات
ليلى مراد ★ يوسف بك وهبي ★ نجيب الريحاني
أنور وجدي
وغناء موسيقار الجيل
عبد الوهاب
بالاشتراك مع
سليمان بك نجيب
محمود المليجي
فردوس محمد
زينات صدقي
عبد الوارث عسر
سعيد ابو بكر
فريد شوقي
عبد المجيد شكري
عبد الحميد زكي
عبد المنعم اسماعيل
فؤاد الرشيدي
تأليف وإخراج
أنور وجدي
التصوير
عبده نصر
الصوت
عزيز فاضل
الحوار: بديع خيري نجيب الريحاني
انتاج وتوزيع : شركة الافلام المتحده (انور وجدي وشركاه) عمارة الايموبيليا - بالقاهرة

His dogged seriousness in the face of misfortune only makes him funnier. We laugh at him, but also frequently with him, and our hearts break a little for him, too. In *Ghazal al-banat* he is Hamam, a poor Arabic-language teacher who gets sacked from a girls' elementary school for not being able to control mischievous students. But then his friend, an employee working for a pasha, finds him a job as a private teacher for the pasha's only daughter, Layla (Layla Murad), who requires help to pass an exam.

Sadly, this would be al-Rihani's last film (he died in June 1969, aged sixty), but what a parting gift he left us. Take, for example, the scene in which Hamam goes to the pasha's mansion for an interview. He is seated in the waiting room, waiting to meet the pasha himself for the first time. A number of smartly dressed servants file in, one after the other, leading to increasingly funny moments as Hamam mistakes each in turn for the pasha, when in reality they are the butler and the veterinarian. When the man himself enters, fresh from gardening in a dirty shirt and straw hat, Hamam gives him a tongue-lashing. It is a scene every bit as funny today as it was back in 1949 and every bit as funny watching it for the twentieth time as it was the first. ★

KEY SCENE

The pathos in this film stems from the old, penniless teacher's love for his young pupil, Layla Murad. Guest-starring as himself, superstar Yusuf Wahbi tells Layla that Hamam is madly in love with her. They are listening to a song by Mohamed Abd al-Wahab—also guest-starring as himself—about unrequited love. Hamam tells her, drying his tears, that his eyes are watering because it's so stuffy inside, but admits that Abd al-Wahab's singing is touching. She apologizes for anything she may have said or done to upset him. He tells her she could never do anything to hurt him, and that she is what brought him back to life, bringing him back happiness and hope after he had given up. Weeping, he apologizes for dreaming of something that he should never have allowed to cross his mind. She joins him in tears, and he embraces her like a father, trying to cheer her up by saying silly things. He asks her about Wahid (Anwar Wagdi), the young man who caught her eye and disappeared. "Maybe he went home," says Layla. "If he did, he's an idiot," grumbles Hamam. "If I were him, I wouldn't have budged from this spot." Sure enough, Wahid pops up from his hiding place, having heard everything that they had said. He declares that he would never build his happiness on another's misery, meaning Hamam. Layla also pledges never to marry without Hamam's blessing, echoed by Wahid. Hamam, gratified by their loyalty, tells them that they must first get home before her father wakes up. In the car, the young lovers laugh together, while the final shot—that remains fresh even today—is of Hamam smiling a little bitterly as they drive home.

Al-Usta Hassan

Master Hassan | 1952

An honest laborer is corrupted by a rich seductress and then finds himself accused of her murder

Director Salah Abu Seif

Screenplay Sayyid Bedeir

Story Farid Shawqi

Produced by Hilal Films

Director of photography Francois Farrakache

Editor Emile Bahari

Set design Waliyy al-Din Samih

Starring Huda Sultan, Farid Shawqi, Zuzu Madi, Rushdi Abaza, Hussein Riyad, Mary Munib, Sayyid Bedeir, Abd al-Warith Assar, Suleiman al-Gindi, Shukuku, Adli Kasib, Abd al-Ghani al-Nagdi, Sa'd Ardash

Running time 123 minutes

First screening 23 June 1952

Black and white

THE STORY OF *al-Usta Hassan* was dreamt up by Farid Shawqi. When he shared it with Huda Sultan, who was his wife at the time, she fell in love with the idea and the film was born, gaining Shawqi his first starring role. It is the story of a good man going astray and then realizing the folly of his ways. Usta Hassan rebels against his settled life with his wife and son, and their life in the alley, and goes to live with a wealthy seductress. His hoped-for happiness fails to materialize when the woman is killed and he finds himself accused of the murder. Later his innocence is proved and he returns repentantly to his old life.

To fully realize Shawqi's story, director Salah Abu Seif, working closely with editor Emile Bahari, made use of a symbolism that transcended the dialogue, as well as neatly getting around some

LEFT Kawthar (Zuzu Madi, *center*), Esmat (Rushdi Abaza, *left*), Hassan (Farid Shawqi, *right*)

KEY SCENE

Al-Usta Hassan climaxes with the trial of Hassan for the murder of Kawthar. Ibrahim Hamdi, the disabled husband of the murdered woman, is called to the stand. From his wheelchair he recounts the story of his unhappy marriage but, he says, he is at a loss to know who might have killed his wife. The prosecution then makes its case for Hassan as the murderer and calls for his execution. Cue scenes of hysteria from the accused's wife and son, who have to be escorted from the courtroom. Ibrahim Hamdi retakes the stand and speaks out in Hassan's defense. He becomes the mouthpiece for the filmmakers' vision: Hassan, says Ibrahim Hamdi, is a greedy man who "thoughtlessly chased riches, forgetting that true happiness lies in health, faith in the Almighty, and being satisfied with your lot in life." However, Hamdi concludes, the accused has now realized this for himself and regrets his transgressions. And then he drops the bombshell: it was he, he confesses, who murdered his wife. "But what of the murder weapon?" the prosecutor asks. In a crowning melodramatic flourish, the husband produces the gun and shoots himself. Hassan emerges from the courtroom reborn.

social taboos. A good example of this is when the wealthy socialite Kawthar attempts to lure Hassan into her bedroom. It would have been unacceptable to shoot any kind of sex scene at the time, so the filmmakers got around this in humorous fashion. In a previous scene, Hassan had asked his would-be seductress about a particular statue in the corner of the room. "It whistles when I'm having fun," Kawthar answers. When the couple go into the bedroom, the film cuts to the statue whistling.

Also noteworthy is the way in which the filmmakers play on the great contrast between the poverty of Bulaq and the opulence of nearby Zamalek. All the poor characters are morally upstanding, solicitous toward their fellow human beings, and rally around each other in times of trouble; conversely, the wealthy are avaricious and cruel. Shawqi and Abu Seif were inspired in their choice of a traditional craftsman's workshop as Hassan's place of labor—what better symbolizes the idea of honorable toil in the service of practical utility? This was the first time a workshop setting took center place in an Egyptian drama and it proved enormously popular with a working-class demographic, helping *al-Usta Hassan* become a smash hit at the box office.

As the femme fatale Kawthar, Zuzu Madi also deserves notice or the extraordinary feat of becoming a sex symbol without ever disrobing or saying anything explicit. Through her body language, eyes, and sultry tone of voice, she completely convinces as a temptress with the power to lure Hassan away from his wife and beloved son. ★

أفلام الهلال
تقدم
أنور وجدى
فريد شوقى
شكرى سرحان
نجمة ابراهيم
زوزو حمدى الحكيم
فى
ريا وسكينة
RAYA ET SEKINA
انتاج وتوزيع أفلام الهلال بمصر
اخراج
صلاح ابو سيف
س ت ٧٧٠٧٢

Raya wa Sakina

Raya and Sakina | 1953

A police officer hunts the infamous serial-killer sisters of Alexandria

IT IS COMMON knowledge that Salah Abu Seif and Naguib Mahfouz based the screenplay of this movie on the true story of Raya and Sakina, two serial-killer sisters who lived in Alexandria in the 1920s. Anwar Wagdi, already a superstar, was recruited to play the police officer Ahmad, but it was Nigma Ibrahim, as the sister Raya, who made the most powerful impact on audiences of the era, chillingly convincing as a woman without conscience. The role established Ibrahim as the face of evil in Egyptian cinema, and the look in her eyes still chills viewers' blood more than half a century later.

The film also benefits from Abu Seif's thrilling and pacey direction. The chase scenes, in particular, are astonishingly suspenseful for the time. Many of these are filmed on location in Alexandria, including the highly charged scene in which Ahmad and his fellow officers are in hot pursuit of Farghalli, a member of Raya and Sakina's gang. Farghalli leads the police past Pompey's Pillar, across a site of Roman ruins, and down backstreets until he reaches a cemetery, where he shelters behind a gravestone and starts shooting. Other similarly gripping scenes also utilize the Alexandrian streetscape, including one in which the police are pursuing a gang member known as the One-Eyed Man: an officer sends a little boy out of a house to fetch the rest of the officers, but the deadbolt on the inside of the door is too high and heavy for the child to open, and as he struggles with it the One-Eyed Man appears. The ensuing scene in which the One-Eyed Man chases the boy still has audiences on the edge of their seats, even today.

Abu Seif allowed Sayyid Bedeir free rein with the dialogue, which smartly captures the flavor of 1920s Alexandria, and this ended up being one of Bedeir's best-ever screenplays. Certain lines of dialogue became popular catchphrases of the time. Anwar Wagdi

Released internationally as *Raya and Sekina*

Director Salah Abu Seif

Screenplay Naguib Mahfouz

Story Naguib Mahfouz

Produced by Hilal Films

Director of photography Wahid Farid

Editor Emile Bahari

Set design Waliyy al-Din Samih

Starring Anwar Wagdi, Farid Shawqi, Shukri Sarhan, Nigma Ibrahim, Zuzu Hamdi al-Hakim, Berlanti Abd al-Hamid, Samira Ahmad, Riyad al-Qasabgi, Zinnat Ilwi, Said Khalil, Abd al-Alim Khattab, Suleiman al-Gindi, Mohamed Ilwan, Malak al-Gamal

Running time 97 minutes

First screening 23 February 1952

Festivals Berlin Film Festival

Black and white

ABOVE One-Eyed Man (Farid Shawqi, *right*), Officer Ahmad (Anwar Wagdi, *left*)

puts in an outstanding performance as the heroic officer who will stop at nothing to catch the killers; Farid Shawqi is a fitting counterpart as the One-Eyed Man, and together the pair ensured that the movie raked in the receipts at the box office. ★

KEY SCENE

The murder of the gypsy woman Warda is one of the tensest sequences in the film. It starts with Warda's entrance into Raya and Sakina's darkened house. The air is fogged with incense and she comments on how unwelcoming it is. Warda's apprehension intensifies when she bumps into a coarse-featured man; Raya reassures her that it's only her husband and leads her inside. Raya instructs Warda to stand before a censer—to ward off the Evil Eye, she says, and commences chanting words that fill Warda with fear. Sakina places her hand on Warda's gold jewelry; Raya sharply admonishes her sister and takes Warda into a gloomy room filled with men. Warda, now thoroughly terrified, tries to retreat, but the sisters reassure her. Musicians start to play the song "Daughter of Our Alley" and Warda is told to dance. Raya brings a drink for Warda and the camera zooms in on the glass like a screeched warning: we, the audience, understand that it is drugged. As Warda dances, one of the sisters sets the chandelier swinging so that the light strobes across the room, and the camera lurches, heightening the hallucinatory effect. The song reaches the verse, "The Salt Flats," climaxing at the line, "Poor girl! Poor girl!" and Warda is murdered.

Hamidu

Hamidu | 1953

A seemingly pious boat captain is secretly a womanizing drug dealer

THIS WAS THE first Egyptian movie to tackle drug addiction as a main theme and a bold venture for Farid Shawqi's first project as producer with his new production company, Aflam al-'Ahd al-Gadid. There was plenty of insurance, however, in the pairing of Shawqi and Mahmud al-Miligi, which all but guaranteed the film was going to be a hit.

The story centers on the titular Hamidu (Shawqi), a fisherman whose main haul is drugs. He has a relationship with Sa'diya (Huda Sultan), whom he has promised to marry, but instead he rapes and abandons her to take up with Fawzeya (Tahiya Carioca), the girlfriend of gang leader al-Akta' (Mahmud al-Miligi). When Sa'diya turns out to be pregnant and threatens to get her revenge by exposing Hamidu's illegal activities, he takes her out on a boat ride of no return.

Released internationally as *Hamido*

Director Niazi Mustafa

Screenplay Sayyid Bedeir, Bertie Baddar

Story Farid Shawqi

Dialogue Sayyid Bedeir

Produced by Aflam al-'Ahd al-Gadid (New Era Films)

Director of photography Wahid Farid

Editor Albert Naguib

Set design Waliyy al-Din Samih

Starring Huda Sultan, Farid Shawqi, Tahiya Carioca, Mahmud al-Miligi, Mary Munib, Fardus Mohamed, Sayyid Bedeir, Said Abu Bakr, Abd al-Ghani al-Nagdi, Ni'mat Mukhtar, Anwar Zaki, Hassan Hamid, Suleiman al-Gindi

Running time 103 minutes

First screening 9 September 1953

Black and white

LEFT Hamidu (Farid Shawqi, *center*)

هدى سلطان ★ فريد شوقي
SVassiliou
مع تحية كاريوكا
محمود المليجي
فردوس محمد
ماري منيب
سيد بدير
سعيد ابوبكر
سليمان الجندي
حميدو
(HAMIDO)
اخراج
نيازي مصطفى
توزيع: شركة دولار فيلم ٣ شارع بهلر بمصر

However, she is rescued from his attempted drowning by a passing fishing boat. From this point on, it is a matter of who will settle with Hamidu first, the back-from-the-dead Sa'diya or vicious rival drug boss al-Akta'. Having come up with the character of Hamidu, Shawqi fleshes him out to create a complex persona that audiences could believe in and even like (he has a dry wit), despite his being a complete villain. It is an excellent script, too: Hamidu's confrontation with his mother (Fardus Mohamed) after she finds out that he has made Sa'diya pregnant and is dealing drugs is a masterpiece of dialogue.

Niazi Mustafa's vérité-style camerawork grounds the action in the patterns of daily life in a fishing village, with documentary-like scenes of boats going out to sea, and workers sorting the catch and packing it for market. The location shoots were matched by a fidelity in the studio, particularly in the recreations of the huts in which the fishermen lived. There is great footage, too, of the bars and other social arenas of 1940s and '50s Alexandria, with crowd scenes thronged with extras.

Such was *Hamidu*'s impact that it led to the country's lawmakers introducing an amendment to increase the jail time for drug dealing to twenty-five years. ★

KEY SCENE

The movie's key scene is a clever reveal of the duplicity at the heart of its main character, Hamidu. We begin with a close-up of a wall clock showing 8 pm. Fawzeya comes in with a bottle of liquor, which she places on the table in front of the seated Hamidu and al-Akta'. Also present are several of al-Akta''s men. The boss asks everyone to recite the Fatiha. While saying the prayer, Hamidu's eyes stray to Fawzeya's legs as she pulls up her stockings. He raises his hands to the Lord in supplication, eyes never leaving her legs. Al-Akta' then asks his subordinates to leave, as he has important business to discuss with Hamidu. Only Fawzeya, her aunt, and her maid remain. Al-Akta' then pulls out a rosary and begins to run it through his fingers as he proposes that Hamidu join him in his drug business. Hamidu pulls an even bigger rosary out of his pocket and rejects the offer, declaring that he will never go down that path. Al-Akta' attempts to convince him, and Fawzeya joins in. Hamidu eventually agrees to work with al-Akta', but insists that he is only joining the enterprise out of goodwill and friendship. He wants nothing in return, he says—as we see a shot, from his point of view, focused intently on Fawzeya's bust.

Sira' fi-l-wadi

Struggle in the Valley | 1954

Among the sugar cane a wealthy pasha indulges in skulduggery but young love wins out in the end

Released internationally as *The Blazing Sun*

Director Youssef Chahine

Based on an idea by Hilmi Halim

Screenplay Ali al-Zurqani

Dialogue Ali al-Zurqani

Produced by Gabriel Talhami

Music Fu'ad al-Zahiri

Director of photography Ahmad Khurshid

Editor Kamal Abu al-Ila

Set design Maher Abd al-Nour

Starring Fatin Hamama, Omar Sharif, Farid Shawqi, Zaki Rostom, Abd al-Warith Assar, Abd al-Ghani Qamar, Hamdi Gheith, Mansi Fahmi, Rafi'a al-Shal, Serag Gum'a

Running time 111 minutes

First screening 1 March 1954

Festivals Cannes, where the film won an Award of Merit

Black and white

THIS WAS CHAHINE'S sixth film and it explores a theme much loved by the director, that of social injustice. The story concerns Ahmad (Omar Sharif), a lower-class engineer whose father, Saber Effendi, is a resourceful farmer who has succeeded in increasing the production of sugar cane on his land. This is a cause of much envy to Tahir Pasha (Zaki Rostom), a wealthy landowner, who also farms sugar cane. Complicating matters, Ahmad is in a secret, mismatch-of-classes relationship with Tahir Pasha's daughter, Amal (Fatin Hamama). In short order, Saber Effendi is convicted of the murder of a business partner and executed, and Ahmad flees and hides out in some ancient ruins (this was the first Egyptian film to shoot in the Valley of the Kings).

RIGHT Riyad (Farid Shawqi, *right*), the pasha (Zaki Rostom, *left*)

جبرائيل تلحمي يقدم
فاتن حمامة
عمر الشريف
في
صراع في الوادي
مع
زكي رستم فريد شوقي
تصوير
خورشيد
اخراج
يوسف شاهين
"DAR EL TEBAA" CAIRO
توزيع : شركة افلام النيل س. ت ٣٤١١٣

Despite the presence of several giants of Egyptian cinema, if this film can be said to have a main protagonist, then it is the crowd. Chahine directs his mass of extras to act as one unified body, whether expressing joy and jubilation (when the sugar crop is purchased by the sugar factory), or registering silent pain as they later stand broken before their ruined crops. At the trial of Saber Effendi, Chahine has the crowd act as prosecutor, leveling charges at the accused, presenting evidence, and demanding the ultimate penalty of death.

In the same way Chahine manipulates the crowd, you feel his presence in the disciplined performance of Omar Sharif (making his big-screen debut), who is almost a proxy for the former actor turned director. Zaki Rostom is equally impressive as the sly, domineering pasha, while Abd al-Ghani Qamar gives what is arguably the best performance of his career. The musical score also plays a vital role in conveying the director's intentions, especially the moaning and wailing choral compositions that soundtrack Ahmad's conversation with his father in prison, and the heartbeat-like drumbeat that accompanies Saber Effendi's walk to the noose. ★

KEY SCENE

There is one scene in particular that lays bare the depths of Tahir Pasha's black soul. The pasha walks in from the balcony, having just spoken with the assembled inhabitants of the neighborhood outside: they have told him that Saber Effendi has killed Sheikh Abd al-Samad. In fact, Abd al-Samad's murder was planned by Tahir Pasha and carried out by his son Riyad. At this moment, Saber Effendi is in the pasha's house, where he has taken refuge from the crowd. The pasha accuses Saber Effendi of the murder, and he, of course, denies it. But you were seen running away, says the pasha. He was chasing the murderer, says Saber. "Your weapon was found at the scene of the crime," says the pasha. Riyad, who is also present, exclaims, "How could you kill that man? And for no reason!" Should he hand Saber over to the people, ponders the pasha, and see a man who has worked for him for thirty years killed, or should he let him escape? Riyad suggests that Saber run away but he refuses, preferring to go outside and face his accusers. When Tahir Pasha tries to stop him, Riyad tells him, "Let him go out and face them."

Al-Wahsh

The Beast | 1954

A police officer and his son are kidnapped by a notorious countryside gangster

THIS FILM WOULD have been banned by the censor if Salah Abu Seif had not eventually given in to the stipulation that he introduce it with a title card reading "Long Ago In the Countryside...," in order to avoid the impression that the subject of the film was contemporaneous. The story was based on real-life police reports of a criminal in Upper Egypt named al-Khot. In the film he becomes the feared al-Wahsh, "the Beast." A police officer is sent to put an end to his reign of terror; however, the gangster manages to kidnap the policeman's son and eventually the officer himself.

Abu Seif chose to shoot in the real-life village of Dariot, which closely resembled the location of the original events. Here, he made

Director Salah Abu Seif

Screenplay Naguib Mahfouz with Salah Abu Seif

Story Naguib Mahfouz

Dialogue Sayyid Bedeir

Produced by Hilal Films

Music Fu'ad al-Zahiri

Director of photography Abd al-Halim Nasr

Editor Emile Bahari

Set design Abd al-Fattah al-Biyali

Starring Samya Gamal, Anwar Wagdi, Mahmud al-Miligi, Abbas Fares, Samiha Ayyub, Mohamed Tawfiq, Omar al-Gizawi, Said Khalil, Abd al-Ghani Qamar, Nazim Sha'rawi, Abd al-Hafiz al-Tatawi, Suleiman al-Gindi

Running time 110 minutes

First screening 5 March 1954

Festivals Cannes, where it received the Jury Prize

Black and white

LEFT Abd al-Sabur (Mahmud al-Miligi)

افلام الهلال
تقدم
انور وجدى
سامية جمال
محمود المليجى
عباس فارس
اخراج
صلاح ابو سيف
الوحش
Solly
انتاج وتوزيع افلام الهلال س.ت ٧٧٠٧٢

good use of wide shots of natural locales, such as fields, country roads, and traditional dwellings, which he combined with scenes filmed on skillfully constructed studio sets. As the villainous al-Wahsh, Mahmud al-Miligi is required to alternate between acts of violence and murder, and an appearance of piety and virtue suitable to his standing as a pillar of the community. He pulls off this trick beautifully. Abbas Fares is similarly enjoyable as the powerful, wealthy bey with friends in high places and strong ties to those at the highest levels of government. He manages to inject some welcome comedy into his role, such as the dagger-like glances he throws at al-Wahsh, when the latter manipulates him into supporting his criminal enterprises by embarrassing him in public. Anwar Wagdi does good work with the over-familiar role of the beleaguered policeman, committed to bringing a dangerous criminal to justice no matter the personal cost. ★

KEY SCENE

Al-Wahsh's theme of evil lurking behind a friendly face is encapsulated in the scene in which the police officer, Ra'uf, welcomes Abd al-Sabur to the police station. The honored Abd al-Sabur is the man who recently saved Ra'uf and his family from a gang of thugs. Unknown to Ra'uf, he is also none other than the criminal mastermind that the police officer is pursuing. The detectives at the station recognize Ra'uf's guest for who he is and so do the criminals being detained there, but when the latter start to speak out in astonishment Ra'uf tells them to settle down or he will throw them into the cells. "We shall make the world safe for honest men like yourself," he tells Abd al-Sabur. The conversation turns to al-Wahsh: "Who is al-Wahsh?" he asks a junior policeman. Abd al-Sabur jumps in to announce he should be leaving but is cut off after just the word "I. . . ." After his guest has gone, Ra'uf asks again, "So who is this al-Wahsh, then?" to which the perplexed underling responds, "Your guest of a few minutes ago, sir." The camera holds on Ra'uf's astonished face and the background laughter of a clown from the next scene seeps onto the soundtrack.

Gaʻaluni mugrim

They Made Me a Criminal | 1954

A young man fresh out of juvenile detention is framed by his uncle for a crime he did not commit

Director Atif Salim

Screenplay Naguib Mahfouz

Story Farid Shawqi with Ramsis Naguib

Dialogue Sayyid Bedeir

Produced by Aflam al-ʻAhd al-Gadid (New Era Films)

Director of photography Wahid Farid

Editor Atiya Abdu

Set design Waliyy al-Din Samih

Starring Farid Shawqi, Huda Sultan, Yahya Shahin, Rushdi Abaza, Serag Munir, Nigma Ibrahim, Hassan al-Barudi, Mohamed Rida, Hamdi Hafiz, Suleiman al-Gindi

Running time 104 minutes

First screening 18 October 1954

Awards Special Prize to Farid Shawqi from the Ministry of Social Affairs. Award of Merit at the International Festival for Best Cinematography and Best Screenplay

Black and white

OPPOSITE Yasmine (Huda Sultan, *right*), Sultan (Farid Shawqi, *left*)

THE TITLE OF THIS film tells you everything you need to know. It is angry and polemical, and it knows just whom to blame. The driving force behind it is actor Farid Shawqi, well known for his championing of the poor, who supplied the story. In this instance, the particular injustice at the heart of the narrative is the unforgiving nature of society. Sultan, played by Farid Shawqi, finds himself at odds with the authorities when his uncle disowns him and has him thrown into juvenile detention. On his release, he finds a job with the help of his friend Sheikh Hassan, played by Yahya Shahin, only to be framed for a crime by his uncle. Before his innocence can be proved, he murders his uncle, finally becoming the criminal he was formerly accused of being. The moral is that a compassionate society produces moral citizens, while a society that is ruthless in its treatment of the underprivileged risks turning them into outcasts and criminals.

The dialogue (by Sayyid Bedeir) misses few opportunities to hit the message home. When Sultan speaks bitterly to Sheikh Hassan about the injustice he has suffered, the holy man replies, "No, Sultan, brother! You do them a disservice to speak that way!" In another scene, Sultan rails at his wife Yasmina: "You were treated unfairly by a few people; I was treated unfairly by an entire society." When toward the end of the film Sultan is cleared of the murder he did not commit, it is too late, by now he has become a killer and the verdict of "Not guilty" mocks him. Just in case anyone misses the point, he spells it out: "Only now has social justice caught up with me, far too late. Society closed its eyes and only opened them when I was already a murderer." The movie ends with Sultan being re-arrested, this time for the murder of his uncle, followed by a shot of street children and a narration in Sultan's voice: "Poor things. Will they share my fate? Or will they find someone to take care of them and raise them up? May

God protect them, may God protect them." The message got through: Egypt's legislative powers acted on one of the film's central demands, which was that the first criminal offense be struck from a juvenile's record to avoid the taint of criminality coloring the rest of their life. Who knows, the film may ultimately have been responsible for many early offenders being able to choose a better path in life, which is definitely not to be sneered at. ★

KEY SCENE

Having just murdered his uncle, Sultan bursts onto the rooftop where Sheikh Hassan lives and where he is met by an ecstatic Yasmina, played by Huda Sultan. She excitedly tells him that the police have caught the man who committed the earlier murder of which Sultan was falsely accused. "You're a free man!" she rejoices. "Your name is cleared!" Sultan grabs her in a fury, wild with rage that this news has come too late to save him. "Go back to the police," he sneers, "and tell them I have no use for their verdict. I have a gun now and I've learned how to use it. My heart has turned to stone. I won't show mercy from this day on." He runs.

Hayah aw mawt

Life or Death | 1954

A pharmacist accidentally issues poison and it becomes a race against time to find the patient before he takes his deadly medicine

THIS FILM IS regarded by many as Kamal El-Cheikh's masterpiece. When El-Cheikh planned his work, he was aware that it was fresh and novel but the jury is still out on whether he knew that he was creating something completely new, a turning point in Egyptian cinema. Nothing was ever the same after *Hayah aw mawt*. All the scenes take place outside on the streets of Cairo, not in enclosed spaces, such as in rooms or set-up studios, which allowed the camera to move around and shoot characters within realistic areas. Many critics believe that if El-Cheikh had had the opportunity, such as specialized and practical means, he would have joined the ranks of the foremost American and European filmmakers.

The plot is beguilingly simple: it is a race to prevent a man from unknowingly drinking an inadvertently poisoned medicine. All the

Director Kamal El-Cheikh

Screenplay Ali al-Zurqani with Kamal El-Cheikh

Story Kamal El-Cheikh

Dialogue Ali al-Zurqani

Produced by Lotus Film

Director of photography Ahmad Khurshid

Editor Amira Fayid

Set design Maher Abd al-Nour

Starring Yusuf Wahbi, Imad Hamdi, Madiha Yusri, Rushdi Abaza, Hussein Riyad, Adli Kasib, Doha Amir, Abd al-Ghani al-Nagdi, Ali Issa, Abd al-Badie al-Arabi, Rafi'a al-Shal

Running time 77 minutes

First screening 6 December 1954

Festivals Cannes. Awarded Best Picture at the Catholic Egyptian Film Festival, State Award of Merit Fourth Class

Black and white

LEFT Ahmad (Imad Hamdi, *left*), Samira (Doha Amir, *right*)

لوتس فيلم تقدم
يوسف وهبي
مديحة يسري
عماد حمدي
حسين رياض
رشدي اباظة
مع الطفلة
ضحى
إخراج
كمال الشيخ
حياة أو موت
تصوير
خورشيد
انتاج
اسيا
توزيع شركة لوتس للتوزيع "أسيا وشركاها" عمارة الايموبيليا بالقاهرة
س-ت ٦٢٩٤٢
مطبعة الرغائب

events in the film take place in the span of just eight hours, or one single working day. Given that the whole issue could be solved today with one phone call, it is astonishing how little the film has dated. Instead, it stands as a testament to El-Cheikh's skill in crafting a thriller built entirely on suspense. As El-Cheikh himself pointed out in an interview, *Hayah aw mawt* "has no crime, struggle, nor chases in the traditional sense of the word"—it has only people and the various apparatuses of the state desperately working together to try and avert an impending disaster. From these elements El-Cheikh masterfully orchestrates seventy-seven minutes of finely tuned Hitchcockian tension that keeps the audience on the edge of its seat.

In what the director describes as "cinematic reportage," the entire film was shot on the streets of Cairo, with the bare minimum of studio footage. The director of photography gave the camera free rein to move and record places, people, and events in an almost documentary fashion. Front and center, however, are Madiha Yusri and Imad Hamdi, as the estranged couple brought together by disaster. Hamdi plays Ahmad, a depressed invalid beset by financial woes, while Yusry plays Wafaa, a woman who is compassionate and loving at her core, and who, despite the couple's separation, risks a great deal to save her husband's life. However, the real heroes of this film, who are on screen for almost the entire duration of the movie, are the child star, the chief of police, and Hussein Riyad as the pharmacist who mixed the fatal concoction. ★

KEY SCENE

Samira arrives home with her father Ahmad's medicine. She brings him a glass and opens the bottle. Suddenly, there is a loud rapping at the door: "Samira! Open the door, now!" It's her mother, Wafaa. Without waiting for a response, Wafaa smashes the glass of the door panel, reaches inside, turns the handle, and rushes in to knock the glass out of her daughter's hand. Wafaa collapses onto the couch and bursts into tears. Ahmad, still mystified as to what is going on, presses his handkerchief to her bleeding hand. Just then, the chief of police bursts in with a company of men and begins to admonish Ahmad for the trouble he has put him through. "But what's going on?" asks Ahmad. For an answer, the chief turns on the radio: "The medicine contains a deadly poison. The medicine contains a deadly poison." So powerful is the scene that the broadcaster's alarming warning became a popular catchphrase for years afterward. The pharmacist then arrives, relieved to discover Ahmad alive, and presents him with a new bottle of medicine. The wife thanks the police chief for his trouble: "All in a day's work," he reassures her and exits, leaving the family happily reunited.

Darb al-mahabil

Alley of Fools | 1955

When the village idiot wins big in the lottery it creates resentment and conflict in the alley

Director Tawfiq Salih

Screenplay Naguib Mahfouz with Tawfiq Salih

Story Naguib Mahfouz

Dialogue Abd al-Hamid Gouda al-Sahhar

Produced by Anwar Wagdi, Sharikat al-Aflam al-Muttahida (United Film Company)

Music Abd al-Aziz Mohamed

Director of photography Abd al-Aziz Fahmi

Editors Said al-Sheikh and Hussein Afifi

Set design Maher Abd al-Nour

Starring Shukri Sarhan, Berlanti Abd al-Hamid, Abd al-Ghani Qamar, Nadia al-Sab', Tawfiq al-Diqin, Abd al-Aziz Ahmad, Hassan al-Barudi, Sa'd Ardash, Ahmad Abaza, Ilham Zaki, Rafi'a al-Shal, Shafiq Nur al-Din, Abd al-Ghani al-Nagdi, Ahmad al-Hariri

Running time 89 minutes

First screening 25 July 1955

Festivals National Film Festival. Second Prize for Best Picture.

Black and white

THIS WAS THE ONLY collaboration between two giants of Egyptian culture, the director Tawfiq Salih and novelist Naguib Mahfouz. Expectations were high, but when the movie was released it was met with disappointment. Over six decades later, however, it is now regarded as one of the top Egyptian films of all time. The action takes place in a space that is dear to Mahfouz, the archetypal Egyptian alley. But rather than Mahfouz's usual celebration of the characters that inhabit such worlds, Salih's movie illuminates the hatred that can lie behind friendly façades. In the film, Darb al-mahabil is a quiet and peaceful alley. One day a lottery ticket is bought by Taha, a young man who hopes to win in order to marry his fiancée, Khadiga. But by chance the ticket ends up in the hands of the village idiot, Quffa. The ticket wins, which triggers a wave of resentment and even hatred, until the inhabitants eventually come to their senses and settle back into their old lives.

One of the delights of the film is the way in which the director marries the images to the soundtrack. For example, during the song "Mabruk ya Quffa" ("Congratulations, Quffa"), shots of Quffa being fêted by the people of the alley alternate with shots of Khadiga crying, her mother weeping, then more scenes of dancing and celebration. This technique of cutting between successive scenes with contrasting emotional tones that alternately harmonize and clash with the soundtrack was quite new, and contributed to the film's popularity with audiences.

Equally memorable are the enraged shrieks of Abdu, played by Tawfiq al-Diqin, as he alternately threatens and pleads, "Where's the money, Quffa?" His is a character completely consumed by greed, prepared to sacrifice everything for wealth. The leads are backed by a powerful and memorable supporting cast of characters: Khadiga's father, Azuz, is wholly convincing in his anguish at having made his

افلام النجاح
محمد محمد فرج وشركاه
تقدم
شكري سرحان
برلنتي عبد الحميد
و عبد الغني قمر
درب المهابيل
قصة
نجيب محفوظ
حوار
عبد الحميد جوده السحار
تصوير
عبد العزيز فهمي
اخراج
توفيق صالح
توزيع شركة الشرق لتوزيع الافلام

RIGHT Tahir (Shukri Sarhan, *left*), Khadiga (Berlanti Abd al-Hamid, *right*)

daughter throw away her lottery ticket and in the crisis of faith he suffers as a result (*see* the Key Scene box). Shukri Sarhan does equally fine work as Taha, the carefree lover-boy turned reckless and grasping, while Abd al-Ghani Qamar turns in one of the most powerful performances of his career, as the slow-witted shepherd Quffa. ★

KEY SCENE

We are in the alley's small mosque following dawn prayer. Azuz is sitting with the imam. Why should Quffa have all this money when he is mentally unequipped to handle it? asks Azuz. The imam responds that the why is known to God and God alone, for it is He who gives to whom He wishes and takes from whom He wills. If he had the money, says Azuz, he would use it to help people. He would marry his daughter to Taha and open a shop for them, rebuild the old mosque, and give Saniya, the local prostitute, enough money to support herself in a proper profession. The imam tells him that anyone who wants money should not wait to get it from a lottery ticket. His job will never make him the sum that fell into Quffa's lap, retorts Azuz. The imam advises him to work hard. "Nobody works as hard as I do!" says Azuz. The imam quotes the Prophet's sayings that emphasize the value of hard work, to which Azuz responds with a proverb about giving wealth to the undeserving. The imam rebukes him: "Ask God's forgiveness at once!" he snaps. "And don't quote blasphemous proverbs." He then quotes the Qur'anic verse, "Wealth and children are [but] adornments of the worldly life. But the enduring good deeds are better to your Lord for reward and better for [one's] hope." "Nobody understands this stuff," says Azuz, "especially not Quffa." To which the imam responds that it is not only Quffa; many are given wealth that they misuse.

Shabab imra'a

Youth of a Woman | 1956

A young student from the country is corrupted by a worldly older woman

THE STORY ON WHICH this film is based was written by novelist Amin Yusuf Ghurab, a man with a refreshing outlook on life. He had no time for platonic love and held that sex was the basis for any healthy relationship. *Shabab imra'a* contrasts the honorable love the young student Imam (Shukri Sarhan) has for the innocent Salwa with the considerably less virginal liaisons he enjoys with the wealthy, mature business owner Shafa'at (Tahiya Carioca). Sex would seem to be winning the day until the prevailing conventional morality kicks in with the death of Shafa'at—a shift in power that was inevitable given the casting of box-office darling Shadya as the good girlfriend. Unsurprisingly, for a film that has as its core subject something that cannot be shown on screen, director Salah Abu Seif made great use

Director Salah Abu Seif

Screenplay Amin Yusuf Ghurab with Salah Abu Seif

Story Amin Yusuf Ghurab

Dialogue Sayyid Bedeir

Produced by Wahid Farid and Ramsis Naguib

Music Fu'ad al-Zahiri

Director of photography Wahid Farid

Editor Atiya Abdu

Set design Waliyy al-Din Samih

Starring Tahiya Carioca, Shadya, Shukri Sarhan, Abd al-Warith Assar, Serag Munir, Fardus Mohamed, Mary Izz al-Din, Suleiman al-Gindi

Running time 126 minutes

First screening 9 January 1956

Festivals Cannes, where it was awarded the Critics' Prize. Best Film at the International Competition. Salah Abu Seif won Best Director and Shukri Sarhan the First State Award of Merit for Best Actor.

Black and white

LEFT Shafa'at (Tahiya Carioca, *right*), Imam (Shukri Sarhan, *left*)

SVassiliou
شادية
تحية كاريوكا
شكري سرحان
في
شباب امرأة
اخراج
صلاح ابو سيف
انتاج
وحيد فريد رمسيس نجيب
توزيع : شركة دولار فيلم

of symbolism. A sequence showing Imam's hurried escape from temptation to sin with Shafa'at is followed by a shot of a pigeon loft with a (presumably male) pigeon climbing skyward toward clear, open skies. Later, not long after which they start their affair, Shafa'at covers Imam's eyes with her hands and the screen cuts to a shot of a mule turning a grindstone at the mill, its eyes also covered. Can't Imam see this affair is going nowhere! This dear old mule has a significant role in the symbolism that freights the film: when Shafa'at asks Hasabo, her old boyfriend, where the mill's mule has gone, he responds, "The mule? Run away and he's not coming back!" Hasabo's meaning is double-edged because he has seen Imam slip off to meet Salwa behind Shafa'at's back. Later, when the mule is back in harness, one of the workers beats it and Hasabo asks him to show some mercy to the animal, to which the worker retorts, "The boss-lady doesn't care! She wants to keep him at it day and night!"

In a movie with much to be entertained by, the greatest fun is in the company of Tahiya Carioca. It is impossible to imagine anyone else playing the rich widow Shafa'at with quite as much aplomb. She is a borderline sex addict as her Shafa'at quite brazenly tempts her lovers with financial favors, new clothes, not to mention her own sultry charms. When her conquests weaken and fail to perform, her contempt is palpable, and she throws them out of her bedroom and goes on the hunt for fresher meat. It is to his credit that Shukri Sarhan more than holds his own on screen and, in fact, he should have won an award for the vigor and interest he brings to the clichéd role of the man who strains against temptation—but not always too hard, otherwise where would the fun be? ★

KEY SCENE

We open with Shafa'at sashaying down the staircase leading from her house to the mill downstairs. She asks her employees why the mule is not working. "Hasabo wanted him to take a break and rest," one of them replies. There follows a conversation between Hasabo and Shafa'at, on the face of it about the mule but the audience is clued in enough to know the subject is really Imam. "He needs a break from time to time! He's exhausted!" says Hasabo. "How do you know? Did the mule complain to you?" says Shafa'at. "If he wasn't a mule, he'd have left the house and run away!" says Hasabo. Shafa'at orders one of the workers to tie the mule up again and set it off on the treadmill, and "Disregard his elder brother"—a cutting reference to Hasabo, who used to fill Imam's position as Shafa'at's lover until he grew too old to perform.

Sira' fi-l-mina

Struggle on the Docks | 1956

A sailor returns after three years at sea only to discover his beloved has fallen for another

Released internationally as *Dark Waters*

Director Youssef Chahine

Screenplay Youssef Chahine with Mohamed Rif'at and Lisette Fayid

Story Youssef Chahine with Mohamed Rif'at and Lisette Fayid

Dialogue Sayyid Bedeir

Produced by Gabriel Talhamy

Music Fu'ad al-Zahiri

Director of photography Ahmad Khurshid

Editor Kamal Abu al-Ila

Set design Maher Abd al-Nour

Starring Fatin Hamama, Omar Sharif, Ahmad Ramzi, Hussein Riyad, Fardus Mohamed, Aziza Hilmi, Tawfiq al-Diqin, Mohamed Subeih, Riyad al-Qasabgi, Abd al-Hamid Badawi

Running time 100 minutes

First screening 16 January 1956

Black and white

MUCH LIKE *Hayah aw mawt (see page 41), Sira' fi-l-mina* is a movie whose events take place in the space of a single day—although in this case it is a full twenty-four hours, rather than *Hayah aw mawt*'s frantic eight. Even with the extended time frame, the film is so condensed, so packed with events, that it is hard to imagine them all taking place in a single day. When Ragab (Omar Sharif), a young fisherman, returns home after three years away raising money for a dowry, he finds his intended, Hamida (Fatin Hamama), has taken up with his old friend Mamduh (Ahmad Ramzi). Meanwhile, there is a feud brewing between the dockworkers and the company.

Chahine is a great technical director and he takes care to remind us of the ticking clock; when Ragab alights from the boat at about eleven in the morning, the sailors tell him that the boat is due to cast off at 10 am the next day. The span of the movie is established. Over the next one hundred minutes of screen time, the camera is hardly ever still. In a way not previously seen in Egyptian cinema, it is constantly in motion as it follows the characters as they move about their business. It is rare in this film to find a shot with characters seated or even standing still. Ragab arrives on a boat, then strides off it to meet his mother, then Hamida; he goes home, then meets Mamduh, then the foreman, then Mamduh, before going home again in search of Hamida. Failing to find her, he returns to Mamduh's home and paces outside, waiting for Hamida. He returns to the docks to meet Amm Ismail and then off again, this time in search of Mamduh once more. Having met Mamduh, he heads back home. There follows a talk with his mother on the subject of Ragab's lack of finances, which is the reason Hamida has left him for Mamduh. Even in conversation Ragab constantly paces throughout. That night, he goes to a bar and later heads home drunkenly with Hamida's murder in mind. He goes to the office of Mamduh's father, the company boss. Later he races out to save

جبرائيل تلحمي يقدم
فاتن حمامه عمر الشريف
صراع في الميناء
احمد رمزي
حسين رياض
فردوس محمد
تصوير
احمد خورشيد
اخراج
يوسف شاهين
إنتاج وتوزيع: جبرائيل تلحمي ٢٠ شارع عدلي باشا بالقاهرة س.ت ٦٧٨٧٣
SVassiliou
دار الطباعه

RIGHT Hamida (Fatin Hamama, *right*), Ragab (Omar Sharif, *left*)

Mamduh from being burned alive on a boat set alight by dockworkers enraged at their treatment by the boss, Fadel, who happens to be Mamduh's father.

With its taut, ticking narrative, *Sira' fi-l-mina* is a fantastic piece of filmmaking but one that, amazingly, the director would better just two years later with another story of an explosive love triangle, this time in a busy railway station. ★

KEY SCENE

As if discovering his girl has left him for his best friend was not misery enough, one key scene late in the movie hits Ragab with an even more seismic emotional shock. We are in the office of Mamduh's father, Fadel, who is the company boss down at the docks. He is calming the workmen and reassuring them that what they have heard—that Fadel will fire the dockers and hire others in their place—is only a rumor. Ragab is present and Fadel asks him to come in urgently. Ragab rebuffs him coldly. He tells him that he can no longer stand the sight of him or of his son Mamduh, and that his mistreatment of his workers will ultimately hurt him. Fadel tells him to keep a level head and not listen to the lies that are being spread. He then begs Ragab to save Mamduh from the burning boat and adds, "He's your brother." This is news to Ragab, who flies into an uncontrollable rage at the revelation that the man speaking to him is his father. "You cut me out of your life for twenty-five years! You left me and my mother to rot in poverty!" Fadel repeats his plea for Ragab to save Mamduh, but it only incenses Ragab to listen to his father be so afraid for his favored son Mamduh.

Ayna 'umri

Where Did My Life Go? | 1956

A woman married at a young age attempts to reclaim her lost youth after her elderly husband dies

ALI AL-ZURQANI scored a box-office hit when he transferred Ihsan Abd al-Quddus's novel to the big screen. Abd al-Quddus's tale was of a girl, Aliya, who is married at sixteen against her wishes. When, after ten or so years, her husband dies, she returns home feeling liberated and determined to regain the youth she feels she has lost.

Director Ahmad Diya' al-Din

Screenplay Ali al-Zurqani

Story Ihsan Abd al-Quddus

Dialogue Ali al-Zurqani

Produced by Magda Films

Director of photography Victor Anton

Editor Albert Naguib

Set design Anton Polysius

Starring Magda, Yahya Shahin, Ahmad Ramzi, Amina Rizq, Zaki Rostom, Mimi Shekib, Fardus Mohamed, Ihsan Sharif, Aziza Hilmi, Adli Kasib, Fu'ad Ga'far, Mohamed Nabih, At'uta, Anwar Zaki

Running time 128 minutes

First screening 6 February 1956

Festivals Berlin, where Magda received an Award of Merit. Best Picture at the Catholic Film Festival

Black and white

All this, al-Zurqani transferred to the screen with skill, successfully replicating the depths of character found in the novel. The screenplay and dialogue (both by al-Zurqani) are particularly good. Before marriage, Aliya is a child: she calls her future husband "Uncle" Aziz and heeds her nurse like an obedient little girl. But once she is married to a man who has no regard for her feelings, does not reciprocate her desires, and locks her up with his two sisters, her language is transformed and she rapidly comes to sound like an embittered woman, much older than her twenty-something years. Audiences were easily able to sympathize with Aliya, and it helped that she was played by box-office favorite Magda. As Aziz, Zaki Rostom was equally convincing as a charming suitor turned flint-hearted husband. But more than either, the pivotal role is that played by Amina Rizq as Aliya's mother, whose over-protective maternal instincts only cause misery. Happiness, she believes, comes from following a mother's commands to the letter. No word is too harsh, no admonishment too severe, when it is all for Aliya's own good. Her overbearing attentions drive Aliya to look for an escape, which she thinks she finds in marriage. She is only a child and the man is more than old enough to be her father, but the mother consents because he has money and status—what more could a young girl need? Later, the mother realizes her error and attempts to make amends. Rizq's mastery in giving flesh to this role (a role she would, in fact, reprise frequently) provides the springboard for the excellent performances of Magda and Zaki Rostom. ★

OPPOSITE Aziz (Zaki Rostom, *left*), Aliya (Magda, *right*)

KEY SCENE

Aziz and Aliya are at the stables at his ranch. They stand before a beautiful mare. He tells her that this mare is a rare Arabian steed and the jewel of his collection. Aliya tells him that she, too, loves horses. "This mare once ran away from the stables," he tells her. "Some of the men brought her back. I almost lost her." Aliya asks why the mare ran off. "She doesn't like being kept tied up," replies Aziz. Aliya says that this is understandable but Aziz disagrees: "She's fed only the best of everything and she's housed in a stable the likes of which cannot be found in the entire governorate!" With that, Aziz leads Aliya off to dinner in the lovely house he has provided for her.

Rasif nimra khamsa

Platform No. 5 | 1956

The ringleader of a drug-running gang plots to kill a police officer and kidnap his son

Director Niazi Mustafa
Screenplay Bertie Baddar and Niazi Mustafa
Story Farid Shawqi and Sayyid Bedeir
Dialogue Sayyid Bedeir
Produced by Aflam al-'Ahd al-Gadid (New Era Films)
Music Fu'ad al-Zahiri
Director of photography Alfizi Orfanelli
Editor Galal Mustafa
Set design Anton Polysius
Starring Farid Shawqi, Huda Sultan, Zaki Rostom, Mahmud al-Miligi, Malak al-Gamal, Hassan Hamid, Mohamed Shawqi, Fakhir Fakhir, Suleiman al-Gindi, Na'ima Wasfi, Anwar Zaki, Abd al-Ghani al-Nagdi, al-Tukhi Tawfiq
Running time 104 minutes
First screening 13 February 1956
Black and white

WITH THIS MOVIE, Farid Shawqi, who supplied the story, creates a gripping tale of drug running and the authorities' attempts to thwart it. The heart of the story revolves around an officer of the law, Khamis (Shawqi), who is fooled by the outward piety and uprightness of Mi'allim Bayyumi (Zaki Rostom), unaware that he is the ringleader of a drug-running gang. Bayyumi plots to kill Khamis but instead kills his wife and kidnaps his son. Eventually, Khamis uncovers the gangster's true identity and goes after him.

Sayyid Bedeir's dialogue contributed greatly to the film's success and, even now, just to mention *Rasif nimra khamsa* triggers lines of dialogue from the film that were long ago lodged in the popular consciousness. Similarly memorable is Rostom's performance as

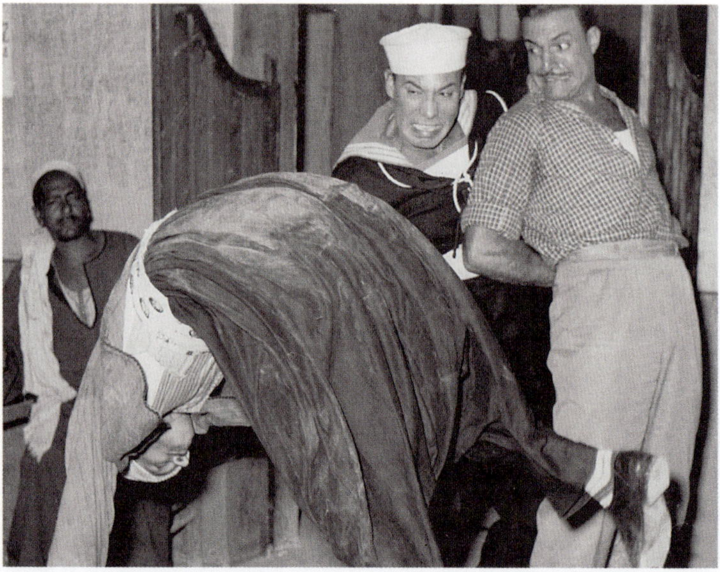

RIGHT Khamis (Farid Shawqi, *left*), Bayyumi (Zaki Rostom, *right*)

افلام العهد الجديد
تقدم
رصيف نمرة ٥
هدى سلطان
فريد شوقي
اخراج
نيازي مصطفى
تصوير القيزي
توزيع دولار فيلم ٣ ممر بهلر القاهره

the crime boss Bayyumi. It would be hard to imagine another actor playing the character with the same guile and cunning. Rostom's Bayyumi manages to conceal his true identity as the ringleader of the drug gang not only from Khamis, but the audience as well. Even when they knew the surprise twist, people still flocked back to the theater for repeat viewings. Another significant aspect of the film was that it remains one of the few movies to feature a disabled character in a major role; this is the mute Bahana (Na'ima Wasfi), who is the key to the discovery of the gangster's true identity, and his last victim before his arrest. No one who has seen the movie can forget her terrified look when she offers Bayyumi a cup of coffee and recognizes who he is. Wasfi was so good in the role that many people at the time thought that the actress really had a speech impediment. Her character is one of the things that lifts this film above the ordinary and raises it to classic status.

Niazi Mustafa worked closely with his director of photography to shoot in a number of real-life locations, especially docks, which were used for many of the chase sequences. The editing is also notably tight, avoiding unnecessary dialogue or lingering, indulgent shots. Stuntmen (for Shawqi and Rostom) were used effectively in the truck scene that comes at the end of the film, and in such a skillful way that for a long time, there were rumors that the two actors had played the scene themselves, which certainly did not hurt box-office receipts. ★

KEY SCENE

In addition to its thrilling action, the film's success and popularity owed much to the character of Bayyumi, who gave the outward appearance of morality and uprightness, but in reality was the leader of the drug-running gang. In the key scene, Khamis exits the police station to find Bayyumi sitting at a café smoking a waterpipe. The two men exchange greetings and Bayyumi insists Khamis join him. Khamis tells him of his recent heroic capture of his own brother-in-law, sent to him by the smuggling ring to convince Khamis to steal an important file. Khamis tells Bayyumi how he pretended to go along with the scheme, then sprang the trap and arrested him. Bayyumi seems to respond with great glee. "Did he inform on any of the gang?" he asks. Khamis says he did not—"But he'll talk," he says. Bayyumi then tells Khamis how proud he is of him for taking on the members of this gang, "who deal in things that God forbids!" He then enthusiastically prays for Khamis's continued success. Khamis looks up at the sky; a flock of doves is flying past. "How great are the ways of the Lord," says Khamis, to which Bayyumi fervently agrees.

Al-Futuwwa

The Thug | 1957

A muscled hick from the country rolls up at a Cairo market and throws down a challenge to the established hierarchy

THIS IS ONE of Farid Shawqi's most important works, as both actor and producer. The movie is based on the true story of a trader at Cairo's old fruit and vegetable market in the Rod al-Farag district who ran a monopoly, artificially inflating the prices for basic produce and unfairly putting the squeeze on those elements of society that could least afford it. For his director on this project, Shawqi enlisted the pioneer of realism, Salah Abu Seif, who masterminded the building of an exact replica of the original marketplace. However, as soon as the finished film was released all screenings were blocked by a lawsuit brought by the real-life trader on whom the story was based, who sued for defamation of character. Shawqi fought the case successfully and the film went on to be shown to wide acclaim.

It was lauded for its realistic depiction of the day-to-day activities at the market, which was helped enormously by Wadid Sirry's fluid camera work, and the superb set, props, and costume design. Shawqi

ABOVE Haridi (Farid Shawqi, *left*), Abu Zeid (Zaki Rostom, *right*)

Director Salah Abu Seif

Story Farid Shawqi with Mahmud Subhi

Screenplay Sayyid Bedeir, Mahmud Subhi, Salah Abu Seif, and Naguib Mahfouz

Dialogue Sayyid Bedeir

Produced by Aflam al-'Ahd al-Gadid (New Era Movies)

Music Fu'ad al-Zahiri

Director of photography Wadid Sirry

Editor Galal Mustafa

Set design Anton Polysius

Starring Farid Shawqi, Tahiya Carioca, Zaki Rostom, Mimi Shekib, Tawfiq al-Diqin, Abd al-Alim Khattab, Mahmud al-Sabba', Fakhir Fakhir, Lutfi al-Hakim, Hassan al-Barudi, Salwa Mahmud, Na'ima Wasfi, Abd al-Ghani al-Nagdi, Ahmad al-Hamaki, Kamal Yassin, Mohamed Rida, Nazim Sha'rawi, Hanaa, and guest starring Huda Sultan and Mahmud al-Miligi

Running time 122 minutes

First screening 29 April 1957

Festivals Berlin, Moscow.

Black and white

افلام العهد الجديد
تقدم
فريد شوقي
تحية كاريوكا
زكي رستم
ميمي شكيب
توفيق الدقن
محمود السباع
فاخر فاخر
الفتوة
اخراج المخرج الواقعي
صلاح ابو سيف
توزيع شركة افلام مصر الجديدة

is on top form as the country greenhorn Haridi, visibly struggling in his attempts to earn an honest living—literally so in his first job, which is to take the place of a sick donkey in pulling a heavily laden cart around town. As he learns the ropes around the market, he crosses paths with Abu Zeid (played with gleeful aplomb by Zaki Rostom) who, with the backing of political allies, runs the fruit and vegetable business like his personal fiefdom. The film portrays Haridi's attempts to break Abu Zeid's stranglehold on the trade, in which he is assisted by a gutsy market girl played by Tahiya Carioca. The battle is not without cost and by the end Haridi has become no better than the tyrant he has sought to displace. In a film of so many fine scenes, standouts include Haridi's frenzied attempts to survive being locked in the cold storage, and the auction in which Haridi is cruising to a successful purchase until the surprise appearance of Abu Zeid, who goads his rival into bidding himself into bankruptcy.

The climax is a wonderfully choreographed battle waged throughout the market between the followers of the two men. In the chaotic melee, the signs of both men's businesses are splattered with thrown tomatoes and both fall to the ground. As the fighting continues, Salah Abu Seif pulls away the camera to catch the arrival of a new man turning up at the market. His entrance mirrors that of Haridi at the start of the film, complete with a slap on the back of the neck dealt him by one of the market lowlifes and unasked-for advice from a market girl that if he wants to survive around here he needs to stand up for himself. And so it begins again: the faces may change but the story remains the same. It remains a brilliant moment in Egyptian cinema. ★

KEY SCENE

During the mass brawl in the market, Abu Zeid seizes his chance to take a shot at Haridi. He only wings him before running out of bullets. He flees and Haridi gives chase. He corners him outside the cold storage room and as they fight they end up inside. When the refrigerator door is knocked closed by another brawling couple Haridi and Abu Zeid awake to the danger of their situation; they stop trying to kill each other and start shouting for help. They pound the door, but in their already exhausted state they quickly succumb and collapse—more or less the final screen moments in what stands as a landmark performance for the two actors involved. Eventually, someone opens the door and, for a second time, Haridi is hauled out of this particular room on the verge of expiration. Abu Zeid is not so fortunate. It is at this point the camera retreats from the chaos to show us the arrival of the newcomer. The message is clear: Haridi may have survived but his time is over.

Inta habibi

You Are My Love | 1957

While plotting to get out of a marriage arranged by their families, a couple find themselves falling in love

Director Youssef Chahine

Screenplay Abu al-Su'ud al-Ibyari

Story Abu al-Su'ud al-Ibyari

Dialogue Abu al-Su'ud al-Ibyari

Produced by Farid al-Atrash Films

Music Farid al-Atrash

Director of photography Ahmad Khurshid

Editors Said al-Sheikh and Hussein Afifi

Set design Hago Aslanian

Starring Farid al-Atrash, Shadya, Hind Rustum, Serag Munir, Abd al-Mun'im Ibrahim, Abd al-Salam al-Nabulsi, Zinnat Sidqi, Abd al-Aziz Ahmad, Mimi Shekib, Abd al-Ghani al-Nagdi, Sayyid Suleiman, Abd al-Nabi Mohamed

Running time 111 minutes

First screening 29 April 1957

Black and white

OPPOSITE Farid (Farid al-Atrash, *left*), Yasmine (Shadya, *right*)

TAKING A BREAK from the tragedy-laced social dramas with which he had made his name, in the mid-1950s Youssef Chahine decided to try his hand at something a little less dark and gritty. So it was that he came to be directing singing stars Farid al-Atrash and Shadya in a couple of delightful musical comedies, the first of which was *Wadda't hubbak (I Said Goodbye to Loving You)* in 1956, and the second, the following year's *Inta habibi*. The story is simplicity itself: two sets of parents arrange for their offspring, Farid (al-Atrash) and Yasmina (Shadya), to get married, which the pair consider a fate worse than death. Eventually they figure the best thing is to give in but follow up with a quick divorce—until, that is, they fall in love for real. It really does seem like Chahine had fun. He got to try out a different style of directing and new ways of using the camera, and tossed in whimsical elements, such as when Farid spanks Yasmina and the scene cuts to fireworks, and when Yasmina's mother smashes a vase over the head of Semsem, who had entered her chamber thinking she was Yasmina, fireworks again.

The directorial vision was more than aided by the screenplay and dialogue of Abu al-Su'ud al-Ibyari, a towering figure in the comic canon of Egyptian cinema. He excels here, as he always did, at serving up complex lines in simple and accessible language, occasionally employing the doggerel that was so popular with audiences. Al-Atrash, in particular, is given some terrifically wry lines, making this easily his most successful comic role. Chahine may be the director but the success of the movie can be laid squarely at al-Ibyari's door. The film also boasts several memorable songs. "Ya salam 'ala hubbi wa hubbak" ("Just Look at Our Love"), for example, is a comic masterpiece, in which the words are ostensibly loving and romantic but have a double meaning, allowing Farid and Yasmina to express their mutual distaste, praying to the Lord to take away

their "too-deep" love that can bring nothing but disaster. It is a song that remains popular to this day. Similarly, "Ahliflak matsadda'shi" ("You Don't Believe My Oaths"), in which Farid declaims his deep love to an incredulous Yasmina. As the love interest and comic foil to al-Atrash, Shadya is also brilliant, and together the couple represent the embodiment of glamour, wit, and sophistication. ★

KEY SCENE

The scene begins with the valet carrying a breakfast tray to Farid's room. There he finds a large hand-lettered sign that reads, "Do Not Disturb Until I Awake." Farid's mother comes to take a look, and then his father. The mother tells the father to wake his son as he ought to go to the hospital to visit his bride-to-be (who is faking appendicitis in order to get out of the wedding). Instead he starts talking loudly outside Farid's door with the idea of waking him. At this point the milk seller announces his arrival with a cry. "Shout louder," they implore him. Finally, they send the valet in. He's not there, he tells them. "You're not looking properly," shouts the mother. A phone call delivers the information that their son has been out all night at a club, the Tick Tock Boom. Meanwhile, Farid returns. His parents confront him. Yes, he was out all night, he says, but he was at the hospital visiting his fiancée, Yasmina. She's very bad, he says, still under anesthetics, and he was up all night worrying. "Yes, his heart was going tick tock boom," says his mother. She won't be able to leave the hospital for a week, insists Farid. At which point, a perfectly healthy-looking Yasmina makes her entrance.

Tamr Hinna

Tamr Hinna | 1957

A young man schemes to transform a gypsy dancer into a fine society lady to fool the pasha

THE MOVIE STARTS with a title card stating that the events to follow are based on a true story that "took place in Sharqiya Governorate." Which seems like a wild claim, given the story that follows, and only adds to the mystique of the wonderful and beguiling *Tamr Hinna*. This is one of the very rare works in Egyptian cinema that includes gypsies *(al-ghagar)*. Dialogue writer Galil al-Bendary happened to be extremely knowledgeable about gypsy culture, and his study of their dialect is reflected in the speech used in the film. When Tamr Hinna brings some chickens for a meal, one of the gypsy girls asks for her share of the banquet, saying, "Enthigh me and embreast yourself, the other idiots can be enwinged. And leave me a bit of the fat and skin, and make sure that it's unsinged."

Director Hussein Fawzi

Screenplay Hussein Fawzi

Story Hussein Fawzi

Dialogue Galil al-Bindari

Produced by Hussein Fawzi

Music Hussein Ahmad Ali

Director of photography Mahmud Nasr

Editors Said al-Sheikh and Hussein Afifi

Set design Anton Polysius

Starring Na'ima Akif, Rushdi Abaza, Ahmad Ramzi, Kariman, Serag Munir, Zinnat Sidqi, Stephan Rosti, Fayza Ahmad, Kamil Anwar, Abd al-Ghani al-Nagdi, Hafiz Amin, Hussein Ismail

Running time 117 minutes

First screening 1 July 1957

Black and white

LEFT Hassan (Rushdi Abaza, *right*), Tamr Hinna (Na'ima Akif, *left*)

أفلام حسين فوزى
تقدم
نعيمة عاكف
احمد رمزى
رشدى أباظه
والمطربة
فايزه احمد
تمر حنة
إنتاج وإخراج
حسين فوزى
توزيع : منتخبات بهنا فيلم
مطابع النصر
الاسكندرية - القاهرة - الخرطوم

It is the tale of a rich man, Ahmad, who falls in love with a gypsy bellydancer, the Tamr Hinna of the title. He transforms her, Pygmalion-like, into a socialite in order for her to be accepted by his family, and so he can win a bet. Meanwhile, the carnival strongman Hassan searches for his former lover. Na'ima Akif secured cinematic immortality as Tamr Hinna; the role was written specifically to showcase her dancing and singing performance. For the ladies in the audience, the film had Rushdi Abaza as Hassan, who memorably suffers having Tamr Hinna's image tattooed on his chest—a graphic scene that combined machismo with rugged sex appeal. The sets were artfully constructed, particularly those for the *mulid* scene in which Ahmad meets Tamr Hinna. In contrasting the burlap tents of the gypsies with the silks and satins of Ahmad's home, the sets also helped convey the film's clear political message, which was one of a new, post-Revolutionary social mobility. "From this day on," says Ahmad, "every human being has dignity, and there's no difference between rich and poor except what they wear." In fact there is a very funny line in which a village boy asks the local tattoo artist to "give me a tattoo of the Suez Canal, and make sure to nationalize it!"

Mention should also be made of the music. There are few songs in the movie but it has an incredibly memorable soundtrack, still widely listened to today and still favored by bellydancers. ★

KEY SCENE

The pivotal scene occurs at a party when "Yasmine"—as Tamr Hinna is now known—overhears Ahmad talking about the bet he made that he could remodel a gypsy girl to fool his father. The ruse had been so successful that Ahmad's father was actually planning to propose to Yasmine at this very party—partly out of infatuation, but also partly because he believed she possessed a fortune. Having found out that Ahmad never loved her, Yasmine brings the whole charade crashing down. The father is furious at the deception. Yasmine counters that he was happy to deceive her, dyeing his hair to appear younger. He retorts that she has taken his money; she takes off the ring he gave her and hands it back. He mocks her, calling her "Yasmine Hanim"; she retorts proudly, "My name is Tamr Hinna, dancer and chicken thief." "You admit it?!" he says incredulously. "I'm proud of where I came from," she replies. "I'm made of better stuff than you bigwigs." At this point, Ahmad appears to protest his love. "Congratulations on winning your bet," she says coolly. She slaps him in the face, saying that this is for fooling her into leaving her family and ruining her reputation, and departs to remove the clothes of Yasmine and put on "clean clothes—the clothes of Tamr Hinna."

Bur Sa'id

Port Said | 1957

A war drama that follows two Egyptian officers in the struggle against British occupation in Port Said

Director Izz al-Din zu-l-Fiqar

Screenplay Izz al-Din zu-l-Fiqar

Story Izz al-Din zu-l-Fiqar

Dialogue Ali al-Zurqani

Produced by Aflam al-'Ahd al-Gadid (New Era Films)

Music Fu'ad al-Zahiri

Director of photography Abd al-Halim Nasr

Editors Albert Naguib and Hussein Ahmad

Set design Abd al-Mun'im Bahnasi

Starring Farid Shawqi, Huda Sultan, Layla Fawzi, Shukri Sarhan, Zahrat al-Ula, Amina Rizq, Hussein Riyad, Zeinab Sidqi, Rushdi Abaza, Tawfiq al-Diqin, Adli Kasib, Na'ima Wasfi, Nur al-Dimerdash, Serag Munir, Ahmad Mazhar

Note Farid Shawqi was granted a special award by President Nasser

Running time 133 minutes

First screening 7 July 1957

Black and white

RIGHT Tulba (Farid Shawqi, *right*), Wafiya (Huda Sultan, *left*)

THIS MOVIE WAS made at the request of the president of Egypt. Gamal Abdel Nasser wanted a film that would inform the world of the Tripartite Aggression of 1956 and specifically highlight the heroism of the people of Port Said. He personally asked for the assistance of cinematic royalty Farid Shawqi, and charged Anwar Sadat with the task of liaising between the filmmakers and the presidential office. The film was duly made. It did not do well at the box office and Shawqi, as the producer, sustained heavy losses. He was left with studio and equipment-rental debts of five thousand Egyptian pounds—at the time, a truly astronomical sum—which he could not pay and for which he risked going to jail. He was rescued by Sadat, who provided him with a letter that basically read, "Do not collect this sum from

أفلام العهد الجديد
تقدم
القصة التي خلدتها المدينة الباسلة في مقاومة الأعداء
هدى سلطان
فريد شوقي
ليلى فوزي
شكري سرحان
أمينة رزق
حسين رياض
والطفل سليمان الجندي
المدينة الباسلة
بور سعيد
تأليف وإخراج: عز الدين ذو الفقار
مطابع النصر
توزيع: شركة أفلام مصر الجديدة
1957

Farid Shawqi. He has lost enough money already. It is enough that he made this film."

The film follows two Egyptian officers, Tulba and Fathi, during the defense of Port Said against British invasion. Shawqi brought together over twenty stars of the silver screen to make up the cast, while the job of directing the film was handed to the great Izz al-Din zu-l-Fiqar. Not only was zu-l-Fiqar a great director, but he had been in Port Said during the invasion. He experienced firsthand the people's suffering and witnessed the atrocities committed by the aggressors. He was the perfect man to tell this story. Zu-l-Fiqar also acted in the film, playing the part of James, head of the spies. Most of the external scenes were shot on location in Port Said, where the events actually took place, or as close to the actual places as possible. In terms of look, feel, and direction, the film could hardly have been any more authentic. In fact, despite being a box-office flop in Egypt, *Port Said* was shown to rave reviews and was a big hit with audiences in numerous other territories, including Syria and Lebanon. The ensemble cast performed admirably, while Shawqi himself gripped his weapon and defended the city with heartfelt patriotism. His grief when his lifelong best friend Fathi is killed is palpable. ★

KEY SCENE

One of the subplots of the film is the idea the enemy within may be more dangerous than the enemy from without. The scene starts at Hamida's café, which is used as a base for the popular resistance. Someone has been identifying the members of the resistance to the British Army and has also passed on the information that Tulba is currently in the neighborhood. "Perhaps the patrol just happened to see you," says the barber Chico. Hamida says she does not believe that the patrol just passed the café by chance. "Some traitor must have told them," she says. But no one could have alerted them, says one of the other men present, because the phone lines are all down. At which point they hear the sound of a telephone ringing. It is coming from inside Chico's barbershop. Tulba goes into the shop and finds a telephone secreted in a corner of the shop. "Answer it," he commands, "and tell the British that Tulba escaped before the patrol could get here." Later, he makes Chico call the British army officer Morehouse and sets up an ambush. Chico begs Tulba not to kill him.

Al-Wisada al-khaliya

The Empty Pillow | 1957

Two young lovers are separated by circumstances beyond their control and forced to marry other people

IT IS AN INNOCUOUS tale of first love, but director Salah Abu Seif received a lot of criticism for this film. He was accused by sycophants of the Nasser regime of turning his back on socialist realism and of betraying the working classes. Abu Seif argued otherwise: realism did not equate to socialism, and the cinema of realism was not confined to singing the praises of the revolutionary government. Realistic representation of a romantic or emotional subject was still realism in his book. So what if the protagonists in this film are upper class? What matters is that they and the situations they find themselves in are completely believable. Audiences agreed, and judging by its success at the box office, *al-Wisada al-khaliya* struck a chord with a great many lovers in the 1950s.

Director Salah Abu Seif

Screenplay Sayyid Bedeir

Story Ihsan Abd al-Quddus

Dialogue Sayyid Bedeir

Produced by Ramsis Naguib

Music Fu'ad al-Zahiri

Director of photography Mahmud Nasr

Editor Atiya Abdu

Set design Anton Polysius

Starring Abd al-Halim Hafiz, Lubna Abd al-Aziz, Zahrat al-Ula, Ahmad Ramzi, Omar al-Hariri, Abd al-Mun'im Ibrahim, Abd al-Warith Assar, Serag Munir, Rafi'a al-Shal, Aziza Hilmi, Kawthar Shafiq, Layla Karim, Aida Kamil, Esmat Mahmud, Ibrahim Hishmat

Running time 127 minutes

First screening 7 October 1957

Black and white

LEFT Salah (Abd al-Halim Hafiz, *right*), Samiha (Lubna Abd al-Aziz, *left*)

The story is based on a novel by Ihsan Abd al-Quddus in which young lovers Salah and Samiha are separated by circumstances, and each marries someone else. From then on they meet only socially in the company of their respective partners. Salah is under the impression that Samiha is still in love with him and he is in love with her. Each night when he goes to bed (the couples sleep in separate beds) it is Samiha's face he sees on his pillow before he falls asleep. But at the end of the movie, he finds out that his so-called love has been nothing but an illusion: he realizes that he is in love with his wife, who is devoted to him above all else.

The casting of Lubna Abd al-Aziz as Samiha was inspired. She was no flaxen-haired, European-style beauty, nor did she have the voluptuous sex appeal of the more glamorous screen goddesses; she was the Egyptian girl next door, slim, pretty, and possessed of a sultry, hoarse voice and dreamy green eyes. Her presence grounded the movie and lent it great credibility. Similarly, her counterpart was no Greek god with chiseled features and bulging muscles; Salah, played by Abd al-Halim Hafiz, is a college student with a modest wardrobe. The film starts out with him trying and failing to scrape together enough money to buy a pastry with some left over for the admission to a public garden. Aided by his friends—played by Ahmad Ramzi and Abd al-Moneim Madbouli—he resorts to a trick that most young men of the time would have found completely plausible. They would have seen themselves in the characters on the screen and this helped the film become one of the smash hits of the era. The actors playing the "lesser halves" of the two couples also put in terrific performances, with Zahrat al-Ula winning audience sympathy even in the face of competition from Lubna Abd al-Aziz, and Omar al-Hariri making such an ideal husband that you almost could see how he could displace Abd al-Halim Hafiz in Samiha's heart. ★

KEY SCENE

Salah is sitting in the hospital waiting for news of the outcome on the surgery being performed on his pregnant wife, Durriya. The news comes: the baby is dead but Durriya survives. Later, Salah goes to bed, as we have seen him do throughout the movie, and looks over at the empty pillow beside him. Previously he had always seen the face of his lover Samiha beside him, but now he sees the pale face of Durriya. He is overwhelmed with his love for her. He embraces the pillow.

عبد الحليم حافظ
لبنى عبد العزيز
الوسادة الخالية
قصة احسان عبد القدوس
سيناريو وحوار السيد بدير
تصوير محمود نصر
انتاج رمسيس نجيب
اخراج صلاح ابو سيف
شركة دار الطباعة
ستوديو عدلي
توزيع شركة الشرق لتوزيع الافلام ٣٣ شارع عرابي بالقاهرة

عبدالحليم نصر يقدم
فاتن حمامه
يحيى شاهين
بالاشتراك مع
مريم فخر الدين
عماد حمدي
هند رستم
رشدي اباظه
و
عمر الشريف
لا انام
بالألوان الطبيعية
اخراج
صلاح ابو سيف
قصة
احسان عبد القدوس
توزيع شركة دولار فيلم
مطابع النصر

La anam

I Don't Sleep | 1957

A scheming and spoiled daughter plots to ruin her father's relationships with women

SALAH ABU SEIF had already adapted one story by Ihsan Abd al-Quddus in 1957, with *al-Wisada al-khaliya* *(see page 71)*. That same year he took the same author's novel *La anam* and turned it into cinematic gold. This story centers on Nadia, a vindictive villainess who manages to destroy her father's and stepmother's happiness with her underhanded scheming. In a bold example of casting against type, Abu Seif chose Fatin Hamama to play Nadia. This was an actress who usually milked audiences for sympathy in poor-little-me roles such as the unrequited lover or ill-treated daughter. Hamama rejected the part at first, afraid of losing her adoring public. Abu Seif worked on her and eventually convinced the actress that she would be a sensation as the character audiences loved to hate. Sure enough, at the film's première, someone in the audience jumped to his feet and yelled,

Director Salah Abu Seif

Screenplay Sayyid Bedeir and Salah Izz al-Din

Story Ihsan Abd al-Quddus

Dialogue Salih Gawdat

Produced by Abd al-Halim Nasr

Music Fu'ad al-Zahiri

Directors of photography Abd al-Halim Nasr and Mahmud Nasr

Editors Emile Bahari and Hussein Ahmad

Set design Abd al-Fattah al-Biyali

Starring Fatin Hamama, Yahya Shahin, Maryam Fakhr al-Din, Imad Hamdi, Hind Rustum, Rushdi Abaza, Omar Sharif, Rafi'a al-Shal

Note The film won Salah Abu Seif the Best Director prize in the International Competition

Running time 122 minutes

First screening 31 October 1956

Color

LEFT Nadia (Fatin Hamama, *right*), Ahmad (Yahya Shahin, *center*), Safiya (Maryam Fakhr al-Din, *left*)

"You bitch!" Hamama was not impressed. Abu Seif and the critics, however, were delighted and reassured her that this proved how brilliant she was in the role.

In fact, it was astute casting because Hamama shared many of the attributes of Ihsan Abd al-Quddus's Nadia: in the novel she is a deceptively graceful and beautiful young woman whose many admirers fail to see beyond her feminine attributes to the intellect beyond—except in the case of Nadia it is a twisted intellect, seeped in wickedness and devoid of anything resembling a conscience. As in the novel, Abu Seif had Nadia narrate events in her own words, using voice-overs to convey her internal monologue. Those events stuck fairly faithfully to the storyline in the novel, and the onscreen characters were for the most part almost direct lifts from the page. Where the film departs from the source novel is in the impact derived from Fu'ad al-Zahiri's music, which greatly enhanced the impact of many scenes. Then there were the moments of pure cinematic genius, achieved in collaboration with the directors of photography Abd al-Halim Nasr and Mahmud Nasr, notably several sequences of innovative, expressive camera work, such as when Nadia's father finally turns on his wife, a key scene described below. ★

KEY SCENE

It begins with Nadia descending the staircase of the large family home. Her father has just told her to leave her stepmother's room, where he has set about ripping his new wife's clothes off their hangers and throwing them into a heap on the floor. This is Nadia's doing: she has told some malicious lies against her stepmother, Safiya, and her father, believing what he has been told, is now in a rage. Nadia sees Safiya, just arriving home, completely oblivious of what has been going on. Nadia flings her arms around her and bursts into tears. Safiya, shocked, thinks something has happened to her husband and rushes to him. She is halfway up the stairs when her husband appears on the top landing, hurling abuse down on her, ordering her to get out of his house, and three times repeating the phrase "I divorce you." Nadia observes from the foot of the stairs. As Nadia's father repeats the phrase "I divorce you," the camera cuts three times to Nadia's ashen face. The father's voice is manipulated to sound like a gunshot and because of the camera we feel it striking Nadia like three bullets. The red carpet around her looks like one big bloodstain.

Tuggar al-mawt

Merchants of Death | 1957

A murderous gangster turns his back on crime when he falls in love with his intended victim

ALI AL-ZURQANI apparently based his script for *Tuggar al-mawt* on incidents from real-life police reports. The story he came up with concerns a Dr. Abbas (Mahmud al-Miligi), whose observance of the Hippocratic Oath is a little shaky, to say the least. He conspires to commit insurance fraud, then does away with the claimant and shares the payments with the beneficiaries. Murad (Farid Shawqi) is in a similarly shady line of business, only he is a little light on funds, having had to pay for care for his ailing mother. When a session at the gaming tables plunges him even further into debt, he tries to strong-arm Abbas into giving him money, but the crooked doctor turns the tables and offers an alternative plan: Murad will marry, insure his wife, and then do away with her and the pair will split the payout. Murad agrees and goes ahead and marries Layla (Iman), the wife of a dead colleague. Except when the time comes to kill her, he cannot go through with it and betrays Abbas to the police instead.

Director Kamal El-Cheikh

Screenplay Ali al-Zurqani

Story Ali al-Zurqani

Produced by Nile Cinema

Director of photography Abd al-Halim Nasr

Editor Amira Fayid

Set design Maher Abd al-Nour

Starring Farid Shawqi, Iman, Mahmud al-Miligi, Rushdi Abaza, Said Abu Bakr, Fardus Mohamed, Ahmad Luxor, Aziza Hilmi, Ahmad Abaza, Abd al-Aziz Ghoneim

Running time 107 minutes

First screening 26 November 1957

Black and white

LEFT Ra'uf (Rushdi Abaza, *left*), Murad Husni (Farid Shawqi, *right*)

In adapting al-Zurqani's tale, director Kamal El-Cheikh sought to shock and astonish audiences by unmasking the cancers beneath the skin of Egyptian society. Although there are lots of complexities to the plot, al-Zurqani makes a virtue of the countless tightly shot scenes of scheming, agreements being made, logistics being organized, and spoils divided. These are contrasted with atmospheric nighttime exteriors and expansive day scenes on busy Cairo streets, including a rare sequence of the train to Helwan, with mob-like crowds struggling to get on as others attempt to get off. The directorial style is fast-paced and positively zips along, but never loses the thread. Along the way, El-Cheikh offers us a number of romantic scenes between Murad and his intended victim Layla. He also skillfully weaves in frequent cutaways to the ongoing police investigation that serve to ramp up the tension.

Abbas is given no motivation for his crimes, and he is clearly meant to garner no sympathy or forgiveness whatsoever from audiences. When Murad changes his mind about murdering Layla, Abbas very coldly reminds him of what may happen to him. (A mention here for Rushdi Abaza, normally seen as a heartthrob, but in this case playing the hit man, a cold-blooded killer, untouched by emotion or sympathy toward his victims.) Miligi, as Abbas, exudes a sinister and commanding presence, and manages to evince effortless evil, especially in the scenes where he dreams up elaborate plots to do away with his victims. It is doubtful whether the movie would have achieved the same degree of popularity if audiences had not totally believed in the evil genius of Abbas. Farid Shawqi is equally good as the dissolute and irresponsible libertine whose gambling losses force him to go along with Abbas's criminal enterprise. Although her career was short-lived, Iman's performance gives an idea of what might have been. ★

KEY SCENE

Abbas is highly intelligent and plans his crimes meticulously. This is most evident in the scene in which Murad goes to Abbas's home. Abbas asks Murad to give him the key to his house so that he can make a copy, in accordance with their previous plan in which Abbas will send someone to murder Murad's wife and make it look like a robbery. They have arranged to meet at the prestigious sporting club of which Abbas is a member, in front of dozens of witnesses, providing both of them with a perfect alibi. The one thing Abbas has not been able to plan for, however, is the unpredictable heart of Murad who, having genuinely fallen in love with his wife, now attempts to thwart Abbas.

Marcel
شركة النيل للسينما تقدم
فريد شوقي
ايمان
محمود المليجي
رشدي اباظه
فيلمسكوب
رصيف الموت
سيناريو
على الزرقاني
تصوير
عبد الحليم نصر
اخراج
كمال الشيخ
توزيع : شركة النيل للسينما

رد قلبى
قصة حب ...... وقصة شعب ... !!!
سينما سكوب
بالألوان الطبيعية
رُد قلبى
اخراج عز الدين ذو الفقار
انتاج آسيا
انتاج وتوزيع لوتس فيلم عمارة الايموبيليا بالقاهرة س.ت ٣٩٤٤٢

Rudda qalbi

Return My Heart | 1957

A poor gardener's son turned army officer falls in love with the pasha's daughter

THE FRIENDSHIP BETWEEN Yusuf al-Siba'i, novelist and army officer, and Izz al-Din zu-l-Fiqar, director and army officer, resulted in this movie. Al-Siba'i wrote a story that was an army officer's take on the 1952 Revolution. His view was that the coup and all that followed had changed the face of Egyptian society. Zu-l-Fiqar was of the same mind, so it was natural he should direct the screen adaptation of his colleague's book. There had already been films about the Revolution but they were propaganda works that unquestioningly glorified the events of 1952 and vilified everything that had come before. *Rudda qalbi* was less preachy and intended to appeal to a far broader audience. The moral message—and the movie is undoubtedly moralistic—is sugared for easy consumption. The fact that the film was made five years after the Revolution allowed for a more measured view.

Rudda qalbi was one of the first Egyptian movies to use both color and Cinemascope, the state-of-the-art British technology at this time. The director capitalized on this to the full, paying meticulous attention to the aesthetics of every frame. On occasion, this can be overdone: even in a modest peasant hut, there are vases of flowers and Ancient Egyptian artifacts. But zu-l-Fiqar outdoes himself in the exterior shots, employing some of Egypt's most attractive scenery as a backdrop—Qanatir, Marsa Matruh, a sunset on the sea at Alexandria. Shukri Sarhan excels in his role as Ali, the poor gardener's son who loves the pasha's daughter, Injy, but whose suit is cruelly dismissed by the pasha. In fact, when Ali does his military service the pasha makes sure he is sent as far from Cairo as possible. He becomes a patriotic officer who sacrifices everything for his country's honor and glory, reserving his love for Egypt. Egypt's sweetheart, Maryam Fakhr al-Din, is Injy, the modest girl from a high-class family who falls hard for the working-class boy, but is equally constrained by societal values. Light

Director Izz al-Din zu-l-Fiqar

Screenplay Izz al-Din zu-l-Fiqar

Story Yusuf al-Siba'i

Dialogue Yusuf al-Siba'i

Produced by Assia

Music Fu'ad al-Zahiri

Director of photography Wahid Farid

Editor Kamal Abu al-Ila

Set design Anton Polysius

Starring Maryam Fakhr al-Din, Shukri Sarhan, Hussein Riyad, Ahmad Mazhar, Salah zu-l-Fiqar, Rushdi Abaza, Zahrat al-Ula, Hind Rustum, Fardus Mohamed, Ahmad Allam, Kamal Yassin, Adli Kasib, Fakhir Fakhir

Festivals Brussels. Also won Second Prize for Directing and Best Actor for Shukri Sarhan at the State Awards

Running time 150 minutes

First screening 9 December 1957

Color

RIGHT Ali (Shukri Sarhan, *right*), Injy (Maryam Fakhr al-Din, *left*)

relief from the frustrated longings comes in the form of Salah zu-l-Fiqar as Hussein, son of the gardener Abd al-Wahid, whose comic presence adds laughs to the pathos and patriotism on display. ★

KEY SCENE

A detachment of soldiers of the Revolution arrives at Injy's villa to confiscate the family's fortune. Injy is instructed by her brother to go out and talk to them. When she comes outside, down the mansion's sweeping staircase, she finds Ali is the officer in charge. She reproaches him for never coming back, only visiting now to take away all their property. He says he is sorry but he is only following orders. She accepts his apology with ill grace, and starts to take off her jewelry and hand it to him. "All you want from me is my jewelry." He tells her she can keep what she likes of her jewelry, but she refuses his charity. "It's not charity," he says, "it's orders." She will not listen to anything further he has to say: "No explanations. No excuses." He starts to walk away, instructing the rest of the committee to start work, but she calls him back. "There is something of sentimental value I want to keep. It means a lot to me and I'll pay you what it's worth." She pulls out the chain with a heart-shaped locket that Ali once gave her, long ago. It breaks Ali's resolve and he blurts out his true feelings for her, telling her he has never forgotten her, never stopped loving her. Overcome with joy, she accepts his proposal of marriage and he leads her away from the mansion. The comic touch that de-sugars the schmaltz is a line from Ahmad Mazhar, playing the role of Alaa, the pasha's son, as he accompanies Injy outside: "Hey, Officer! Is she part of the confiscated goods too?"

Bab al-hadid

Cairo Main Station | 1958

A disabled newspaper vendor's dreams of possessing a beautiful lemonade seller end in horror and tragedy

THE RAILWAY STATION is not only a setting in this movie, it is a central metaphor. It shapes the character of impulsive and flighty Hannuma, the main female character; it instills in Abu Sree' the strength to take a stand against the oppressive head of the porters' guild. The station dictates the pattern of life for the ever-watchful

Released internationally as *Cairo Station*

Director Youssef Chahine

Screenplay Abd al-Hayy Adib

Story Abd al-Hayy Adib

Dialogue Mohamed Abu Yusuf

Produced by Gabriel Talhamy

Music Fu'ad al-Zahiri

Director of photography Alfizi Orfanelli

Editor Kamal Abu al-Ila

Set design Abbas Hilmi

Starring Farid Shawqi, Hind Rustum, Youssef Chahine, Hassan al-Barudi, Abd al-Aziz Khalil, Said Khalil, Abd al-Ghani al-Nagdi, Lutfi al-Hakim, Abd al-Hamid Badawi, Sayyid al-Arabi, Ahmad Abaza, Hanaa Abd al-Fattah, Safiya Tharwat

Festivals Berlin, Boston. Chahine won Best Actor and Best Director

Running time 74 minutes

First screening 20 January 1958

Black and white

BELOW Abu Sree' (Farid Shawqi, *left*), Qinawi (Youssef Chahine, *right*)

Madbouli, the newsstand owner, a man of trademark calm and patient demeanor. The station also shapes the character of crippled, slightly retarded Qinawi, whose resentment at his cruel fate grows daily as he watches the crowds coming and going, filled with health, finely clothed, with beautiful women meeting friends, lovers, and husbands. Qinawi (played by the director) sells newspapers at the

station, living by the tracks, and spending his days fantasizing about the sexy Hannuma (Rustum), a lemonade seller engaged to macho porter Abu Sree' (Shawqi).

Bab al-hadid was initially ignored by audiences and banned by critics on release. It may be that they were not interested in a film that takes place almost entirely in a railway station. More likely is that it was just too daring. The public could not relate to a rag-clad male lead who stuttered, shuffled, and hobbled, and exhibited some unsavory traits, such as cutting pictures of scantily clad women out of the magazines he is supposed to be selling and never bathing. Neither was the sexy female lead that easy to love, revealing herself to be cruelly manipulative.

But *Bab al-hadid* is that rare thing, a true masterpiece on pretty much every level. Everything about it is sublime, from the noirish photography to the railway-carriage rock'n'roll number. The crowning glory, though, is the character of Qinawi, the first protagonist in Egyptian cinema to have both a mental and a physical disability, and a character played, let us not forget, by the film's director. Such was his performance in front of the camera that many critics assumed that Chahine shared some characteristics with Qinawi. He had the last laugh when, many years after its original release, *Bab al-hadid* was rediscovered and garlanded with the acclaim it was due. ★

Toward the end of the movie, scorned and spurned by the object of his desire, the unfortunate Qinawi suffers an emotional breakdown, screaming and howling in public. In desperation he seizes Hannuma, presses a wicked-looking knife to her skin, and drags her down the railway track. Activity in the station comes to a halt as everyone watches to see what will happen next. The authorities nominate Qinawi's employer Madbouli to the role of hostage negotiator. He cautiously approaches the equally terrified kidnapper and his victim. "I'll marry her to you," says Madbouli. "I have the dowry right here, with me. I even brought you your wedding jacket." Of course, it is no wedding garment, it is a straitjacket, but Qinawi puts it on willingly. Meanwhile, Abu Sree', who has crawled along the tracks, grabs the knife. As reality dawns, Qinawi lets out a terrible scream and begs Madbouli to help him. Madbouli weeps for Qinawi.

Al-Tariq al-masdud

The Closed Path | 1958

A young girl struggles to do what is right but finds that the moral path is not always easily followed

Director Salah Abu Seif

Screenplay Naguib Mahfouz

Story Ihsan Abd al-Quddus

Dialogue Sayyid Bedeir

Produced by Ramsis Naguib

Music Fu'ad al-Zahiri

Director of photography Mahmud Nasr

Editor Atiya Abdu

Set design Anton Polysius

Starring Fatin Hamama, Ahmad Mazhar, Shukri Sarhan, Zuzu Madi, Tawfiq al-Diqin, Khairiya Ahmad, Riyad al-Qasabgi, Fardus Mohamed, Qadriya Kamil, Widad Hamdi, Malak al-Gamal, Ihsan Sharif, Na'ima Wasfi, Adli Kasib, Lutfi al-Hakim

Running time 118 minutes

First screening 21 April 1958

Black and white

THE FILM BEGINS with a quote from novelist Ihsan Abd al-Quddus: "Sin is not born with us. We are driven to it by society." It is a familiar theme in Egyptian cinema but tackled here with such mastery of the medium that we are willing to go through it all over again. Fatin Hamama plays Fayza, a young student whose father is dead and whose mother (Zuzu Madi) allows their home to be used as a gambling den to bring in some much-needed income. Offended by this, Fayza leaves to take up a post as a schoolteacher in the countryside. But things do not go well as the villagers resent her presence and wage a campaign to smear her reputation by claiming she is having an affair (*see* the Key Scene box). Ultimately, it seems that, like her mother, Fayza will have to compromise her morals in order to survive.

If he had only ever made this one film, Salah Abu Seif would still have merited a place alongside the world's great directors. Witness the scene in which Fayza is waiting for Ahmad, played by Shukri Sarhan, next to an abandoned waterwheel. She is worried because he is late, and she paces back and forth. She stands still for a few moments, looking straight ahead, then turns toward the camera for a few seconds. In just a few brief, wordless shots Abu Seif has established her innocence, vulnerability, and anxiety. When Ahmad walks up behind her, she is so tense that he has to say her name twice before she realizes he is there and breaks into a relieved smile. The precise placing and movement of the actors and camera are superb. It is unshowy and nothing that would be noticed by the audience, but without such tight direction the scene would not have had half the impact it does.

Much credit also goes to Fatin Hamama as the metamorphosing Fayza: at first virginal and upright; then shattered by a barrage of false accusations; then broken and reduced to a "life of sin" by the

الشركة العربية للسينما
تقدم
قصة
احسان عبد القدوس
بطولة
فاتن حمامه
حافظ مظهر
زوزو ماضي
شكري سرحان
الطريق المسدود
انتاج
رمسيس نجيب ٥ جمال الليثي
اخراج صلاح ابو سيف
توزيع: الشركة العربية للسينما ٨٣ شارع رمسيس

RIGHT Fayza (Fatin Hamama, *left*), Munir (Ahmad Mazhar, *right*)

calumnies of an unjust society. Eventually, there is redemption as she returns to the straight and narrow under the guidance of her old friend Munir (Ahmad Mazhar). Each of these stages is played with great conviction. Mazhar was the type of actor Abu Seif frequently used in this kind of story: a serious and honorable person, a good man to have at your side in a crisis, but not without a sense of fun. Mazhar lent credibility to his character, endearing him to audiences, which translated into good box-office receipts. ★

KEY SCENE

The film preaches virtue (especially of the female sort) and the struggle to retain it in a society that rewards wrongdoing. This is exemplified in the interrogation scene at the police station. The police officer asks Sa'diya, Fayza's co-worker, to tell him everything she knows about Fayza and Mohamed, a student that adores her. Out of spite and jealousy, Sa'diya pretends that she wants to safeguard Fayza's reputation, and tells the officer that Fayza let Mohamed kiss her. "I saw it myself," she says. She accuses Fayza of being a flirt. Another co-worker claims Fayza was often away from school grounds ("There's something about the way that girl acts that I don't like," she says). The most damning statement comes from one of the parents: "Ever since that Fayza came to our town, I've feared for my own virtue. If that girl stays in the village, well, it's either her or me." The lone voice of protest for the defense comes from an honest co-worker who maintains that Fayza is a decent, upright person, innocent of all the accusations being heaped on her. "This is so unfair," she says, and bursts into tears.

Sahir al-nisa'

The Ladies' Man | 1958

A con man fresh out of jail uses his ability to charm to go into business as a so-called spiritual healer

STORIES ABOUT CONFIDENCE tricksters and identity theft filled the crime pages of the newspapers and magazines around this time. They inspired Naguib Mahfouz to write the story on which director Fatin Abd al-Wahab based this movie. It begins with Hamza, a small-time swindler played by Farid Shawqi, leaving prison. Another inmate has

Director Fatin Abd al-Wahab

Screenplay Mahmud Subhi, Abbas Kamil, and Kamil al-Tilmissani

Story Naguib Mahfouz

Dialogue Mahmud Subhi, Abbas Kamil, and Kamil al-Tilmissani

Produced by Abbas Hilmi

Director of photography Mohamed Abd al-Azim

Editor Kamal Abu al-Ila

Set design Abbas Hilmi

Starring Farid Shawqi, Hind Rustum, Tawfiq al-Diqin, Riyad al-Qasabgi, Widad Hamdi, Suhair al-Babli, Khairiya Ahmad, Hassan Hamid, Mohamed Ilwan, Rafi'a al-Shal, Fikriya Kamil, At'uta, Hussein Qandil, Mohamed al-Dib

Running time 106 minutes

First screening 21 April 1958

Black and white

told him about two individuals with stashed wealth, and Hamza poses as a wild-haired holy man to con them both out of their cash. He uses these funds to become a swindler of a higher class, dressing in a smart suit and groovy shades, and posing as a "spiritual researcher" who can cure people by invoking intervention from the spirits. His targets this time are a disabled businessman and his wife, Aziza (Hind Rustum). But things get tricky when Hamza's former cellmate is released from prison and turns up to demand a share of the spoils.

Although the subject is crime, Abd al-Wahab casts it as a comedy. To ensure it complied with the prevailing practice of "art as moral lesson," he had Hamza caught and sent back to jail at the end. Until then, his escapades are steeped in the Egyptian lightheartedness in which, as a director, Abd al-Wahab excelled. The dialogue is nothing short of brilliant, with its rapid-fire pace, short sentences, and playfulness. Hamza says, with his back turned to his cellmate al-Kawakbi, "What is your complaint?" The response: "Love." Hamza asks: "You're in love?" Kawakbi: "Unrequited." Hamza: "Poor fellow!" Kawakbi: "I'm a wreck!" For Shawqi the role of Hamza was a big departure from type and, in a long career spent mostly playing resolute heroic types, it is exciting to see him stretch himself a little. In this case, the challenge was to play the sort of loathsome person who makes a living from preying on society's most vulnerable and gullible (and the treatment that Hamza subjects the businessman to is needlessly cruel), yet make audiences happy to spend time in his company. To his credit, Shawqi manages it admirably. ★

OPPOSITE Hamza "al-Bahlawan" (Farid Shawqi, *left*), Aziza (Hind Rustum, *right*)

KEY SCENE

At the core of this movie is the tendency of Egyptians to confer an aura of holiness upon any mentally disabled, ragged man who shambles around and babbles incomprehensibly. This is at the heart of a scene that begins with a close-up of a broom being wielded by a street sweeper, who brushes the dirt off a discarded mackerel tin but leaves the tin where it is. Mursi (Tawfiq al-Diqin) is sitting on a bench smoking a waterpipe. Hamza appears wearing the traditional garb of the blessed idiot, and is immediately welcomed and invited to sit with Mursi, who believes that he brings good fortune. Hamza has learned all about the drug-dealing Mursi from his former cellmate and uses the information to make himself appear all-knowing: "Why, this is true! How did you know that, O Holy Man?" says a dazzled Mursi. Hamza tells him that a neighbor wants to buy Mursi's house because, unknown to him, it contains a great treasure. "I'll help you dig it up," he tells Mursi. "Bring a pail, a hoe, and three thousand pounds." Mursi thanks Hamza and kisses his hand.

Sultan

Sultan | 1958

A downtrodden soldier is accused of stealing from a senior officer and escapes into a den of criminals

Released internationally as *Soltane*

Director Niazi Mustafa

Screenplay Niazi Mustafa and Abd al-Hayy Adib

Story Galil al-Bindari

Dialogue Sayyid Bedeir

Produced by Ramsis Naguib

Director of photography Alfizi Orfanelli

Editor Galal Mustafa

Set design Maher Abd al-Nour

Starring Farid Shawqi, Berlanti Abd al-Hamid, Rushdi Abaza, Nadia Lutfi, Fakhir Fakhir, Abd al-Ghani Qamar, Hassan Hamid, Mahmud Farag, Tawfiq al-Diqin, Adli Kasib, Aziza Hilmi, Riyad al-Qasabgi, Ahmad Luxor, Abd al-Ghani al-Nagdi, Mohamed Badr al-Din, Abd al-Aziz Ghoneim, Nahid Samir

Running time 102 minutes

First screening 6 October 1958

Black and white

SUPPOSEDLY BASED ON the true story of a criminal named Abbas al-Aswad, this movie brings together longtime collaborators Niazi Mustafa and Abd al-Hayy Adib, both action aficionados. Mustafa was an experienced director of action sequences, while Adib learned to incorporate them into his scripts when he started working regularly with Mustafa. In *Sultan*, however, the action is largely emotional and psychological.

The details of the story may differ but essentially *Sultan* makes the same point as Atif Salim's movie of four years previously, *Ga'aluni mugrim* *(see page 38)*; this is spelled out in opening titles that read, "Each of us has good and evil within; it is the society in which we

RIGHT Sultan (Farid Shawqi, *left*), (Berlanti Abd al-Hamid, *right*)

رمسيس نجيب
يقدم
فريد شوقي
والوجه الجديد
نادية لطفي
سلطان
توزيع
شركة الشرق لتوزيع الأفلام
٨٧ شارع رمسيس
إخراج : نيازي مصطفى

live that shapes our character, leading us now to good, now to evil." When the audience first sees the character Sultan (Farid Shawqi) he is an errand boy at the Cairo home of a senior army officer. We are left in no doubt as to his naïve and unspoiled nature as he drops the shopping he has been carrying to salute Officer Essam and refuses to stand at ease until Essam commands him to.

Later we see scenes of the country village where Sultan was born and raised. It was, we learn, anything but an idyllic upbringing. Sultan was raised by an abusive stepfather who whipped him for the slightest transgression. He did this while wearing a brass-buttoned coat, instilling in the poor boy a deep-seated fear of uniforms. Back in Cairo we learn that even though Sultan is now an enlisted man in the army, his situation is hardly any better. Instead of completing his military service he is a virtual slave of the officer. Later he is accused of stealing and once again he is flogged. Inevitably, he rejects society and joins a den of criminals, becoming their leader. The story ends in tragedy as Sultan is hunted by the police and dies at their hands. ★

KEY SCENE

Sultan stands accused of stealing the gold stars belonging to the officer in whose house he serves as an errand boy. He finds himself locked in a cell, with the sentence "Twenty-five lashes" ringing in his ears. Once again he relives the agonies of his youth. He sees himself as a little boy, being brutally beaten by his stepfather in his night-watchman's coat with its glinting brass buttons; the buttons merge with those sported by the soldier who carried out his sentence and gave him the lashing; they merge with the bright brass buttons on the suit of the officer who kicks him with army-issue boots for daring to request a short furlough to visit his mother on her death bed. He hears the officer's voice in his mind again: "No furloughs permitted! No travel allowed!" Sultan snaps out of his trance with a scream: "Enough!" It is a scream directed at an entire society.

Shari' al-hubb

Love Street | 1958

A young musician dons facial hair in order to get a job, then loses it as a result of a bet between two college girls

Director Izz al-Din zu-l-Fiqar

Screenplay Izz al-Din zu-l-Fiqar

Story Yusuf al-Siba'i

Dialogue Yusuf al-Siba'i

Produced by Hilmi Rafla Films

Director of photography Wahid Farid

Editor Albert Naguib

Set design Anton Polysius

Starring Abd al-Halim Hafiz, Sabah, Abd al-Salam al-Nabulsi, Hussein Riyad, Munira Sonbol, Hassan Fayiq, Fattuh Nashati, Abd al-Mun'im Ibrahim, Zinnat Sidqi, Riyad al-Qasabgi, Nur al-Dimerdash, Ahmad al-Haddad, Ahmad "Biju" Ratib, Mohamed "Shakal" Yusuf, Nagwa Fu'ad

Running time 144 minutes

First screening 13 October 1958

Black and white

THIS LIGHTWEIGHT ROMANTIC comedy is all about providing a vehicle for singing superstar Abd al-Halim Hafiz and his Lebanese co-star Sabah. Al-Halim Hafiz plays a young musician, Abd al-Mun'im, who is offered employment as a music teacher on the condition that he grows a beard and moustache, in order to make him appear suitably senior. Among his students are Karima (Sabah) and Mervat, who make a bet with each other that they can make him lose his beard. It is a very slight story but what elevates the movie is the supporting cast of top comic talent, not least Abd al-Salam al-Nabulsi as egocentric musician Hasaballah—or, as he insists on being called, "Hasaballah the Sixteenth"—and Zinnat Sidqi as Saniya Terter (or "Sequins"). The actors are assisted by some superb dialogue, so good that one might swear it came from the mind of Abu al-Su'ud al-Ibyari,

LEFT *Left to right* Saniya Terter (Zinnat Sidqi), Karima (Sabah), Abd al-Mun'im (Abd al-Halim Hafiz), Hasaballah (Abd al-Salam al-Nabulsi)

افلام حلمي رفله
تقدم
عبد الحليم حافظ
صباح
SVassiliou
شارع الحب
حسين رياض عبد السلام النابلسي منيره سنبل
عبد المنعم ابراهيم زينات صدقي حسن فايق
اخراج عز الدين ذو الفقار انتاج حلمي رفلة توزيع شركة الشرق لتوزيع الافلام

writer of such gems as *Inta habibi* *(see page 62)*, as it bears all his hallmarks—in fact it was, astonishingly, written by Yusuf al-Siba'i. Take, for example, when Abd al-Mun'im discovers that all Karima's attentions toward him were just part of a game. "She won our bet," says Mervat maliciously. "Whichever of us was the first to make the music teacher fall for her and shave off his mustache and beard won a Coke." Of course, by this time Karima has fallen for Abd al-Mun'im for real. Karima grabs Hasaballah and begs him to tell Abd al-Mun'im that she truly is in love with him. "Please, Hasaballah!" quickly adding, "the Sixteenth!" "Please let go of my suit," he says. "It belongs to someone else."

With his slight build and dreamy demeanor, al-Halim Hafiz is perfect as Abd al-Mun'im, particularly when he attempts to make himself appear older than he really is. This is also one of the roles for which Sabah is most fondly remembered, as she plays the kind of romantic heroine that audiences loved to watch. Al-Salam al-Nabulsi is just perfect in his well-judged balance of selflessness (seen in his efforts to keep his band going) and ridiculous self-importance. Whenever the name Hasaballah is mentioned even today the first thing that leaps to mind is still "the Sixteenth." ★

Abd al-Mun'im has just been humiliated. He jumped into water to save Karima, who had threatened to kill herself when he wouldn't cut off his beard, only to have to be rescued himself—by Karima—because he could not swim. Then, to top it all, he discovers he is the unwitting subject of a cruel bet between the girls. He returns home dejected where he finds the members of his band quick to offer their moral support, chanting, "Down with women!" To which Saniya Sequins responds, "Curse you all!" His art, they tell him, is the one thing that will never turn on him or stab him in the back. Hasaballah assures him that Maestro Aziz, the director of the Opera House, had admired Abd al-Mun'im's artistic ability at his recent audition. One of the band members suggests they rent a hall, print up tickets, and hold a concert. "And where will we get the money for that?" asks Abd al-Mun'im. Each of the band members pledges to work day and night to raise the money, while Sequins says she will pawn her jewelry, and mortgage the house, café, and everything she owns. Abd al-Mun'im thanks them all, assuring them that he has already forgotten Karima.

Al-Akh al-kabir

The Elder Brother | 1958

A drug dealer tries to rescue his young brother from the clutches of his own ex-girlfriend

Director Fatin Abd al-Wahab

Screenplay Ali al-Zurqani

Story Ali al-Zurqani

Dialogue Ali al-Zurqani

Produced by Mohamed Afifi Films

Music Mohamed Hassan al-Shuga'i

Director of photography Cello Cicivelli

Editor Fathi Qasim

Set design Abbas Hilmi

Starring Farid Shawqi, Hind Rustum, Ahmad Ramzi, Farida Fahmi, Fardus Mohamed, Said Abu-Bakr, Mohamed Tawfiq, Riyad al-Qasabgi, Mahmud al-Sabba', Mohamed Rida, Mahmud Azmi, Said Khalil, al-Tukhi Tawfiq

Running time 80 minutes

First screening 24 November 1958

Black and white

ALTHOUGH MOST OF Fatin Abd al-Wahab's works were comic—he is considered by many to be the father of situation comedy in the Arab world—he was no less adept at handling drama and tragedy. Exhibit A in support of this is *al-Akh al-kabir*.

It is a movie in which Awad (Farid Shawqi) is the elder in his family, taking care of his mother (Fardus Mohamed), his younger brother Ahmad (Ahmad Ramzi), and his niece Dawlat (Farida Fahmi). The family believes him to be a respectable tradesman but in reality he is the head of a gang of drug peddlers. He had a girlfriend, Rawhiya (Hind Rustum), a dancer who was also involved in drugs, who wanted to marry Awad but he refused. So secretly, in a vicious act of revenge, she turns her attentions to Ahmad, who is in his final year of law school, and introduces him to her brother's product.

RIGHT Awad (Farid Shawqi, *right*), 'Ubad (Mohamed Tawfiq, *left*)

افلام محمد عفيفي تقدم
فريد شوقي . هند رستم . احمد رمزي
S Vassiliou
الأخ الكبير
اخراج فطين عبد الوهاب
فردوس محمد
فريده فهمي
سعيد ابو بكر
قصة على الزرقاني تصوير كليليو مدير الانتاج كامل التلمساني توزيع دولار فيلم ٨٥ شارع رمسيس

The script skillfully points up the contrast in Awad as he is with his family—uprightness personified—and his dissolute and debauched life as a gang leader. The double life is hardly a novel concept, and similar scenarios crop up in countless movies of the era, but here it is leavened by humorous touches that provide relief from the darker moments. Few parts are darker than those featuring Mohamed Tawfiq as a drug addict. Tawfiq is a fine actor, but with the help of some terrific lines this is a performance that takes him onto a whole other plane. The pain of his suffering moves *al-Akh al-kabir* from just being a conventional cautionary tale about the dangers of drug addiction. His face as he tells Awad's mother that her son cruelly refused him a fix is as pathetic an expression of strung-out addiction as you are likely to see, crying and begging for drugs as he suffers and writhes. It is unlikely any other actor of his generation could have equaled Tawfiq's performance in this scene. Fardus Mohamed was similarly at the top of her form, while Farid Shawqi carries his emotions close to the surface throughout: witness his stricken eyes when his little brother, whom he is striving so hard to protect, slaps him across the face. Hind Rustum is by turns sexy, sympathetic, and despicable as the dancer in love with Awad and prepared to go to any lengths to have him. It is always fun to have an actress play someone playing someone else, and Rustum does a star turn as a lowlife street dancer masquerading as a high-class lady on her deathbed. ★

KEY SCENE

"Evil always comes home to roost" is the moral of this particular cautionary tale. The key scene is when Awad rings the doorbell of the apartment where his brother, Ahmad, is staying. He is unaware that it belongs to his own ex-girlfriend, Rawhiya, who swore vengeance on him for refusing to marry her. She opens the door, to their mutual shock. Awad enters the apartment, and realizes that it is Rawhiya who has been giving Ahmad drugs at the café he frequents. With a look of contempt, he flings the dregs of a cup of coffee in her face, then bursts into the room where his brother is being kept, and grabs his hand to lead him away. An enraged Ahmad turns on his brother and they argue violently. Awad tries to convince him of Rawhiya's true intentions and describes her as a debauched lowlife. Ahmad strikes Awad in the face. "Ahmad!" cries a heartbroken Awad. At this, his brother snaps out of it. Rawhiya tells Ahmad that what his brother says is true. Ahmad rushes out, followed by Awad.

Djamilah Bu-Hreid

Djamilah Bu-Hreid | 1958

A pioneering slice of new realism in which a common man of the alley fights against prejudice to succeed in business

A ONE-EYED FRENCH officer, Béjart, serves as the face of French colonial occupation in Algeria in this movie. Played brilliantly by Rushdi Abaza, the patch-wearing officer is symbolically blind to justice. He is unrelenting in his tyranny, unable to see the extent of his wrongdoing. With his one good eye, all he can see is France's divine right to rape, plunder, and pillage Algeria, and bring its people to its knees.

The counterpoint to Béjart is the Djamilah for whom the film is named. She is a young Algerian woman living in the Qasaba area of Algiers. Her nationalist spirit is awakened when she witnesses French soldiers attempt to arrest a classmate who kills herself rather than be taken. She joins the ranks of the National Liberation Front (FLN) and takes part in a series of operations before she is wounded and

Released internationally as *Jamilah*

Director Youssef Chahine

Story Yusuf al-Siba'i

Script and dialogue Naguib Mahfouz, Abd al-Rahman al-Sharqawi, Ali al-Zurqani, al-Tukhi Nagib

Produced by Magda

Director of photography Abd al-Aziz Fahmi

Editor Mohamed Abbas

Set design Anton Polysius

Starring Magda, Ahmad Mazhar, Rushdi Abaza, Salah zu-l-Fiqar, Kariman, Hussein Riyad, Fakhir Fakhir, Zahrat al-Ula, Farida Fahmi, Mahmud al-Miligi, Salah Nazmi, Fattuh Nashati, Adli Kasib, Abd al-Ghani Qamar, Said Khalil, Ahmad Lutfi, Ahmad Abaza, Suleiman al-Gindi, Mohamed Hamdi, Tahani Rashid, Nadia al-Gindi

Running time 125 minutes

First screening 8 January 1958

Black and white

LEFT Djamilah Bu-Hreid (Magda, *right*), Yusuf (Ahmad Mazhar, *left*)

Note This film was screened at the Moscow International Film Festival, where actress Magda received an award from the Moscow Women's Association, and the movie was awarded the prize for Best Screenplay. In addition, it walked off with the awards for Best Picture, Best Director, Best Actor, and Best Cinematography at the Cinema Foundation's International Competition.

captured by Béjart. She is tortured in an attempt to get her to give up the names of other resistance fighters and ultimately sentenced to death. Djamilah Bu-Hreid was a real person and this movie is her story.

The actress Magda plays the title role with aplomb. She seems too slight and feminine to be involved in such violence, but it helps her carry the audience. Knowing that the events portrayed on screen actually happened makes it doubly hard to watch the scenes in which Djamilah is brutally tortured by the French. Her physical and mental torment when Béjart twists her broken arm is shockingly realistic. As for the scene in which her brother is tortured before her eyes, it remains uncomfortable to watch even today. ★

KEY SCENE

Djamilah is in court, faced with the members of the tribunal and the military officials acting for the prosecution. The court is filled with French soldiers howling for Djamilah's blood, calling for the death sentence. The charges are read out: they include planting explosives, murder, attempted murder, and the destruction of property. Again the soldiers call for the death penalty. She admits that she is a member of the FLN, but this is only doing her duty as an Algerian. She rejects the lawyer appointed by the court and insists on a privately appointed French lawyer. She also insists on not being called "the criminal" by the judge, who tells her she is out of order and must ask permission by raising her hand before addressing the court. She tells him that her hand has been crippled from torture, and rejects the tribunal as invalid. The court calls a witness for the prosecution, her friend Bu-Azza. The latter is completely distraught from the effects of extreme torture; she lapses into incoherent shouting and eventually has to be escorted out of the courtroom. "No one wants to speak in your defense," the court tells Djamilah. Suddenly, the French lawyer Jacques Vergès strides into the courtroom. He is there to defend her and her right to defend her homeland. The French soldiers scream that he is a collaborator and a traitor in the enemy's pay. "This is no trial," Vergès says. "It's a pack of wild animals gathered around their prey." He asks to speak to his client in private. The court refuses. Djamilah speaks to him in public, in the courtroom where everyone can hear. She tells him about the torture. The lawyer then calls some witnesses to verify this. The prosecutor says that they have killed themselves. Vergès calls on the court to appoint a doctor to examine the defendant and asks for an adjournment. He also demands that the court safeguard his life: "I would prefer not to 'commit suicide' between now and tomorrow morning," he says.

جميلة
DJAMILAH

Imra'a fi-l-tariq

Woman on the Road | 1958

A love triangle between two brothers and a sex-crazed woman leads to a double murder

Released internationally as *A Woman on the Road*

Director Izz al-Din zu-l-Fiqar

Screenplay Abd al-Hayy Adib

Story Abd al-Hayy Adib

Dialogue Mohamed Abu Seif

Produced by Hilmi Rafla Films

Music Andre Ryder

Director of photography Wadid Sirry

Editor Albert Naguib

Set design Anton Polysius

Starring Huda Sultan, Rushdi Abaza, Shukri Sarhan, Zaki Rostom, Amal Farid, Abd al-Ghani Qamar, Mohamed Tawfiq, Shafiq Nur al-Din, Salwa Mahmud, Hassan Hamid, Mahmud Farag, Mohamed Subeih, Mohamed Badr al-Din

Running time 119 minutes

First screening 22 December 1958

Black and white

THIS MOVIE TOWERS above other similar works that deal with the sexual fervors that boil beneath the cover of tradition, convention, and, above all, religious observance. Here, the covers are stripped away and sexual passion is front and center in this exceptionally popular yet occasionally cheap and tawdry melodrama. Sex drives the plot, which revolves around a love triangle between the two sons of Mi'allim Farag—Saber, the elder, and Hassanein, the younger—and the seductress Lawahiz, the main generator of sexual tension in the film. She starts out by marrying Hassanein, who is unable to control his wife's irrepressible sex addiction. She then turns to his brother, Saber, who rebuffs her, but this only increases her ardor. She takes the drastic step of removing Hassanein from the picture by murdering him. Ironically, it is Saber who then protects the now widowed Lawahiz from the rapacious advances of the sex-crazed men of their alley,

RIGHT Lawahiz (Huda Sultan, *right*), Saber (Rushdi Abaza, *left*)

افلام حلمي رفله تقدم
هدى سلطان شكري سرحان
رشدي اباظه زكي رستم
امرأة في الطريق
اخراج عز الدين ذو الفقار
تصوير وديد سري
توزيع دولار فيلم
SVassiliou

even as he steadfastly refuses to be the one to satisfy her cravings. Saber has a girlfriend of his own, a woman worthy of his love, but he protects Lawahiz out of respect for his brother's memory. The film does a convincing job of presenting a set of characters whose actions are motivated by baser instincts. Izz al-Din zu-l-Fiqar could have found no actress better suited to the role of the sex-crazed, murderous wife than Huda Sultan, who flirts and seduces with a serpent's demonic smoothness. Audiences had no trouble believing that here was a woman for whom a man would gladly sell his soul. Zaki Rostom, as the boys' father, is similarly convincing as the strong and chivalrous Upper Egyptian patriarch. Rushdi Abaza, as Saber, is full of filial piety toward his father and brother. ★

KEY SCENE

The film's basic message is that treating one of your children better than the other will come to no good. The key scene is when Hassanein visits his now blind father. Taking his younger son's hand, Farag asks why he doesn't come more often. Hassanein is building up to telling Farag that it is his fault that his father is blind. Farag was blinded while working on a car with his sons; he was lying under the vehicle when a piece of metal hit him in the head. Farag assumed it was Saber's doing but it was actually Hassanein who caused the accident. Hassanein thinks Farag knows the secret he has been keeping; however, Farag then says, "I know the reason why you don't come; you're uncomfortable seeing your father blind and knowing that Saber is an ungrateful murderer." He goes on to say that if Saber is allowed to stay on in the family home, he will likely murder Hassanein and his father as well. Farag will not listen to Hassanein's pleas on Saber's behalf, and is pleased to learn that Saber has left the house for good. He asks Hassanein to bring his mother's photograph. Farag takes the photo and asks Hassanein to sit. "Thirty years ago," he says, "I made that unfortunate marriage to Saber's mother. She made my life a living hell." He goes on to tell him that this was what motivated him to move away from Upper Egypt and settle in Alexandria, working as a porter at the docks. In Alexandria, he tells him, he met Hassanein's mother, who made his life a heaven on earth: he was well-off then, he tells Hassanein, and his mother was such an angel that she insisted they bring Saber and Saber's mother to live with them. But Saber's jealous mother poisoned the new wife's tea; the latter died begging Farag to take care of his son, lest he too be murdered by Saber's mother, or Saber himself. Saber's mother was sentenced to life imprisonment, and she died in jail. Farag always feared for Hassanein's life, afraid Saber would murder him. Farag imagines that he has been blinded due to an abortive murder attempt by Saber. "Don't trust Saber," he implores Hassanein. He repeats his warning again, unaware that Hassanein has left the room.

Ana hurra

I Am Free | 1959

A young girl's desire for emancipation leads her to fall in love with a revolutionary

"IN 1936, AT 7 AM, a fifteen-year-old girl with dark skin and fiery red cheeks and lips was standing at the window of 3 Ganzuri Street, Abbasiya, eyes darting back and forth, unsure where to look." With these words, Ihsan Abd al-Quddus begins his novel *Ana hurra*. Director Salah Abu Seif fell in love with the book and resolved to bring it to the silver screen. The movie he made is a faithful expression of the main thrust of the novel, which is essentially the conflict between young and old that repeats itself with each new generation, even if some of the details had to be changed in order to bring the work to the screen. In the novel, Amina, a rebellious young woman who has gone to university in Cairo to escape the strictures of living with her aunt and uncle, graduates and gains her financial independence with a job. She falls for a young man named

Director Salah Abu Seif

Screenplay Naguib Mahfouz

Story Ihsan Abd al-Quddus

Dialogue Sayyid Bedeir

Produced by Ramsis Naguib

Music Fu'ad al-Zahiri

Director of photography Mahmud Nasr

Editor Atiya Abdu

Set design Anton Polysius

Starring Lubna Abd al-Aziz, Shukri Sarhan, Hussein Riyad, Zuzu Nabil, Kamal Yassin, Hassan Yusuf, Mohamed Abd al-Quddus, Gamal Sami, Layla Karim, Gamil Izz al-Din, Victoria Hebe'a

Festivals Venice Film Festival. Awarded Best Screenplay.

Running time 110 minutes

First screening 12 January 1959

Black and white

LEFT Amina (Lubna Abd al-Aziz, *right*), Abbas (Shukri Sarhan, *left*)

انتاج
رمسيس نجيب
يقدم
لبنى عبد العزيز
شكري سرحان
أجرأ قصة كتبها
احسان عبد القدوس
وأخرجها
صلاح ابو سيف
تصوير محمود نصر
انا حره
مطبعة انور ٤٨١٦٦
توزيع شركة الشرق لتوزيع الأفلام

Abbas and moves in with him. Their relationship is accepted by those around them, just as if they were married. Whenever anyone asks Amina about the nature of her relationship with Abbas, she responds, "I am free." When it came to adapting this for the cinema, screenwriter Naguib Mahfouz knew that, unlike educated readers, moviegoers would not be so accepting of the idea of living in sin, so the cohabitation had to go. For good measure, he also had the couple get married later in the film—in jail, in fact, after they had both been incarcerated for distributing inflammatory pamphlets.

In the book, the target of the couple's political protest was the incumbent Egyptian regime, but for the film this was changed to the colonial rule of the British. For added poignancy, the film has the couple's wedding day falling on 22 July 1952, just one day before the revolution of which they had been dreaming becomes a reality. Lubna Abd al-Aziz is very convincing as the dark-skinned, red-lipped rebel Amina, whose early smoldering insolence blooms, over the course of the movie, into full-blown, freedom-fighting fervor. ★

Amina is at her desk at the oil company where she works. On the walls around her are signs emphasizing the value of time and devotion to the job. She goes off into a daydream in which her conscience starts to interrogate her: Why is she not happy? What is bothering her? "Isn't this," her conscience taunts her, "the freedom you fought for? Didn't you want to graduate and get a job so you wouldn't be dependent on anyone? Don't you come and go as you please and stay out as late as you want? Why are you so full of resentment?" Her inner voice responds: "Something's missing, but I don't know what it is." Her conscience tells her she is living an empty life. Freedom, it says, must be used in the service of a higher goal or purpose. Freedom is a means, it says, not an end. At which point, Amina is snapped out of her daydream by the voice of her boss.

Al-'Ataba al-khadra'

Ataba 'Green' Square | 1959

A country bumpkin falls into the clutches of a con man who tricks him into buying a central Cairo landmark

Released internationally as *El-Ataba el-Khadra*

Director Fatin Abd al-Wahab

Screenplay Galil al-Bindari

Story Galil al-Bindari

Dialogue Galil al-Bindari

Produced by Abd al-Rahim Yazdi

Music Ahmad Fu'ad Hassan

Director of photography Ali Hassan

Editors Emile Bahari and Hussein Ahmad

Set design Maher Abd al-Nour

Starring Sabah, Ahmad Mazhar, Isma'il Yassin, Omar al-Hariri, Huda Shams al-Din, Zinnat Sidqi, Riyad al-Qasabgi, Said Khalil, Fathiya Shahin, Mohamed al-Dib, I'tidal Chahine, Nazim Sha'rawi, Edmund Tweima, Abd al-Ghani al-Nagdi, Abd al-Mun'im Ismail, Ahmad Luxor, Muhsin Hassanein, Mohamed Subeih

Running time 107 minutes

First screening 16 March 1959

Black and white

GALIL AL-BINDARI DREW the inspiration for this movie from a real-life incident in which a professional shyster sold the Cairo tram system to a visiting gentleman from the country. In this fictional case, the con man Yusuf attempts to sell nothing less than a central Cairo square to Mabruk, the simple man from Upper Egypt, and his fame-seeking companion Mona. Al-Bindari crafted the screenplay and dialogue with a great deal of comic flair, which was then taken up by director Fatin Abd al-Wahab, the pioneer of Egyptian comedy. The movie has great sport contrasting its documentary-like footage of the grandeur of Ataba Square, with its Belle Époque architecture, noble institutions, and nonstop commerce, with the mud-hut horizons of the

ABOVE Yusuf Gamil (Ahmad Mazhar, *right*), Mabruk (Isma'il Yassin, *left*)

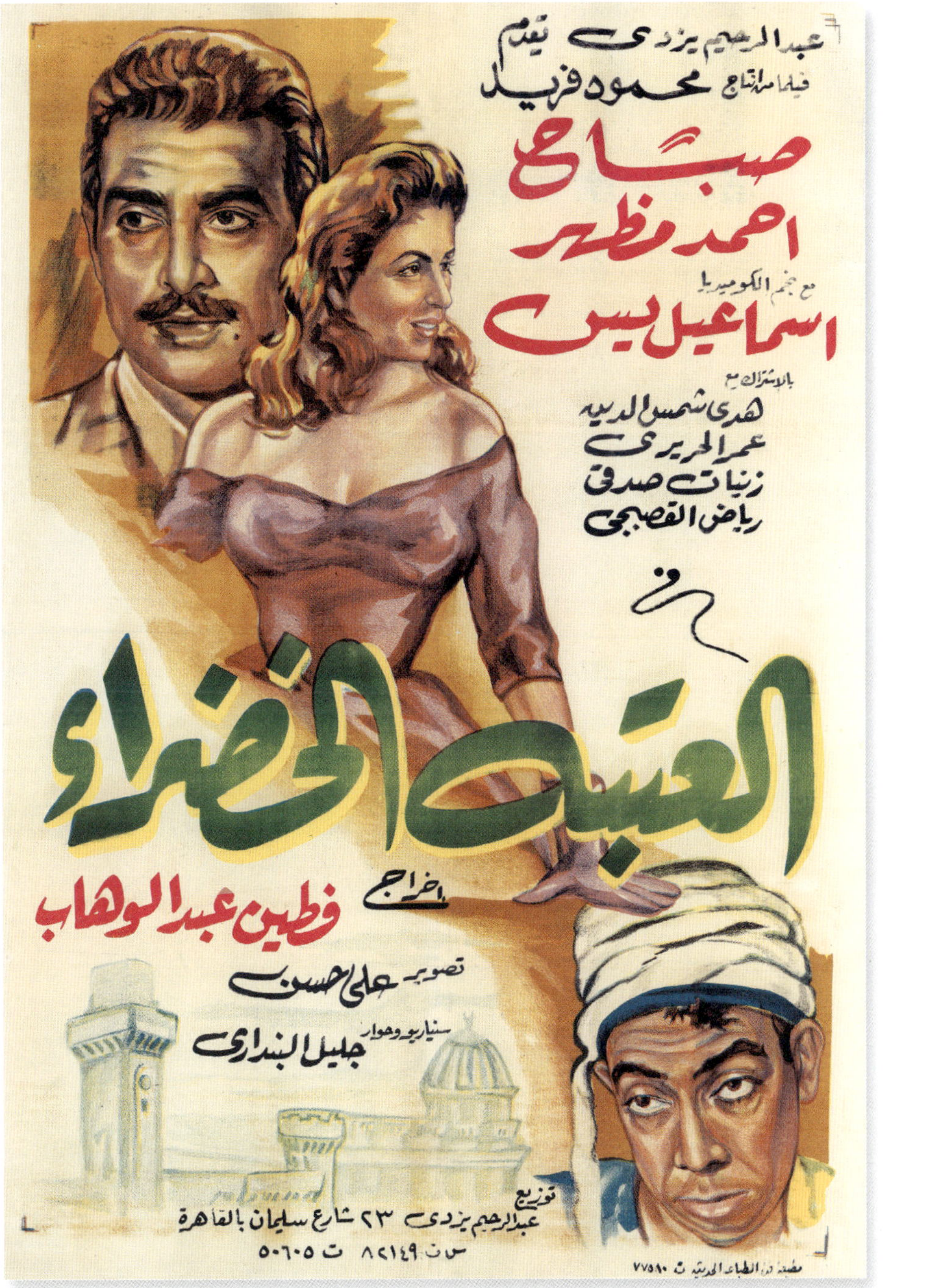
عبد الرحيم يزدي يقدم
فيلما من إنتاج محمود فريد
صباح
أحمد مظهر
مع نجم الكوميديا
اسماعيل يس
بالاشتراك مع
هدى شمس الدين
عمر الحريري
زينات صدقي
رياض القصبجي
في
العتبة الخضراء
إخراج
فطين عبد الوهاب
تصوير علي حسن
سيناريو وحوار جليل البنداري
توزيع
عبد الرحيم يزدي ٢٣ شارع سليمان بالقاهرة
س ت ٨٢١٤٩ ت ٥٠٦٠٥
مطبعة دار الطباعة الحديثة ت ٧٧٥٩٠

dupe Mabruk. The film has its perfect chump in comedy star Isma'il Yassin, who at this point in his career was at the top of his form. Nevertheless, heartthrob Ahmad Mazhar, who played Yusuf, stipulated that his name top the bill, immediately followed by that of Sabah, who played Mona. Yassin did not object, and up on the marquee and posters, his name came third. However, when audiences sat down to watch the movie, they were in no doubt as to who was the star. With his inimitable presence and comic flair, Yassin upstages everyone else on screen. Mazhar was forced to concede that top billing was no measure of how much an artist actually contributes to the movie. Which is not to say that Mazhar performed badly: he is excellent as a comic con man possessed of the glib tongue of a born crook. Sabah, meanwhile, has some fine musical numbers and gets to wear some fabulous dresses. ★

KEY SCENE

The con man Yusuf arrives at his office where he is eagerly met by his dupe Mabruk. "The chief of police sent someone over with the rent for the station but you weren't here," says the admiring Mabruk. "And the fire chief called and says to wait for the rent because they're not getting many fires these days." Yusuf feigns irritation. Mabruk tells Yusuf that he should be more patient. "Do you want the fire chief to go around setting fires just so they can pay the rent?" Impressed by Yusuf's business, Mabruk asks how it is done. "I own all Ataba Square," says Yusuf. He explains that it is an inheritance, but one he has no desire to hold on to. We see scenes of Ataba Square, while in voice-over Yusuf tells Mabruk that his holdings include the Halawa department store, Azbakiya and Ataba gardens, the opera house, and the post office. "What do you charge the post office in rent?" asks Mabruk. Just then, an accomplice of Yusuf's comes in, playing the part of a postal service employee, and hands over a hefty sum. Yusuf counts the money. "Why then would you sell all this?" asks Mabruk. "I want to buy the Pyramids," says Yusuf. Mabruk wants to know the going rate for Ataba. "Twenty thousand pounds," says Yusuf. Mabruk starts haggling: "We're friends! You need to give me a break on the price. You wouldn't begrudge me Ataba, would you?" Yusuf agrees to discuss it.

'Ashat li-l-hubb

She Lived for Love | 1959

A young man with some seriously unresolved issues regarding women struggles in his relationship with a loving girlfriend

FROM A STORY BY Mohamed Abd al-Halim Abdullah originally titled *Shagarat al-liblab (Bindweed)*, the less effectively named *'Ashat li-l-hubb* hinges on the lasting trauma experienced by Husni when he catches his stepmother cheating on his father. The shock of it later threatens to destroy his own relationship with the blameless Zeinab. And what a tragedy that is when Zeinab is embodied on screen by the lovely Zubayda Tharwat, a proper, modest, and understated beauty, rather than one of those vampish sex kittens. Aficionados still consider her the dreamiest romantic female lead in Egyptian cinema. Director Sayyid Bedeir does his best to make the audience understand the roots of Husni's troubles—deprived of a mother's love by her untimely death and of a father's love by his preference for drinking and whoring. Then there is the thing with

Director Sayyid Bedeir

Screenplay Sayyid Bedeir

Story Mohamed Abd al-Halim Abdullah

Dialogue Salih Gawdat

Produced by Abbas Hilmi Films

Director of photography Abd al-Halim Nasr

Editor Albert Naguib

Set design Abd al-Mun'im Ali

Starring Zubayda Tharwat, Kamal al-Shinnawi, Abd al-Mun'im Ibrahim, Layla Tahir, Mary Izz al-Din, Salwa Mahmud, Aziza Hilmi, Abdullah Ghayth, Widad Hamdi, Kamal Hussein, Mohamed Shawqi, Hussein Assar, Abd al-Aziz Hamdi

Running time 104 minutes

First screening 14 September 1959

Black and white

LEFT Husni (Kamal al-Shinnawi, *left*), Zeinab (Zubayda Tharwat, *right*)

his stepmother, after which he develops the belief that no woman is to be trusted. Kamal al-Shinnawi is flawless as the damaged Husni, who nevertheless does fall head-over-heels in love, only to have all his misguided fears confirmed when his adoring girlfriend sleeps with him. With all that inner turmoil to portray and the tricky mood swings, it is on his shoulders that the success of the film rests.

All the anguish is sweetened by some lovely incidental music, particularly the recurring love theme that underscores scenes between Husni and Zeinab. There are also plenty of comic touches lightening the melodrama, as in the scene when little Husni runs away, afraid of being punished by his father, and is brought back home by his uncle. Father is in his room playing cards with his wife. When the wife reaches to pick up the jack—what Egyptians call the "boy"—her husband shouts, "Leave the boy alone!" The uncle, standing outside, naturally thinks the father's words are addressed to him. ★

KEY SCENE

Husni is on a train. Poor Zeinab has just shared his bed and rather than delighting her lover, this has sent him into a rage, screaming at her, "You're no different from any woman!" He has accused her of having sex with him only as a way of trapping him in marriage. Now, he conducts an internal monologue. The poor soul wanted a woman who would love only for love's sake. He had pinned his hopes on Zeinab being the one who could erase the predatory image of women from his mind. He has tried, he tells himself, to banish the distrust seared into him by his stepmother but Zeinab's willingness to commit sin with him has brought it all back: all women, he cannot help but believe, from his stepmother to Ghanim the milkman's wife to Zeinab, are equally treacherous in his eyes. Audience sympathies at the time presumably lay with Husni, although one would hope anyone watching today would be firmly in Zeinab's camp.

أفلام الاتحاد
عباس حلمي
تقدم
زبيده ثروت
كمال الشناوي
ليلى طاهر
عبد المنعم ابراهيم
في
عاشت للحب
عن قصة (شجرة اللبلاب)
اخراج
السيد بدير
مدير التصوير
عبد الحليم نصر
قصة
محمد عبد الحليم عبد الله
توزيع شركة الشرق لتوزيع الأفلام

Ihna al-talamza

We, the Students | 1959

The failings of society set three young men on a path that leads to the courthouse

Director Atif Salim

Screenplay Naguib Mahfouz

Story Tawfiq Salih and Kamil Yusuf

Dialogue Mohamed Abu Yusuf

Produced by Hilmi Rafla Films

Music Ahmad Fu'ad Hassan

Director of photography Bruno Salvi

Editor Hassuf

Set design Anton Polysius

Starring Shukri Sarhan, Tahiya Carioca, Omar Sharif, Yusuf Fakhr al-Din, Zizi al-Badrawi, Mahmud al-Miligi, Amal Farid, Tahani Rashid, Nagwa Fu'ad, Kamal Hussein, Abd al-Ghani Qamar, Fardus Mohamed, Mimi Shekib, Abd al-Aziz Ahmad, Fu'ad Shafiq

Running time 114 minutes

First screening 12 October 1959

Notes State Award of Merit

Black and white

DIRECTOR ATIF SALIM tackles three separate social issues in this movie: revenge killing, child abuse, and child neglect. One of these blights the childhood of each of the three young men at the heart of the movie, ultimately driving them to crime. Events come to a head in a grand courtroom scene in which the director (with no small help from his screenwriter Naguib Mahfouz and dialogue writer Mohamed Abu Yusuf) puts his own opinions on the matter into the mouth of the lawyer: "These three are no doubt guilty but, in essence, they are also innocent victims." *Ihna al-talamza* was one of the most daring of many similar-minded movies of the time to tackle such subjects, all taboos that were not otherwise widely discussed in general society. What raises it above the field is the stellar constellation of talent Atif Salim gathered for his cast. They were so successful in

RIGHT Samir (Yusuf Fakhr al-Din, *left*), Adil (Omar Sharif, *center*), Hassanein (Shukri Sarhan, *right*)

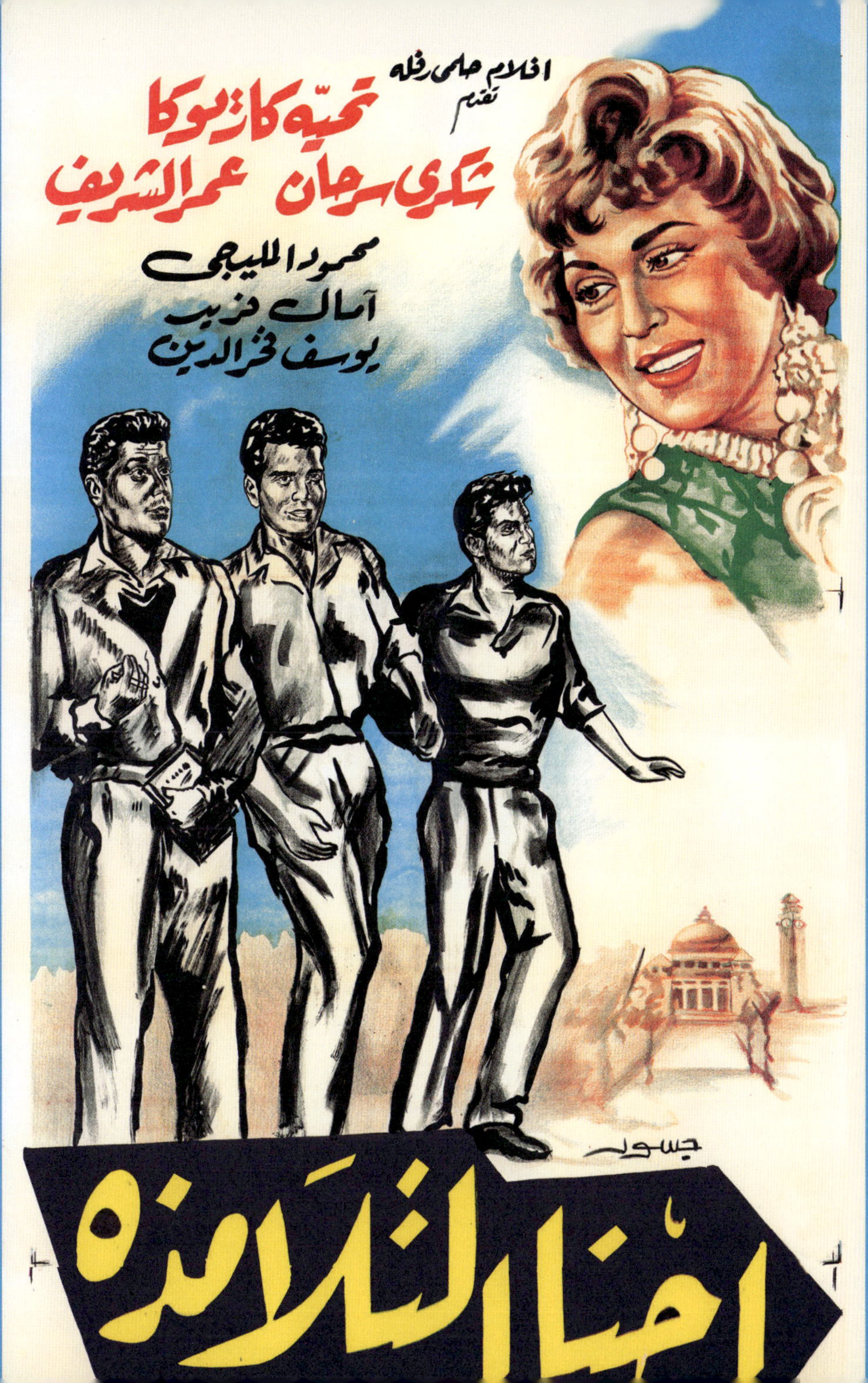

افلام حلمي رفله
تقدم
تحية كاريوكا
شكري سرحان عمر الشريف
محمود المليجي
آمال فريد
يوسف فخر الدين
جسور
إحنا التلامذة

their roles that in the aftermath of the movie the three lead actors were frequently referred to by their character names. It is difficult now to imagine the parts ever being played by anyone else. Shukri Sarhan is brilliant as Hassanein, the Upper Egyptian student with leadership qualities that had the potential to bring him great success: instead, his abusive family situation turned him into the ringleader of a gang of juvenile delinquents. Despite being in his mid-thirties at the time, Sarhan fizzes with teenage rebellion, all jerky movements and barely suppressed energy. Twenty-seven-year-old Omar Sharif is Adil, the romantic teen who lives by his emotions; crushed by his overbearing father, he follows Hassanein into petty criminality. Yusuf Fakhr al-Din also excels as Samir, the spoiled boy who receives the best of everything but is starved of his parents' love and attention. Tahiya Carioca plays Gamalat, a bellydancing prostitute who exploits the callow youths to satisfy her personal ends. Zizi Mustafa, as the innocent servant girl Sa'diya, is a passionate foil for the boys, and was a hit with audiences, who cried for her and sympathized with her plight. The film also boasts a particularly good musical score by Ahmad Fu'ad Hassan. Listen in the scene when Adil follows his girlfriend into her house and goes up the stairs behind her: the music starts out romantic and sweet, then crescendos into something faster and more urgent, as he ascends the stairs. ★

KEY SCENE

We are in the courtroom and the three teens are in the dock, along with Gamalat, the dancer. They have been accused of two separate murders: one kills with the motive of stealing money owed to him and the other to conceal a pregnancy the result of rape, and the three acting as accessories to crime. The lawyer steps up to speak. The youths are, he says, guilty and deserving of punishment. However, he adds, before any sentence is passed or there is any talk of punishment, the court must first look for the reasons the young men turned to crime. The reason, he states, lies with their parents, guardians, and families. Had they been properly cared for they would not now be in the courtroom. Adil was the victim of constant belittling and derision from his bad-tempered father. Hassanein was goaded by a family forever urging him to commit murder as part of a blood feud. When he refused to comply they cut off their financial support. Samir was the victim of his parents' constant absence, as they spent all their time out at parties and other soirees. "I speak," the lawyer says, "for an entire generation. I defend an entire generation, every father, every mother, every child, every family. Our sense of responsibility and our duty is to find a solution to these problems so that we may build healthy generations that benefit our homeland."

Du'a' al-karawan

The Call of the Curlew | 1959

A Bedouin girl plots revenge against the engineer who took her sister's honor

Director Henri Barakat

Screenplay Henri Barakat and Yusuf Guhar

Story Taha Hussein

Dialogue Yusuf Guhar

Produced by Henri Barakat

Music Andre Ryder

Director of photography Wahid Farid

Editor Mohamed Abbas

Set design Maher Abd al-Nur

Starring Fatin Hamama, Ahmad Mazhar, Zahrat al-Ula, Amina Rizq, Abd al-Alim Khattab, Mimi Shekib, Raga' al-Giddawi, Nahid Samir, Hussein Assar, Edmund Tweima, Lutfi al-Hakim, Kawthar Ramzi, Zaki Abd al-Magid, Hussein Ismail, Abd al-Hamid Badawi, Salwa Izz al-Din

Festivals Berlin, Academy Awards. Nominated for Best Foreign Film at that year's Academy Awards. Awarded a special prize by the Oscars Committee. Best Picture and Best Actress at the Egyptian International Film Festival.

Running time 119 minutes

First screening 22 November 1959

Black and white

THE MOVIE IS a wonderful adaptation of Taha Hussein's masterly novel *Du'a' al-karawan*, which he completed in 1934. For their film, director Henri Barakat and writer Yusuf Guhar fashioned a script that is the equal of the novel's genius. The often poetic language of the screenplay reflects the dialect and local inflections of the three women at the heart of the film, Amna, her elder sister Hanadi, and their mother, who belong to the nomadic desert people of Upper Egypt. They have had to abandon their village because of the adulterous escapades of the father and have arrived in a city where the two sisters take jobs as housekeepers. Hanadi is seduced by her employer, a handsome engineer, and surrenders her virginity, thus

ABOVE Amna (Fatin Hamama, *left*), Ahmad (Ahmad Mazhar, *right*)

افلام بركات
تقدم
قصة
الدكتور طه حسين
الدكتور طه حسين
دعاء الكروان
فاتن حمامه • احمد مظهر
دعاء الكروان
مدير التصوير وحيد فريد
حوار يوسف جوهر
اخراج بركات
مطبعة انور ٤٨١٦٦
توزيع شركة دولار فيلم (اسماعيل الكردى واولاده) ٨٥ شارع عبيس بالقاهرة

sealing her death at the hands of an uncle who values the family honor over the life of his niece. Amna, in turn, swears to avenge herself on the engineer.

Barakat is skilled at portraying the psychological journey undertaken by the sisters; at the start of the film, we see shy girls hidden behind their veils, peeking out from a world confined to themselves and their mother. Later, they walk sans veils with heads held high, no longer cowed by the city, until Hanadi, forgetting where they have come from, takes her boldness further than is wise. Her murder takes place in the desert from whence she came—the harsh and inhospitable setting contrasting with the tame comforts of the city, the sand soaking up the blood to erase all traces that anyone was ever there. Zahrat al-Ula's performance as Hanadi is outstanding and continues to haunt anyone who sees it even today. Fatin Hamama is equally memorable as Amna, who schemes to work her way into the affections of the engineer in order to kill him. Against the odds, Ahmad Mazhar, in the role of the engineer, manages to earn our sympathy as he genuinely falls for Amna and is horror-stricken when he learns why she has come into his life and of the blood that stains his hands. Redemption comes when he throws himself in front of the bullet meant for Amna fired by the ever-vengeful uncle.

The great man of letters himself approved wholeheartedly of the way his novel had been transferred to the big screen, expressing his pleasure by recording a voice-over for the end of the film. ★

KEY SCENE

The key scene is the one in which Amna reveals to the engineer, Ahmad, who she really is. It begins with Amna hurrying toward the house after kissing him. She is ashamed of the kiss, ashamed that she has forgotten what this man did to her sister and how it resulted in her death. She locks herself in her room. She is followed by Ahmad, who stands at the door confessing his sincere love for her. He proposes marriage. She tells him she hates him, which he is at a loss to understand. "I came into this house," says Amna, "to bring you down!" She tells him that the housekeeper he deflowered was her sister who was then murdered by her uncle in an honor killing. Ahmad staggers out of the room in horror. He tells Amna he wishes he were dead. Before the end of the movie his wish will come true and Amna, who has grown to love him, will be left devastated once more.

Al-Rajul al-thani

The Second Man | 1959

The sister of a murdered gangster avenges his death by helping to bring down his double-crossing former crew

Director Izz al-Din zu-l-Fiqar

Screenplay Yusuf Guhar

Story Yusuf Guhar and Izz al-Din zu-l-Fiqar

Dialogue Yusuf Guhar

Produced by Izz al-Din zu-l-Fiqar

Music Andre Ryder

Director of photography Wahid Farid

Editor Albert Naguib

Set design Anton Polysius

Starring Rushdi Abaza, Sabah, Samya Gamal, Salah zu-l-Fiqar, Salah Nazmi, Abd al-Khalek Salih, Hassan Hamid, Mahmud Farag, Qadriya Qadri, Abd al-Ghani al-Nagdi, Mohamed Subeih, Mohamed Badr al-Din, Hussein Ismail, Gamil Izz al-Din, Badr Nofal

Running time 164 minutes

First screening 28 December 1959

Black and white

OPERATING IN THE film noir tradition, which enjoyed its classic period in the 1940s and 1950s, *al-Rajul al-thani* (the title even echoes the classic British film noir of 1949, *The Third Man*) is a superior cops-and-robbers tale in which a detective seeks to bring down a criminal gang. The "second man" is Esmat Kazim, second-in-command of a smuggling operation between Egypt and Lebanon, which uses his cabaret in Cairo as a front. Ibrahim, the smuggling ring's man in Beirut, is murdered in a dispute with Esmat. When the police relay news of the murder to Ibrahim's sister Lamia, a former singer at Esmat's cabaret and an old flame of his, she decides to take revenge by cooperating with the police to bring Esmat to justice.

Director Izz al-Din zu-l-Fiqar employs many of the tropes of crime movies of the period, particularly the chiaroscuro lighting—check out the scene in which he places the police officer, Kamal, in stripes of shadow as he watches Esmat sexually harassing Lamia.

RIGHT Esmat (Rushdi Abaza, *left*), Lamia (Sabah, *right*)

عزالدين ذوالفقار يقدم
الرجل الثاني
سامية جمال
صباح
صلاح ذوالفقار
رشدي اباظه
اخراج
عزالدين ذوالفقار
جسور
حوار
يوسف جوهر
مدير التصوير
وحيد فريد
توزيع
شركة الشرق لتوزيع الأفلام
فن الطباعه الحديثه ت ٧٦١٥٠

As the gangster Esmat, Rushdi Abaza succeeds in portraying the inner and outer life of his character, giving us a criminal who is a true mastermind and a worthy adversary for the police. Salah zu-l-Fiqar plays his role, as Akram, with almost indecent ease, the police officer who would give his life for his country and his duty. Sabah, playing Lamia, and Samya Gamal, playing Samraa, formed a wonderful double female lead. Esmat is the leader of a gang; he has a casino-like shop, and one of the employees there is the dancer Samraa, who manages the finances of those who go to gamble, and who is also Esmat's girlfriend. Lamia was recruited by the police to be part of a complicated ruse to entrap Esmat. Kamal, the police officer, was disguised and sent undercover as Lamia's brother, Akram. Lamia asks Esmat if she can return to work with him, under the ruse of protecting her brother. Esmat agrees because he is in love with Lamia, and confesses to her that he is the Second Man in the gang. ★

KEY SCENE

The key scene sees Esmat tricked by his girlfriend Samraa. When Esmat takes Lamia to Samraa's house, taking advantage of the fact that Samraa is out of town with Kamal (who is actually a police officer, but plays the part of Akram, Lamia's brother, as part of a complicated ruse), Kamal finds out that Esmat plans to introduce Lamia to the First Man. He abandons his travel plans, and hides in the trunk of their car. When they get to the house, Esmat starts to make advances to Lamia. She asks him when the First Man is coming. He tells her that he is not coming that night. She starts to leave; he stops her and starts touching her by force. Kamal, unable to watch, bursts in with his weapon drawn, and berates Esmat for making advances on his "sister" (as she has been presented to the gang). Esmat takes Lamia hostage, and pulls out his own gun, threatening to kill Kamal if he does not explain immediately why he is back unexpectedly from Alexandria. At this point, Samraa emerges from her hiding place. "He came back from Alexandria because he's in love with me!" she declares. "You've neglected me long enough. We're getting married." Kamal picks up the tale, affirming that he did not kill Samraa because she is his bride-to-be. This is another layer of cover-up devised by Samraa to protect Akram. Esmat asks why they really came back. Samraa says that she called the hospital where their daughter is, and they said she was in critical condition and needed an urgent surgery; she came back to the hospital with Kamal, then they both came home to find Esmat being unfaithful to her. Esmat laughs, but Samraa shuts him up: "Our daughter is dead!" Esmat is stunned. The phone rings. He listens and leaves, promising to meet the next day. After he exits, Samraa tells Kamal that she was motivated by revenge on Esmat for the death of their child.

Sira' fi-l-Nil

Struggle on the Nile | 1959

A journey up the Nile becomes a metaphysical rite of passage into manhood complete with violence and sexual pitfalls

THIS MOVIE INTRODUCED several brand-new uses of location and cinematography never before seen in Egyptian cinema. The story follows the waterborne journey of naive young Muhassib, who is tasked by his father, the village chief, with taking a dilapidated sailing boat, the *Bride of the Nile*, down to Cairo, where it is to be sold to raise money to purchase a new motorized vessel. Accompanying Muhassib is the dependable Megahed. However, a ruthless business rival has managed to place his man Hisham among the *Bride*'s small crew, with the job of sabotaging the mission. In addition to the human characters, the Nile looms large on screen, its heavy presence almost threatening to upstage the actors. Equally important is the *Bride* itself, which provides the dramatic setting for much of the action. Filming aboard the boat provided director Atif Salim with some unique

Director Atif Salim

Screenplay Ali al-Zurqani

Story Ali al-Zurqani

Dialogue Ali al-Zurqani

Produced by Gamal al-Leithi Films

Music Fu'ad al-Zahiri

Director of photography Cello Cicivelli

Editors Emile Bahari and Hussein Ahmad

Set design Anton Polysius

Starring Hind Rustum, Rushdi Abaza, Omar Sharif, Ahmad al-Haddad, Hassan Hamid, Mahmud Farag, Hassan al-Barudi, Tahani Rashid, Nazim Sha'rawi, Said Khalil, Mohamed Qandil, Abd al-Ghani al-Nagdi, al-Tukhi Tawfiq, Muhsin Hassanein

Running time 121 minutes

First screening 28 December 1959

Black and white

LEFT Megahed (Rushdi Abaza, *center*), (Mahmud Farag, *left*), (Mohamed Qandil, *right*)

صراع فى النيل
هند رستم
عمر الشريف

problems to overcome, with hardly any room for the bulky and unwieldy camera equipment, particularly those scenes shot in the cabins below decks.

The fine cinematography is beautifully complemented by Fu'ad al-Zahiri's score, one of the loveliest composed for an Egyptian movie. This was not, as much film music of the time was, a mishmash of music appropriated from elsewhere, but an original composition. The romantic scenes between Muhassib and his village love, Warda, were accompanied by the throaty notes of the *nayy*, the traditional Egyptian reed flute. When the boat is being loaded up with traditional Upper Egyptian clay pots, this is soundtracked by the Sayyid Darwish composition "al-Qullal al-Qinawi" ("Pots from Qena").

Omar Sharif is solid in the central role of the feckless Muhassib, who seems determined to bring about ruin for his father and the village, irrespective of the malign scheming of Hisham. Rushdi Abaza is also excellent as Megahed, the strong and chivalrous Upper Egyptian, who does his best to shepherd Muhassib and is forced to step in and right his wrongs on numerous occasions. Most impressive of all, though, is Hind Rustum as the wantonly sensuous Nargis, a dancer who charms her way onboard the *Bride* and becomes a dangerous distraction, eventually driving a wedge between Muhassib—with whom she enters into a quickie marriage—and Megahed that ends in violence. Of course, Nargis gets her comeuppance and the horny and irresponsible Muhassib returns home to his welcoming fiancée as if nothing ever happened. ★

Megahed and Muhassib are summoned by the village foreman Gad, Muhassib's father. "I am old," he tells Megahed, "as old and useless as the *Nile Bride*." The boat has outlived its usefulness, he tells them, and he has decided to sell it and buy a motorized barge to keep up with the changing times. "They," he says, meaning the fishermen in his employ, "are with me in this, and they have sold everything they own to raise the money for the new boat." This money is to be taken on the *Nile Bride* to Cairo, where it and the boat will be handed over in exchange for the new vessel. "I'm trusting you," says Gad, "with the *Nile Bride*, with Muhassib, and with the money." Gad gives the money to Megahed, who tells Muhassib, "You carry it, you're a man now." Gad rips the earring out of his son's ear, indicating that such childish things are finished now. The foreman then reiterates his instruction to Megahed to safeguard the money and Muhassib: "I'm trusting you with both." Inevitably, at the first stop they make, Muhassib loses the money and, soon after, loses himself to the charms of the dancer Nargis.

Law'at al-hubb

Agony of Love | 1960

A neglected new bride finds solace in the arms of her violent railroad-loving husband's assistant

Director Salah Abu Seif

Screenplay Salah Abu Seif, Galil al-Bindari, and Sayyid Bedeir

Story Galil al-Bindari

Dialogue Sayyid Bedeir

Produced by Mohamed Afifi Films

Music Fu'ad al-Zahiri

Director of photography Wadid Sirry

Editor Emile Bahari

Set design Anton Polysius

Starring Shadya, Ahmad Mazhar, Omar Sharif, Layla Karim, Aziza Hilmi, Thuraya Fakhri, Esmat Mahmud, Said Khalil, Salwa Izz al-Din, Shafiq Nur al-Din, Abd al-Ghani al-Nagdi, Hussein Ismail

Running time 110 minutes

First screening 24 March 1960

Black and white

THE PIONEER OF EGYPTIAN cinematic realism, Salah Abu Seif, found great riches to be mined in Galil al-Bindari's tale of a wife-abusing railroad engineer. The camera lens became a microscope through which to examine the engineer's life in intimate detail, poring over his relationships with his wife and his job. The quest for authenticity carries through into the dialogue, which, daringly for the time, is peppered with the vocabulary and speech patterns of the lower classes. The engineer calls a co-worker who treats his wife kindly a *khushni*, which is not quite a curse word but an uncouth way of implying a lack of manhood. The message is also similarly low class: in order to be a man, you need to keep your woman in her place. The dialogue also includes plenty of real-seeming railroad jargon in the conversations that take place between the engine

RIGHT Mahmud (Ahmad Mazhar, *center*), Amal (Shadya, *right*), Hassan (Omar Sharif, *left*)

SVassiliou
افلام محمد عفيفي تقدم
عمر الشريف
شادية
احمد مظهر
لوعة الحب
اخراج صلاح ابو سيف
قصة جليل البنداري
حوار السيد بدير
مدير التصوير وحيد فريد
توزيع دولار فيلم
مطابع الوسيط بمصر ت ٤٢١١٦
Dimitri

drivers. In one scene, a girl comes into the bar where the men are drinking to ask her father to come outside and speak to her mother. He is reluctant to oblige; "He'll arrive on time," one of his comrades tells the girl. Later, someone else says, "Slam on the brakes, Khalil, you need to brake in time!" and a colleague is described as having a really good voice, "Like a diesel engine."

While the engineer is the motor of the movie, its heart is his poor, downtrodden wife Amal. She is played by Shadya, who is wonderful in this movie as a bride expecting love from her new husband but receiving instead only a tirade of verbal and emotional abuse. Her affair with the gentle and soft-spoken young Hassan (Omar Sharif), her husband's assistant, is almost inevitable. Abu Seif even manages to bring the railway into the couple's furtive romance: when the two have a secret date, the place they choose as somewhere they are unlikely to be seen is Cairo's Railway Museum. In the museum, Abu Seif allows the camera to linger on various exhibits. At one point, the couple's wooing is halted by a museum guide who expounds on one of the museum's attractions. As sweet as this romance is, audiences were still largely in approval when at the end of the film the engineer seems to undergo a transformation from tyrant to loving husband and Amal returns to the marital home. ★

KEY SCENE

The pivotal scene comes nearly at the end of the movie, when we begin to see the transformation in the way the formerly brutish engineer now behaves toward Amal. It begins with him extending the unexpected courtesy of informing his wife that he might be late home. He pets the cat his wife is holding—previously he was more likely to kick the animal. "Why are you upset, kitty?" he says pleasantly. "I didn't like that cat at first," he says, "but now I can't live without her." His wife responds: "The cat couldn't stand to live in this house either. She was always wanting to get out." This is as close as she will get to admitting that she wanted to run off with Hassan, the only man who treated her with affection until now. "Does the cat feel happy now living here?" asks the engineer. "Of course she does," his wife replies. "The cat will only grow to like you more, you know. She might end up never leaving the house at all." The husband bids wife and cat a fond farewell.

Suq al-silah

Arms Market | 1960

A bellydancer seeks revenge on the drug dealer who caused the death of her father and brother

THIS CRIME THRILLER pits two cinematic heavyweights against each other and adds a beautiful and vengeful bellydancer into the mix. The story revolves around Shakkura (Mahmud al-Miligi) and the double life he leads. In his native alley, he wears traditional Egyptian garb and plays the role of the *mi'allim*, a boss, commanding the respect of his neighbors and peers. He performs the pilgrimage to Mecca, and his return home is celebrated with dancing and singing. But unknown to these simple folk, he has another life. In his opulent mansion far from the alley, he wears Western suits and silk ties, and acts the part of the modern businessman. Only the business he deals in is drugs. He meets his nemesis in Sayyid (Farid Shawqi), a simple man from

Director Kamal Attiya

Screenplay Galil al-Bindari, Abd al-Hayy Adib, and Bahgat Qamar

Story Galil al-Bindari

Dialogue Galil al-Bindari, Abd al-Hayy Adib, and Bahgat Qamar

Produced by Aflam al-Nagm al-Fiddi (Silver Star Films)

Director of photography Mustafa Hassan

Editor Hussein Afifi

Set design Hilmi Azab

Starring Huda Sultan, Farid Shawqi, Mahmud al-Miligi, Hassan Yusuf, Said Khalil, Mohamed Rida, Abd al-Salam Mohamed, Mohamed Subeih

Running time 111 minutes

First screening 2 June 1960

Black and white

LEFT Sayyid (Farid Shawqi, *left*), Shakkura (Mahmud al-Miligi, *right*)

أفلام النجم الفضي تقدم
سوق السلاح
هدى سلطان
فريد شوقي
محمود المليجي
إخراج
كمال عطيه
تصوير
مصطفى حسن
مدير الانتاج
صالح العوضي
توزيع: عبد الرحيم يزدي
ستوديو
مطابع النصر
Dimitri

the country who has come to the city looking for work. He has little success and eventually settles for joining Shakkura's gang. He has no liking for the drug lord but is smart enough to hide his disdain behind a veneer of sycophancy. For his part, Shakkura quite admires this burly *fallah*, who is able to take on all his men and beat them in a fistfight. As he gains his boss's trust, Sayyid reveals his ambition and negotiates with Shakkura for the chance to conduct a major drug deal himself (*see* the Key Scene box). Matters become complicated when Sayyid falls for bellydancer Bahiya (Huda Sultan), who has more than just love on her mind: she is seeking revenge on Shakkura for causing the death of her father and brother.

The dark and twisty plot inspires some suitably stark and dramatic cinematography, notably a fight between Sayyid and some policemen under a bridge on the Nile, which uses off-kilter camera angles to striking effect. The editing is fast-paced and flowing, and keeps the story rattling along to its ultimate and morally correct end. ★

KEY SCENE

This is where Sayyid plays his hand with Shakkura for the first time. The scene is Shakkura's house. Sayyid asks the boss why he is so preoccupied. "People are like booze," says Shakkura. "Some are a fine vintage, and some are watered-down and low-class." He thanks the Lord that he has managed to let go of some of his men who are of the latter quality. There is a big drug deal coming up on which a lot of money is riding. "So who's going to carry out the deal?" says Sayyid. Shakkura tells him that the candidate for this deal has to be a good man. Sayyid offers himself. Shakkura says why not, but then Sayyid asks for half the profits. Shakkura is stunned at his greed. "I put my whole fortune into this," he reminds him. "Well," says Sayyid, "whoever goes to Shubra with the drugs is putting his whole life on the line." Shakkura rejects Sayyid's offer: "I'll do it myself." Sayyid wishes him good luck. Shakkura walks out onto the balcony, unsure what to do. He does not notice Bahiya's assistant, who has been spying on the pair's conversation.

Bidaya wa nihaya

Beginning and End | 1960

A young man from a poor family succeeds in becoming a police officer only to find his sister has been working as a prostitute to support him

Director Salah Abu Seif

Screenplay Salah Izz al-Din

Story Naguib Mahfouz

Dialogue Ahmad Shukri and Kamil Abd al-Salam

Produced by Dinar Film

Music Fu'ad al-Zahiri

Director of photography Kamal Karim

Editor Emile Bahari

Set design Hilmi Azab

Starring Farid Shawqi, Omar Sharif, Amina Rizq, Amal Farid, Kamal Hussein, Salah Mansur, Sana' Gamil, Abd al-Khalek Salih, Hamid Mursi, Galal Issa, Ya'qub Mikhail, Samya Rushdi, Mukhtar Hussein, Hussein Ismail

Festivals Moscow International Film Festival. Also won the State Award for Best Director.

Running time 130 minutes

First screening 31 October 1960

Black and white

AMINA RIZQ IS key to the success of this movie. She is the widowed matriarch struggling to raise a brood of three sons and their sister Nafisa on next to no money. The oldest son, Hassan, turns to petty crime and consorts with prostitutes, which is tolerated as long as he continues to contribute financially. Another son, Hussein, quits his studies and leaves Cairo to find work elsewhere to earn much-needed cash. The youngest son, Hassanein, is the chief beneficiary of his brothers' earnings, as they are paying for him to train as a police officer. Rizq's steeliness in the face of unremitting hardship and grief had audiences just as in thrall to her as her sons. Audiences never felt it the least implausible that Hassan, Hussein, and Hassanein obeyed

RIGHT Hassan (Farid Shawqi, *left*), Omar (Omar Sharif, *center*), Nafisa (Sana' Gamil, *right*)

دينار فيلم
تقدم
قصة
نجيب محفوظ
بداية ونهاية
بدايه ونهايه
فريد شوقي
عمر الشريف
امينه رزق
امال فريد
كمال حسين
مع نجمة المسرح
سناء جميل
اخراج
صلاح ابو سيف
مدير التصوير
كمال كريم
توزيع : دولار فيلم

this woman without question, showing subservience and sometimes even fear of their mother. A lesser actress could not have commanded the respect of hulking, wayward Hassan but even bad boys are cowed by Rizq.

Omar Sharif is also praiseworthy as the self-centered Hassanein, especially in the final scene (*see* the Key Scene box), while Farid Shawqi, as Hassan, pulls off the trick of concealing a core of gentleness beneath a bullish and aggressive exterior. It is hard to say which of the two actors, Sharif or Shawqi, upstages the other. In fact, why try? The clear winner in this contest is clearly the audience. Interestingly, despite the many story and screenwriting credits already to his name, this was the first adaptation of a Naguib Mahfouz novel for the cinema. The resounding success of *Bidaya wa nihaya* ensured that it would not be the last. ★

KEY SCENE

The brothers' sister, Nafisa (wonderfully played by Sana' Gamil), is a plain but sweet girl whose life is ruined when the object of her affections gets her into bed, then goes off and marries someone else. Before long she has become a prostitute and the money she earns she contributes to the family fund to advance Hassanein's career. One day Nafisa is arrested, which leads to Hassanein finding out about her career path. Terrified that if he kills her his career will be ruined, Nafisa offers to commit suicide to preserve family honor. Hassanein takes her up on the offer and leads her to the Nile, where he commands her to kill herself. As he watches from behind a tree, the soundtrack heavy and tense with Hassanein's heavy breathing, two people pass by, forcing Nafisa to momentarily postpone her death. Hassanein slumps in relief, clearly now wanting some deus ex machina to swoop in and save his sister as he struggles to resolve his own emotional conflict. Nafisa resumes climbing the fence to get to the river, while Hassanein's mind races. His breathing crescendoes as he is overcome with an intense sympathy for his sister. He screams her name—but too late. His self-centeredness comes back to the fore when a policeman asks him if she is any relation to him and he answers no. He watches as her body is pulled from the river, and as he does so he considers her life, crushed by poverty and driven to death by those who were supposed to love her. Hassanein throws himself into the Nile.

Fi baytina rajul

A Man in Our House | 1961

A revolutionary convicted of assassinating the prime minister escapes from a hospital and hides in the home of his apolitical friend

THIS FILM STANDS as one of director Henri Barakat's greatest achievements. It is a glorious piece of nationalist propaganda that stars Omar Sharif as Ibrahim Hamdi, a university student whose desire to see Egypt freed from British rule leads him to murder the Egyptian prime minister. Afterward he takes refuge in the home of a classmate, putting the whole family in danger. Matters become more complicated when Hamdi falls in love with the young daughter of the house, a love that is reciprocated, and even more complicated when a slimy cousin discovers Hamdi is in hiding and blackmails the family.

Barakat sets the historical tone for the movie with a voice-over that booms at the start: "The events of this film took place before

Director Henri Barakat

Screenplay Yusuf Issa and Henri Barakat

Story Ihsan Abd al-Quddus

Dialogue Yusuf Issa

Produced by Henri Barakat

Music Fu'ad al-Zahiri

Director of photography Wadid Sirry

Editor Fathi Qasim

Set design Maher Abd al-Nour

Starring Zubayda Tharwat, Omar Sharif, Rushdi Abaza, Zahrat al-Ula, Hassan Yusuf, Tawfiq al-Diqin, Hussein Riyad, Nahid Samir, Abd al-Khalek Salih, Zaki Abd al-Magid, Yusuf Sha'ban

Festivals New Delhi International Film Festival, India, where it won Best Picture. The film also won the Catholic Center's prize for Best Picture.

Running time 153 minutes

First screening 17 April 1961

Black and white

LEFT Ibrahim (Omar Sharif, *right*), Nawal (Zubayda Tharwat, *left*)

افلام بركات تقدم
قصة
احسان عبد القدوس
زبيده ثروت
عمر الشريف
زهرة العلا
حسن يوسف
الممثل الكبير
حسين رياض
بالاشتراك مع
رشدي اباظه
اخراج
بركات
في بيتنا رجل
سيناريو يوسف عيسى ، بركات
تصوير وحيد فريد
توزيع الاقليم الجنوبي افلام بركات
توزيع الخارج المتحدة للسينما

the miracle of the Revolution, when Egypt was suffering under occupation for over seventy years, and when colonialism insinuated its paid puppets into the highest echelons of government. Colonialism succeeded in its nefarious goal of splitting Egyptians up into factions fighting for political power, and fighting among themselves." This opening narration aside, Barakat otherwise avoids heavy-handed exposition and concentrates on the story. The movie includes some powerful scenes, such as when soldiers open fire on students marching on the bridge; this is so well done that it has an almost documentary-like feel. The camerawork and direction are similarly terrific in the scene in which Hamdi encounters the corpse of a martyr lying in a room. Barakat places Hamdi at the door with the light falling on his face and his eyes ablaze; he casts his shadow into the room, and it is as if Hamdi is standing at the dividing line between the shining life that lies behind him and the death that lies before him in the darkened room.

Omar Sharif reaffirms his star quality, speaking volumes with just a look and making for a truly charismatic revolutionary. Rushdi Abaza also excells as Abd al-Hamid, the man with no principles in life, and cousin of Muhy, played by Hassan Yusuf. The film was a box-office smash and deservedly so. It kindled patriotic feelings as many audience members saw themselves as an Ibrahim Hamdi or an Abd al-Hamid. ★

The film says that every true Egyptian bears a trove of patriotic feeling within their breast. It lies dormant, masked by everyday routine, family obligations, and work, but when the time comes, it shines out. This is most clearly embodied in the scene in which Ibrahim Hamdi, the revolutionary fighter, bids goodbye to the members of the family that have bravely sheltered him at great personal risk. The young daughter Nawal is overcome, having fallen in love with him: she hands him half of a scrap of paper with the Islamic credo scrawled on it (a nod to the popular belief that two such halves will always one day be reunited). Zahir Effendi, the paterfamilias, wishes him safe travels and gives him some money. The mother, visibly moved, gives him a small copy of the Qur'an. The eldest daughter, Samya, wishes him well. In short, the entire family's affections and aspirations go with him, and they are unable to eat their breakfast after watching him, tearfully, until he is out of sight.

Dima' 'ala al-Nil

Blood on the Nile | 1961

A woman seeking revenge for the murder of her husband becomes stranded on an island with his killer

Director Niazi Mustafa

Screenplay Abd al-Hayy Adib

Story Niazi Mustafa

Dialogue Ahmad Shukri, Bahgat Qamar

Produced by Gamal al-Leithi Films

Music Fu'ad al-Zahiri

Director of photography Cello Cicivelli

Editor Hussein Ahmad

Set design Anton Polysius

Starring Farid Shawqi, Hind Rustum, Amina Rizq, Fakhir Fakhir, Hassan Yusuf, Mahmud Farag, Salwa Mahmud, Hassan Hamid, Ahmad al-Haddad, Mohamed Subeih, Said Khalil, Abd al-Ghani al-Nagdi, Hassan Atlah

Running time 100 minutes

First screening 24 May 1961

Black and white

CASHING IN ON the success of Atif Salim's 1959 hit *Sira' fi-l-Nil* *(see page 125)*, Niazi Mustafa decided to recycle many of the same elements for his next movie. Included on his list were Upper Egyptian village locations, scenes in and around ancient temples and ruins, lots of shots of the Nile, scenes set on sailboats and in their below-decks cabins, and, not least, many of the same actors, including Hind Rustum, Mahmud Farag, Hassan Hamid, Ahmad al-Haddad, and Abd al-Ghani al-Nagdi. At least the story is different. For his movie, Mustafa concocted a story dealing with the issue of blood feuds, which at the time was a serious problem that threatened to destroy the villages and even towns of Upper Egypt. The film, which received a state subsidy, sought to play a part in warning against this destructive practice.

In *Dima' 'ala al-Nil*, an out-of-control blood feud between two families has sunk its claws into Ghaliya, who is bound to avenge her murdered husband. The killer is a man called Awad. She intrigues her way onto his boat and makes a couple of failed attempts to do away with him before they end up on an island together, at which point she falls in love him, particularly after Awad enlightens her as to her husband's treachery: "I wish he were alive so I could kill him myself," she says. As a backdrop to the drama, Mustafa's use of exterior locations is masterful: he makes good use of Upper Egypt's profusion of photogenic ancient monuments and even weaves in documentary footage of local folk

افلام جمال الليثي
تقدم
فريد شوقي
هند رستم
امينه رزق محمود فرج
فاخر فاخر سلوى محمود
حسن حامد
حسن يوسف
دماء
على النيل

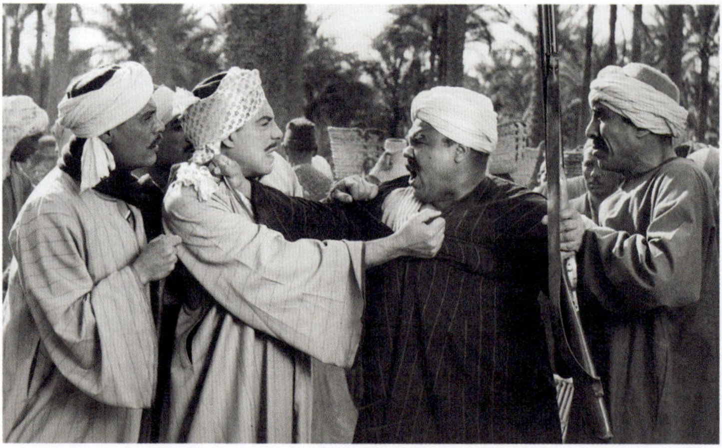

RIGHT Awad (Farid Shawqi, *left-center*), Hamdan (Mahmud Farag, *right-center*)

traditions. Farid Shawqi is good as the "killer" Awad, pulling off the crucial feat of winning the audience over to his side. Hind Rustum is even better as Ghaliya: hers was not an easy role but she manages to convince in her dramatic shift from would-be murderess to protective lover. Fakhir Fakhir, as Sheikh Salim, who harbors animosity against another tribe because he got blinded by a fire which they started on his land, offers up one of his finest roles, showing us the fire in his soul that leads him to exact vengeance for his son, and his father before him. His blindness—caused by an accident planned by the rival family—is a convincing motivation for his continued vocal desire for vengeance and perpetuation of a spiral of violence that will ultimately pull his children down to ruin. He lives in the past and cannot see—quite literally—the good a different course might bring. His performance elevates the movie onto another plane. ★

KEY SCENE

Stuck on the island and having taken refuge in a cave, Ghaliya wakes. Her emotions have undergone a complete transformation: she now cares deeply for the man she had formerly sworn to kill. Seeing him still asleep, she reaches out to touch his forehead tenderly and pulls the covers up over him. Looking up at the mouth of the cave, she sees a wolf standing there and she draws back in fear. She reaches for the rifle, which is loaded with a single bullet. She raises the rifle and fires, killing the wolf. Awad starts awake. He sees the dead wolf. "Why did you waste the bullet?" he asks. "You were going to kill me with it." She tells him, "You don't deserve to die. The one who did deserve to die is already dead." He confesses his love for her and she does likewise. He pulls her to him.

Tariq al-dumu'

Path of Tears | 1961

An aspiring actor stops at nothing to get to the top, jettisoning family and friends along the way

ANWAR WAGDI WAS an actor, director, producer, and all-around colossus of Egyptian cinema until his premature death, aged fifty, of polycystic kidney disease in 1955. Coming from a notably poor background, his rise was fueled by extraordinary ambition and a desire never to experience poverty again. Kamal al-Shinnawi had acted under Wagdi's direction in the 1951 movie *Laylat al-Henna (Henna Night)*, and ten years later those experiences fed into *Tariq al-dumu'*, which is a biopic of Wagdi's life. Al-Shinnawi wrote the story, produced, and played the part of Ashraf Hamdi, which was Wagdi in all but name; he would probably have directed the movie himself if he could, but instead was obliged to hire Hilmi Halim. Wagdi and al-Shinnawi had had a troubled, on-again-off-again friendship, but al-Shinnawi is never less than respectful to his subject. In playing Ashraf

Director Hilmi Halim

Screenplay Sayyid Bedeir

Story Kamal al-Shinnawi

Dialogue Sayyid Bedeir

Produced by Kamal al-Shinnawi

Director of photography Ali Hassan

Editors Albert Naguib and Nabil Abd al-Aziz

Set design Shadi Abd al-Salam

Starring Kamal al-Shinnawi, Sabah, Layla Fawzi, Abd al-Mun'im Ibrahim, Hamid Mursi, Abd al-Aziz Ahmad, Mohamed Tawfiq, Nazim Sha'rawi, Samya Rushdi, Said Khalil, Ni'mat al-Miligi, Layla Fahmi

Festivals Won Best Egyptian Picture and Best Actor (Kamal al-Shinnawi) from the Catholic Center.

Running time 125 minutes

First screening 26 November 1961

Black and white

LEFT Samya Fu'ad (Sabah, *right*), Ashraf (Kamal al-Shinnawi, *left*)

افلام كمال الشناوي تقدم
صباح
كمال الشناوي
ليلى فوزي
عبد المنعم ابراهيم
عبد العزيز احمد
حامد مرسي
محمد توفيق
نعمات المليجي
طريق الدموع
SVassiliou
مدير التصوير
على حسن
انتاج
كمال الشناوي
مصطفى حسن السراج
توزيع
شركة الشرق
اخراج
حلمي حليم
Dimitri
مطبعة الرغائب

Hamdi, he did not mimic Wagdi but treated him as a character in his own right, albeit one whose life follows the same trajectory, starting out poor before accruing riches through a combination of hard work and chicanery. Most of the drama comes from the protagonist's struggle to amass the hundred thousand pounds he dreams of.

Support in the movie comes from Sabah, who plays the woman to whom Wagdi was married and divorced three times, another icon of Egyptian cinema, Layla Murad (although she carries the name Samya in the film). Murad lived until 1995, which might explain why Sabah's portrayal is pleasant but bland—she had no wish to offend. Abd al-Mun'im Ibrahim is his usual charismatic and beloved self as Said, Ashraf Hamdi's one-time roommate and close confidant, until he was washed away in the wake of his ambitious friend. He is the counterpoint to the Wagdi character, holding fast to his morals and not interested in getting rich quick. Credit goes to another cinematic legend, Shadi Abd al-Salam, whose set designs for the movie often speak more eloquently than the script, whether evoking a squalid, shared attic room or the opulence of the office of Ashraf Hamdi. ★

When Ashraf Hamdi visits his friend Said in the impoverished living quarters they once shared together, he finds him tearing into his customary meal of fuul, falafel, and pickled eggplant. Said welcomes him warmly and invites Ashraf to share his meal. Ashraf tells him, "I'm not allowed to eat that kind of thing. Kidney disease." Said is shocked—he hadn't realized Ashraf was so ill. "I wanted to visit you. I just wasn't sure you wouldn't throw me out." Ashraf apologizes for his conduct toward Said. He tells him that his bank account has just hit one hundred thousand pounds. Said congratulates him but wishes him, more importantly, good health. "That's gotten worse," says Ashraf miserably. "At least you can afford the best healthcare money can buy," says Said. Yes, he has made the money he always wanted, admits Ashraf, but he has also managed to lose everyone he ever cared about along the way. Said, he says, has always stood by him and never expected anything in return. Ashraf then asks if he can spend the night. Said agrees and Ashraf suggests they draw lots for the bed, just as they used to do in the old days. Said refuses and tells Ashraf to take the bed, not because he's ill, but because he is a guest and a beloved friend. He finds him some fresh pajamas. Ashraf looks around at his old room, regretting his youth which he spent here.

La tutfi' al-shams

Don't Turn Out the Sun | 1961

An aristocratic Cairo family is torn apart following the death of its patriarch

Director Salah Abu Seif

Screenplay Lucien Lambert

Story Ihsan Abd al-Quddus

Dialogue Ihsan Abd al-Quddus

Produced by Omar Sharif and Ahmad Ramzi

Music Ali Ismail

Director of photography Abd al-Halim Nasr

Editors Hussein Ahmad and Abd al-Aziz Fakhri

Set design Maher Abd al-Nour

Starring Shukri Sarhan, Fatin Hamama, Ahmad Ramzi, Aquila Ratib, Imad Hamdi, Layla Tahir, Nadia Lutfi, Shirin, Samiha Ayyub, Abd al-Khalek Salih, Layla Sidqi, Omar zu-l-Fiqar, Mohamed Hamdi, Mohamed Ilwan, Omar al-Turguman, Adil al-Hilmi

Running time 142 minutes

First screening 25 December 1961

Black and white

OPPOSITE Ahmad (Shukri Sarhan, *left*), Shahira (Nadia Lutfi, *right*)

MADE INTO A HIT TV series for Ramadan 2017, Ihsan Abd al-Quddus's novel *La tutfi' al-shams* first reached the screen in the form of this classic 1961 movie. It follows the fortunes of a wealthy Cairo family following the death of its patriarch. The eldest son, Ahmad, shoulders his responsibilities as the new man of the house, while younger brother Mamduh goes off the rails. There is more trouble with daughter Layla, who pursues a romance with an older, married man. In other hands, this could be a run-of-the-mill soap, but what elevates this family saga is the quality of the writing and, in particular, the dialogue, which was supplied by al-Quddus himself. He was particularly skilled at teasing out character through language. For example, Mamduh's lines embody his rebellious nature in the face of his conservative family; he attempts to convince his brother Ahmad that he was right to sell newspapers and magazines at the gates of his college, speaking in the slang of the time: "I flew to the Faculty of Law," he says. Ahmad, on the other hand, uses words and phrases that are stilted and bound by tradition. The thoughts and words of Layla, their sister, are colored with romance. Meanwhile, another sister, Fifi, is in a relationship with a teaching assistant; their conversation is intellectual, bespeaking a love of ideas. They deliberately avoid talk of romance, treating their relationship as a scientific experiment, one in which the results are not yet in.

Appropriately for a movie that places emphasis on what the audience hears as much as what it sees, the music also speaks volumes. When Ahmad meets his girl Shahira at the sporting club, but is held back by shyness from confessing his love for her, and during Layla's meetings with her paramour Fathi, the music is soft and dreamy; later, it segues into a minor key when Layla is waiting for an oblivious Fathi at his apartment after she has run away from home.

The showy role belongs to Ahmad Ramzi as Mamduh, the young firebrand out to grasp a future filled with excitement and new experiences until, following a fight with his brother, he jumps onto his motorbike and speeds away to his tragic and accidental death. Shukri Sarhan brings to the role of Ahmad a great maturity. Trapped in a job he hates, he nevertheless always does the right thing until, after his brother's death, he starts to see that his more adventurous outlook was not without merit. Meanwhile, Aquila Ratib is superb as the adrift mother trying to do the best for her children. ★

KEY SCENE

Solid, reliable Ahmad is not always as upright as he seems, as his girlfriend Shahira realizes when she discovers him with a prostitute. He goes to her at the sporting club and implores her to listen to him. He loves her and has quit his hated job, he tells her, to start a new life. And he will no longer visit prostitutes! "Don't pay attention to what people say! You and I are the whole world," he tells her. He reiterates his love for her and apologizes for his past actions. He picks up her puppy. "She likes you," says Shahira, using the popular ploy of the pet as proxy *(see page 128 Law'at al-hubb)*. He asks Shahira to marry him but she tells him to wait until he finds a good job. As they are talking, a mutual friend appears and asks Ahmad to join him in fighting the War of Attrition against Israel. Shahira says that her younger brother is going to join up, whereupon Ahmad agrees to go too.

Al-Khataya

Sins | 1962

A son learns he is adopted, only to discover he is actually the offspring of his mother and her cousin

HASSAN AL-IMAM was a prolific director. He began his career in the late 1940s and by the time of *al-Khataya* he had already racked up directorial credits on something like forty movies. What makes this one stand out is its perfect casting of singing star Abd al-Halim Hafiz. The story concerns a troubled relationship between a son, Hussein (Abd al-Halim Hafiz), and his disapproving, authoritarian father (Imad Hamdi). The nature of the beleaguered son, a melancholic, wispy, awkward boy-next-door, is perfectly suited to Hafiz, who led a life equally tragic: Hafiz was born into poverty, raised an orphan, and suffered from bilharzia. Audiences loved to wallow in pity with Abd al-Halim Hafiz.

The key scene, and one which alone secures the movie a place in the annals of Egyptian cinema, is the callous reveal (*see* the Key Scene

Director Hassan al-Imam

Screenplay Mohamed Mustafa Sami with Mohamed Uthman

Story Mohamed Uthman

Dialogue Mohamed Mustafa Sami

Produced by Aflam Sawt al-Fann (Voice of Art Films)

Director of photography Wahid Farid

Editor Albert Naguib

Set design Shadi Abd al-Salam

Starring Abd al-Halim Hafiz, Nadia Lutfi, Hassan Yusuf, Madiha Yusri, Imad Hamdi, Fakhir Fakhir, Kamal Hussein, Galal Issa, Zain al-Ashmawi, Abd al-Ghani al-Nagdi, Muhsin Hassanein, Ahmad Shawqi, Mimi Gamal, Fathiya Ali, Mamduh Shukri

Running time 147 minutes

First screening 4 March 1962

Black and white

LEFT Mahmud (Imad Hamdi, *right*), Ahmad (Hassan Yusuf, *center*), Hussein (Abd al-Halim Hafiz, *left*)

box) when the audience and Hussein learn that he is adopted. As good as Hafiz is, this scene belongs to Imad Hamdi. Questioned by Hussein as to why he has never loved him, his anger escalates until it explodes in an almighty slap.

Madiha Yusri brings pathos to the role of the mother who keeps her secrets locked up inside, determined to do right by both her husband and her son. It is a role that features often in Egyptian cinema, but with this performance she is in a class of her own. The lovely Nadia Lutfi is excellent as the level-headed Suhair, the girl who desires Hussein as a husband even though he is an orphan—this carried a stigma at the time. Another audience favorite was Hassan Yusuf, who provided the comic relief as light-hearted younger brother Ahmad, always ready to make a joke out of everything. Not forgetting, of course, that this is a musical, so as dire as Hussein's life might be, there is always a wonderful song for him to sing, including such classics as "Wehyat albi," "Maghruur," "Ulli haaga," and "al-Helwa." ★

KEY SCENE

Hussein and Ahmad enter the room in which their father sits working. "Where were you?" he asks, and they tell him they were at a party. Hussein is told to be around the next morning as they are going to get a passport for him. Hussein asks why he needs a passport and his father informs him he is going to be sent abroad to study. Hussein asks that the trip be postponed for a year so that he can work and save some money to get married, after which he will happily complete his studies abroad with his wife. "What wife?" asks the father. Hussein tells him it is Suhair, whereupon his father flies into a rage. "You have no right," his father tells him, "to even be in this house." "Why have you been so hard on me all my life?" asks Hussein. "Because I'm not your father!" Ihsan is not his mother nor Ahmad his brother. They adopted him from an orphanage. Seeing his mother at the top of the staircase, Hussein asks her, "Aren't you my mother?" She does not reply. He staggers away, a broken man. (Just so the audience does not leave the cinema too depressed, it later turns out Ihsan is Hussein's biological mother, a fact that even the father did not know.)

افلام صوت الفن تقدم
محمد عبد الوهاب وشركاه
فيلما من اخراج حسن الامام
بطولة
عبد الحليم حافظ
نادية لطفي
حسن يوسف فاخر فاخر
بالاشتراك مع
مديحة يسري
عماد حمدي
الخطايا
مدير التصوير وحيد فريد
مدير الانتاج اديب جابر
توزيع افلام صوت الفن ١٦ شارع عدلي
SVassiliou
Dimitri
مطبعة الرغائب بمصر

جمال الليثي يقدم
شاديه رشدي اباظه
شويكار عبد المنعم ابراهيم حسن فايق
Marcel
الزوجه ١٣
اخراج
فطين عبد الوهاب
قصه علي الزرقاني تصوير كمال كريم
توزيع دولار فيلم
مطابع النصر بمصر والاسكندرية

Al-Zawja raqam 13

Wife No. 13 | 1962

A wealthy womanizer is a serial marrier, but it all stops with wife number thirteen, who decides to institute some reforms

MANY CRITICS REGARD Fatin Abd al-Wahab as the true father of Egyptian comedy. He never resorted to the cheap tricks of many other Egyptian directors, who too often relied on a meanness of spirit to raise laughs, poking fun at gormless stereotypes or, worse, those with an unusual physical appearance or disability. The roots of this tale lie in *The Thousand and One Nights* and, in particular, the story of Sheherazade. That well-worn tale has a succession of wives being led to the sultan's bedchamber and summarily losing their heads the next morning, until one crafty storyteller saves her neck by leaving the king with a cliffhanger. In his movie, Abd al-Wahab has a rich man by the name of Murad Salim marry and divorce his way through twelve women, until the thirteenth breaks the pattern by also holding back.

Director Fatin Abd al-Wahab

Screenplay Ali al-Zurqani and Abu al-Su'ud al-Ibyari

Story Ali al-Zurqani

Dialogue Ali al-Zurqani and Abu al-Su'ud al-Ibyari

Produced by Gamal al-Leithi Pictures

Music Fu'ad al-Zahiri

Director of photography Kamal Karim

Editor Hussein al-Ganayni

Set design Anton Polysius

Starring Shadya, Rushdi Abaza, Abd al-Mun'im Ibrahim, Hassan Fayiq, Zeinab Sidqi, Widad Hamdi, Shwikar, Zinnat Ilwi, Mona Sarhan, Shihab Nisim, Layla Sabri

Festivals Venice, Berlin, Mogadishu, Melbourne

Running time 116 minutes

First screening 5 March 1962

Black and white

LEFT Aida (Shadya, *right*), Murad Salim (Rushdi Abaza, *left*)

To bring his story to the screen he hired two of the best screenwriters in the business: Abu al-Su'ud al-Ibyari, the undisputed king of cinematic comedy, and Ali al-Zurqani, who was a genius with dialogue. In the role of Murad Salim he cast Rushdi Abaza and directed him to new comic heights, courtesy of a series of laugh-out-loud scenarios and set pieces. One of the funniest recurring gags is Salim's repeated attempts to secure a meeting with his wily new wife, whose excuses become increasingly hilarious as the movie progresses. Abaza's pompous self-importance makes every snub and mishap that much funnier. As Aida, wife number thirteen of the title, Shadya is also excellent, but then she was always a wonderful comedienne.

Elsewhere, Hassan Fayiq as Saber Pasha fills the work with his customary lovable lightheartedness. The comedy in his role stems from his status as the former Minister of Religious Endowments and Head of the Council of Elders; his financial situation has deteriorated catastrophically, but not his self-importance and tendency to lord it over others. When a hotel flunky asks that he settle his bill, Saber Pasha looks down his nose at the employee and exclaims, "How dare you? I am one of the masters of this land!" The joke is that he cannot afford to cover the bill. There is a particularly fine bit of fun involving both Rushdi Abaza and Hassan Fayiq as Murad Salim chats with Saber Pasha, the latter remaining blissfully unaware that the flirtatious conversation is directed not at him but at his daughter, Aida. It is a master class in the art of gentle comedy. ★

KEY SCENE

The most memorable part of the movie involves Murad's humiliation at the hands of his gathered exes. They arrive one by one for a surprise birthday party at the home where he lives with his thirteenth wife, Aida. Murad is frantic to conceal their identities from Aida, never suspecting that she is actually orchestrating the proceedings. He offers one ex money to conceal her identity, which she refuses. He pretends another is his sister and another his cousin; a further ex is presented as another sister on the grounds that they shared a wet nurse. The women ply him with liquor and each of them insists on a dance, to his increasing discomfort. More bribes are offered to further ex-wives as they arrive. All the ex-wives take it in turns to dance with Murad until he collapses, drunk and woozy. Nani, one of the wives, picks him up by the hair and goes on dancing with him until he passes out. All the exes leave, and Aida supports him up to their bedroom, barely conscious.

Al-Liss wa-l-kilab

The Thief and the Dogs | 1962

A moralistic thief gets out of jail to find that the world has moved on and left him behind

WHEN NAGUIB MAHFOUZ'S short novel *al-Liss wa-l-kilab* was published in 1961, it was notable for its use of the sort of stream-of-consciousness writing that typically does not lend itself easily to filmic adaptation. Nevertheless, it was only the following year that Kamal El-Cheikh released his film version of the story into cinemas. Despite a dialogue-heavy screenplay, it is a fascinating combination of suspenseful film noir and scathing social commentary, as well as being a work of terrific visual beauty. The movie remains true to the novel's tale of a Robin–Hoodlike thief, Said Mahran, who, after four years in prison, emerges into a changed world: his wife has abandoned him for his former best friend and they are keeping his six-year-old daughter from him. Just as crushing, his former mentor, Ra'uf

ABOVE Said Mahran Bayyumi (Shukri Sarhan, *left*), Nur (Shadya, *right*)

Director Kamal El-Cheikh

Screenplay Sabri Izzat and Kamal El-Cheikh

Story Naguib Mahfouz

Dialogue Sabri Izzat

Produced by Gamal al-Leithi Pictures

Music Andre Ryder

Director of photography Kamal Karim

Editor Said al-Sheikh

Set design Maher Abd al-Nour

Starring Shadya, Kamal al-Shinnawi, Shukri Sarhan, Fakhir Fakhir, Adli Kasib, Salah Mansur, Salwa Mahmud, Zain al-Ashmawi, Nazim Sha'rawi, Salah Jahin, Abd al-Badie al-Arabi, Ibrahim Feteiha, Kamil Anwar

Festivals Academy Awards, where it was nominated for Best Picture of that year, and the Berlin Film Festival. Kamal al-Shinnawi and Shukri Sarhan both received awards of merit from President Nasser.

Running time 125 minutes

First screening 12 November 1962

Black and white

Ilwan, who once taught him that stealing from the rich in an unjust society is an act of justice, is now himself a wealthy newspaper editor. Mahran's confused attempts at revenge backfire and he becomes a hunted man, finding refuge with a prostitute in her flat with a view of a cemetery.

Shukri Sarhan offers a superb performance as the anti-hero Mahran, avoiding the usual bad-guy clichés to deliver a subtle psychological portrait of a man spiraling into self-destruction. Kamal al-Shinnawi is a scintillating Ra'uf Ilwan, a man whose former revolutionary zeal has been co-opted by power and luxury. Shadya also does well with the tired old role of the kind-hearted prostitute, imbuing her character, Nur, with depth and character. The real star, though, is Kamal Karim's carefully composed cinematography, full of moody shadows and atmospheric use of locations in the baladi neighborhoods at the foot of Cairo's Citadel. The visuals are beautifully complemented by Andre Ryder's music, making this an absolute classic of Egyptian cinema. ★

KEY SCENE

The recently freed Said Mahran pays a visit to his former mentor, Ra'uf Ilwan. Ilwan congratulates Mahran on his release from prison. "How's your daughter doing?" he asks, to which Mahran replies that she didn't recognize him. Ilwan attempts to console him: "She'll come to recognize you in due time." Mahran tells him how happy it had made him in prison whenever he heard news of his friend's achievements. He looks around at Ilwan's opulent home: "You don't need to struggle like you used to," he says. Ilwan responds that it's just a temporary truce from his political struggle and that every war has its field of battle. "Pretty comfortable battlefield if you ask me," Mahran says dryly. "I've always earned an honest living," Ilwan responds, tetchily. He tells Mahran that he should start looking for a job at once. Mahran explains that while he learned some tailoring skills in jail, "there's only one profession that makes good money, as you know, and there's nothing I can do but go back to it." "What do you mean by 'as I know'?" demands Ilwan. Mahran apologizes and asks his former friend to help him find a job in journalism. Ilwan says that's not possible for someone just out of jail. He gives Mahran some money and indicates that it's time for him to leave. He will be rather busy from now on, he says, and Mahran should not count on seeing him.

افلام جمال الليثى تقدم
شاديه
كمال الشناوى
وفتى الشاشه
شكرى سرحان
فى قصة نجيب محفوظ
اللص والكلاب
اخراج
كمال الشيخ
سيناريو
صبرى عزت
تصوير
كمال كريم
توزيع دولار فيلم

لوتس فيلم
تقدم مع
المؤسسة المصرية العامة للسينما
احمد مظهر
نادية لطفى
صلاح ذو الفقار
ليلى فوزى
حمدى غيث
ليلى طاهر
عمر الحريرى
حسين رياض
محمود المليجى
توفيق الدقن
زكى طليمات
احمد لوكسر
بالألوان الطبيعية . والتراسكوب
الناصر صلاح الدين
انتاج
آسيا
قصة وحوار
يوسف السباعى
سيناريو وحوار
عبد الرحمن الشرقاوى
مدير التصوير
وديد سرى
مدير الانتاج
مصطفى عبد اللطيف
اخراج
يوسف شاهين
توزيع شركة لوتس للتوزيع آسيا وشركاها س ت ٣٩٤٤٢ القاهرة
تصريح رقم ٢٨٠/١٩٦١

Al-Nasir Salah al-Din

Saladin the Victorious | 1963

An epic historical drama about Saladin's reclamation of Jerusalem from the Christian Crusaders in the 12th century

WHEN THEY SAY "they don't make them like that any more," the prime piece of evidence is this movie, a sprawling, three-hour historical epic with superb production values. *Al-Nasir Salah al-Din* is without doubt the finest Egyptian—and Arab-world—historical movie ever made. It depicts the military campaigns of the Ayyubid warlord Salah al-Din to retake and defend Jerusalem from the European Crusaders commanded by the English king Richard I "the Lionheart," during what is commonly referred to as the Third Crusade. As well as offering a magnificent visual spectacle, Chahine's movie is also a meditation on the struggle between East and West, a struggle that he is remarkably even-handed in portraying. The Christian soldiers, for example, are shown as being driven by a faith equal to that of the

Released internationally as *Saladin*

Director Youssef Chahine

Screenplay Abd al-Rahman al-Sharqawi

Story Yusuf al-Siba'i, adapted for the screen by Naguib Mahfouz, Izz al-Din zu-l-Fiqar, and Mohamed Abd al-Gawad

Dialogue Yusuf al-Siba'i

Produced by Assia

Music Franciscola Vanino

Director of photography Wadid Sirry

Editor Rashida Abd al-Salam

Set design Habib Khuri, Charles Finberg, and Anton Polysius

Starring Ahmad Mazhar, Nadia Lutfi, Salah zu-l-Fiqar, Layla Fawzi, Hamdi Gheith, Layla Tahir, Omar al-Hariri, Hussein Riyad, Mahmud al-Miligi, Zaki Tulaymat, Tawfiq al-Diqin, Ahmad Luxor, Mohamed Hamdi, Salah Nazmi, Badr Nofal

Running time 180 minutes

First screening 25 February 1963

Color

LEFT Al-Nasir Salah al-Din (Ahmad Mazhar)

Festivals Moscow International Film Festival. Best Picture from the Egyptian Catholic Cinema Association, and Production Award in the International Festival.

Muslims. The movie also speaks to the politics of the era in which it was made: this was the early 1960s, the glory years of President Nasser, when he was a unifying figure for the Arab world. During his campaign to recapture Jerusalem, Chahine has Salah al-Din repeatedly telling his army that victory can only be achieved through "Arab unity."

The dialogue is magnificent and Chahine supplements it with wordless visuals that do a neat job of getting the message across. This can be seen, for example, in the scene where Chahine seeks to express that Salah al-Din is the entire army: he focuses Salah al-Din's image prominently in the forefront of the scene, with the Arab armies charging in the background. Similarly, to evoke the massed ranks of Crusaders, he uses a shot of crashing waves, and to evoke the bloodthirstiness of Arthur, one of the leaders of the Crusaders, he has him cast a deep-red shadow across a chessboard. He marks the mass deaths of combatants by showing blood washing over a white garment. Symbolism comes to the fore again in the final scene, in which Issa, one of Salah al-Din's lieutenants, and Luisa, a female Crusader, come together against a background of olive branches, indicating that peace between East and West is possible. ★

KEY SCENE

The nature of the conflict and those who are engaged in it is brought to the fore in a scene in which two trials are shown going on simultaneously. One is of Luisa, who is charged with treason after aiding Issa's escape from the Crusader camp. The other is of the Wali of Acre, who is accused of betraying the Muslim forces. The scene begins with Prince Conrad of Montferrat detailing Luisa's treachery. He stirs up hatred against her among the assembled nobles, describing her as a fallen woman. The film then cuts to the traitorous Wali begging Salah al-Din for mercy. The latter rebukes him: "You killed thousands of children when you opened the gates of Acre to the Crusaders." Cut to Luisa's trial: Prince Conrad labels Salah al-Din a savage, yet Luisa sides with him "as though he were better than her own people! As though the Arabs were not barbarians! And thus, she uprooted the sacred hatred from her heart." Cut to the trial of the Wali: Salah al-Din is telling him that he uprooted the love of his country from his heart and handed it over to the enemy. Now we see both trials on a split screen as though Salah al-Din and Prince Conrad are debating directly. Finally, Richard bursts out, declaring that Conrad himself is a traitor: he offers as evidence Salah al-Din's rejection of Conrad's plot against Richard himself. He calls down curses on him; meanwhile, Salah al-Din sentences the Wali of Akka to death.

Al-Naddara al-Sawda'

Dark Glasses | 1963

An unhappy young woman drifts through life from one liaison to the next, until she meets a man who sparks a transformation

OF ALL THE MANY fine big-screen adaptations of books by Ihsan Abd al-Quddus, this is one of the best. The conceit is simple: sunglasses, or "dark glasses" as the book calls them, are the veil behind which wrongdoers and sinners conceal their guilt. These people, the story preaches, cannot face the world without some form of concealment. They are literally unable to look society in the eye. In the movie, director Husam al-Din Mustafa gets straight down to business in the very first scene, which has our heroine in bed, wrestling with insomnia and suffering terrible nightmares every time she manages to fall asleep. She reaches out to her nightstand and fumbles not for sleeping pills or the nightlight, but for her sunglasses, which she puts on and mercifully finds some sort of release.

Director Husam al-Din Mustafa

Screenplay Lucien Lambert

Story Ihsan Abd al-Quddus

Dialogue Mohamed Kamal Abd al-Salim

Produced by Etihad Films

Director of photography Mahmud Nasr

Editor Fikri Rustum

Set design Abbas Hilmi

Starring Nadia Lutfi, Ahmad Mazhar, Ahmad Ramzi, Sana' Mazhar, Abd al-Khalek Salih, Abu Bakr Izzat, Karima al-Sharif, Khalil Badr al-Din, Fayiq Bahgat

Festivals Best Actress Award for Nadia Lutfi from the Catholic Institute.

Running time 105 minutes

First screening 29 April 1963

Black and white

LEFT Madiha (Nadia Lutfi, *right*), Omar (Ahmad Mazhar, *left*)

افلام الاتحاد
تقدم
احمد مظهر
مع ضيف الشرف
احمد رمزي
مع
سناء مظهر
نادية لطفي
Marcel
النظارة السوداء

This is Madiha, or Maddie as she calls herself (of course, a sinful party girl has to have a Western name). She was once devoted to a man but he let her down and left her, and now to dull the pain she indulges in hedonistic pleasures at all hours of the day and night. This continues until she meets another man (of course), Omar (Ahmad Mazhar), for whom she straightens out and turns her life around. That is, until she loses him, too.

Nadia Lutfi's desperation as Maddie is what makes this film worthwhile. She is, of course, never allowed to descend too far into debauchery, and we are always aware that she is a good girl at heart. However, the audience gets to go on a fabulous ride of highs and lows in her company as the film progresses. The two Ahmads, Ramzi and Mazhar, also acquit themselves admirably. Ramzi is great as Maddie's original lover, an amoral, debauched libertine—a role he played often—who enjoys toying with a naive young girl and reducing her world to pleasure and sex. Mazhar gets the less interesting role of strait-laced Omar, although he does get to stray off the path a little himself later in the film, and then it is Maddie who comes to his rescue, putting aside her dark glasses for good. ★

This is Maddie's conversion scene. Omar comes home in a rage, having just witnessed a totally different Madiha from the one he left behind when he went to Germany. The sight of her laughing and joking in her bathing suit with a group of young men at the club has pushed him over the edge. He rips the flowers he had brought Maddie out of their vase and casts them aside. He picks up his bags to go into his room; the doorbell rings. It is Maddie, who comes in and tries to jolly him out of his rage. He rejects her overtures. She opens a package he brought her, delighted that he brought her back a present; he slaps her in the face, and tells her it's the payment for the time he spent with her. She reproaches him with the accusation, "You drove me to it!" saying that he never answered any of her letters. "Didn't you know I needed you? Temptation was too strong for me!" What he taught her in one month, she tells him, cannot erase the habits of years. She is a person with vulnerabilities he should have appreciated, she tells him. "Why didn't you write to me?" He tells her that he was testing her. "But now you are broken." He then throws her out, not allowing her a word in self-defense: "You know how to help yourself if you want. I'm not wasting any more time with you." She leaves in abject humiliation, with a choice to make about how she wants her life to be in the future.

Umm al-'arusa

Mother of the Bride | 1963

A family attempts to organize their daughter's wedding but the groom's parents have over-the-top demands

Director Atif Salim

Screenplay Abd al-Hayy Adib

Story Abd al-Hamid Gouda al-Sahhar

Dialogue Abd al-Hamid Gouda al-Sahhar

Produced by Nagib Khury

Director of photography Mas'ud Issa

Editor Hussein Ahmad

Set design Habib Khuri

Starring Tahiya Carioca, Samira Ahmad, Imad Hamdi, Hassan Yusuf, Yusuf Sha'ban, Madiha Salim, Adli Kasib, Khairiya Ahmad, Malak al-Gamal, Ihsan Sharif, Suleiman al-Gindi, Alexander Mansi, Abd al-Rahman al-Arabi, Inas Abdullah, Atif Makram

Festivals Best Picture Award from the Egyptian Catholic Center.

Running time 102 minutes

First screening 23 December 1963

Black and white

ON PAPER IT SOUNDS like a surefire hit—a zany comedy in which the harassed parents of seven demanding children find themselves having to improvise to cover the costs of their eldest daughter's wedding, and all the while the groom's parents make ever more costly demands. Except it was rejected by at least two major directors and it was not until Atif Salim fell in love with Abd al-Hayy Adib's screenplay that Abd al-Hamid Gouda al-Sahhar's story finally made its transition to film. Not that the transition was entirely trouble-free. For a long time the creative team could not come up with a suitable way to end the film. The book lacked the kind of memorable finale desired by Salim. It came when al-Hayy Adib attended the wedding of one of the children of a big-time drug dealer. It was raided by the police. The happy affair immediately turned tense with an expectation of arrests,

RIGHT Zeinab (Tahiya Carioca, *left*), Ahlam (Samira Ahmad, *center*), Galal (Yusuf Sha'ban, *right*)

جسور
نجيب خوري يقدم
سميرة احمد
عماد حمدي
حسن يوسف
يوسف شعبان
مديحه سالم
تحية كاريوكا
أم العروسة
إخراج
عاطف سالم
قصة وحوار
عبد الحميد جوده السحار
سيناريو
عبد الحي أديب
مدير التصوير
مسعود عيسى
توزيع افلام صوت الفن ١٦ شارع عدلي
مطابع السينما العربية

maybe even a shoot-out. But the police chief simply directed his men to the speakers and had them removed: some of the neighbors had been complaining about the noise. It gave al-Hayy Adib the inspiration he needed (*see* the Key Scene box).

Some of the extravagant demands put forth by the groom's parents are: that all the bedroom furniture be made of solid *arw*, the most fancy and expensive wood on the Egyptian market, with six mattresses; that the formal reception furniture include two couches and six chairs all of gold lacquer, a dining room for ten people, and other such ludicrous requests. Imad Hamdi puts in a winningly madcap performance as the harried paterfamilias struggling to meet the needs of his family, driven frantic by the wedding, and ultimately resorting to embezzlement to cover the expenses of his daughter's trousseau. The vampish Tahiya Carioca seems an odd casting choice as *umm al-'arusa*, but her maturity (she was in her forties at the time and had already plowed through a fair number of her eventual tally of fourteen husbands) lent her an air of authenticity. Samira Ahmad makes for a delightful daughter, while Madiha Salim, playing another of the daughters, is a deliciously intelligent, naughty flirt. All the characters are Egyptian types instantly recognizable to audiences, and were popular at the box office. ★

KEY SCENE

The father of the bride, Hussein, comes out of his house to check on the preparations for his daughter's wedding. He is alarmed to see a police officer asking for him. He immediately supposes the officer is there to arrest him for embezzling money from his company, which he has used to pay for the event. Resigned to his fate, he tells his wife to take care of the children and goes to face his accuser. But the officer is gone. Hussein asks his colleague Morcos where the police officer has gone and what he wanted. "Oh," says Morcos, "he wanted to give us a ticket for creating a disturbance, but I talked him out of it!" Hussein is a man transformed. He runs off joyously to be part of his daughter's wedding, leaving Morcos behind calling "Hey! Where are you going?"

Al-Aydi al-na'ima

Soft Hands | 1963

An aristocrat dispossessed by the 1952 Revolution is forced to adjust to the new social realities

IT MAY BE PURE propaganda for the 1952 Revolution, but first and foremost *al-Aydi al-na'ima* is an absolute joy, and one of the most beloved movies in the history of Egyptian cinema. Tawfiq al-Hakim's play of the same name was adapted for the screen with such brilliance that it leaves the original in the shade. The story centers on a former aristocrat, Shawkat, "the Prince," who is stripped of his wealth in the wake of the Revolution and who refuses to accept the new state of affairs. While his daughters move on with their lives—one marries a mechanic and another sells off her paintings to make a living—he refuses to work. In fact, he can hardly read Arabic. To help him get over this problem, he invites a professor, Dr. Mahmoud, to share his residence. An unintended consequence of this is that the prince falls in love with the professor's sister, Karima. Ultimately, it is

Director Mahmud zu-l-Fiqar

Screenplay Yusuf Guhar

Story Tawfiq al-Hakim

Dialogue Yusuf Guhar

Produced by al-Sharika al-'Amma li-l-Intag al-Sinima'i al-'Arabi (Arab Public Film Production Company)

Music Ali Ismail

Director of photography Wadid Sirry

Editor Fikri Rustum

Set design Anton Polysius

Starring Sabah, Maryam Fakhr al-Din, Ahmad Mazhar, Salah zu-l-Fiqar, Layla Tahir, Ahmad Khamis, Widad Hamdi, Kamil Anwar, Ahmad Luxor, Abd al-Ghani al-Nagdi, Hussein Assar, Abbas al-Dali, Edmund Tweima, Mohamed Idris

Festivals Berlin

Running time 132 minutes

First screening 29 December 1963

Color

LEFT Karima (Sabah, *right*), Shawkat (Ahmad Mazhar, *left*)

الشركة العامة للانتاج السينمائى العربى
تقدم
صباح
مريم فخر الدين
احمد مظهر
صلاح ذو الفقار
ليلى طاهر
الأيدى الناعمة
بالألوان الطبيعية
قصة توفيق الحكيم
اخراج محمود ذو الفقار
سيناريو وحوار يوسف جوهر
مدير التصوير وديد سرى
توزيع شركة الشرق
رخصة رقم ١٤١٤ - ٢٣/٨/٦٢
مطبعة النور ت ٤٨١٦٦

from Karima that he learns the values of the new classless society, in which everyone has to work.

Screenwriter Yusuf Guhar modified the original plot to make it tighter and more cohesive—and to inject plenty of humor. For example, in the original play, when the prince discovers a ploy by his daughters to give him charity behind his back, he accepts with gratitude; in the movie he loses his temper and rants, which is far more in keeping with his character. The dialogue (also by Yusuf Guhar) is some of the best ever written for the Egyptian screen. The low-class tenants who come to live at the villa speak in the vernacular of the marketplace, offering comic contrast with the speech of Shawkat. Dr. Mahmud's lines are inspired, a brilliant combination of the simplicity of the Egyptian in the street and the linguistic culture that is his métier.

The cinematography is sunlit and bright, especially in the scenes filmed at the Manasterly Palace, on the island of Roda in Cairo, while the achingly beautiful violin score includes a love theme that was hummed on streets around the Arab world. Ahmad Mazhar's performance as "the Prince" is truly exceptional. While the character on the page is obviously written as a comic stereotype intended to skewer the old elite, Mazhar undercuts the puffed-up arrogance and haughtiness with a hint of vulnerability. And he is incredibly funny, with his ridiculous catchphrase, "Traitors!" fired off at anyone who disagrees with or refuses to help him. Equally inspired is Salah zu-l-Fiqar as Hammuda, the Arabic language department graduate with a PhD in the preposition "even." This is possibly also Sabah's best-loved movie: she shines as Karima, a woman so radiant that it is easy to believe that Shawkat could drop his airs for her. ★

In a scene written to showcase the values of Egypt's new regime, Shawkat eats at a basbusa cart, where he has been reduced to trading his precious medals, one by one, in exchange for meals. They are now shown to be so worthless that the basbusa vendor uses them to decorate his cart. As Shawkat is eating, the vendor's son appears. He is a handsome, well-dressed young man. "How can such a figure," Shawkat wonders, "be the son of a street vendor?" Using refined language the young man informs Shawkat that thanks to the hard work of his father, he has been able to graduate from college and is now a diplomat at the foreign office, and engaged to the daughter of a CEO. "Times have changed," says the young man. "It is hard work that gets you places now, not who your family is."

Bayn al-Qasrayna

Palace Walk | 1964

A patriarch rules his family with an iron fist while secretly enjoying dalliances with loose women and dancers

Released internationally as *Bayn al-Qasrayn*

Director Hassan al-Imam

Screenplay Yusuf Guhar

Story Naguib Mahfouz

Dialogue Yusuf Guhar

Produced by al-Sharika al-'Amma li-l-Intag al-Sinima'i al-'Arabi (Arab Public Film Production Company)

Music Ali Ismail

Director of photography Mustafa Hassan

Editor Rashida Abd al-Salam

Set design Shadi Abd al-Salam

Starring Yahya Shahin, Maha Sabri, Salah Qabil, Zizi al-Badrawi, Abd al-Mun'im Ibrahim, Ni'mat Mukhtar, Mohamed Rida, Said Khalil, Zuzu Nabil, Amal Zayid, Hala Fakhir, Suhair al-Baruni, Mimi Shekib, Hamid Mursi, Thuraya Fakhri, Ibrahim al-Shami, Izzat al-Alayli, Wagdi al-Arabi

Running time 128 minutes

First screening 2 March 1964

Black and white

JUST A FEW YEARS after the publication of Naguib Mahfouz's landmark "Cairo Trilogy," the Public Sector for Cinema, the official government filmmaking body, decided to enshrine the works on film. The second and third of the resulting three movies are of questionable quality, but the first, *Bayn al-Qasrayna*, is an absolute classic. For those who do not know the story, Abd al-Gawad is a strict patriarch who has forbidden his wife to go outside the family home for the last twenty-five years and inspires reverence and fear in his children. Meanwhile, he spends evenings carousing with his fellow businessmen, indulging in wine and the company of prostitutes. The drama comes when the children encourage their mother to venture out of the house and the sons discover their father's double life.

The setting of the events is very specific: it is 1919 in Cairo, the First World War has just ended, and resentment against continued British occupation of Egypt is on the rise. The time and place are wonderfully evoked by the sets and costumes of Shadi Abd al-Salam. Meticulous in his attention to detail, he used only materials that were available at the time and had his teams build all manner of period props, such as the open trolley that in one scene revolutionary demonstrators push off the tracks to use as a shield against the British soldiers' bullets. He recreated the interiors of churches and mosques, which were then expertly shot to create memorable intercut scenes of priests and imams making fiery speeches of revolution.

No less expressive of the period was the dialogue. The difficulty for screenwriter Yusuf Guhar was in crafting lines for Abd al-Gawad, because there is such a sharp contrast between how he speaks with his wife and family, and how he expresses himself when he is among the boozers and bellydancers. Not only does Guhar deal with this deftly, he also manages to inject an element of playfulness: for example, watch the scene in which Abd al-Gawad is visited at his

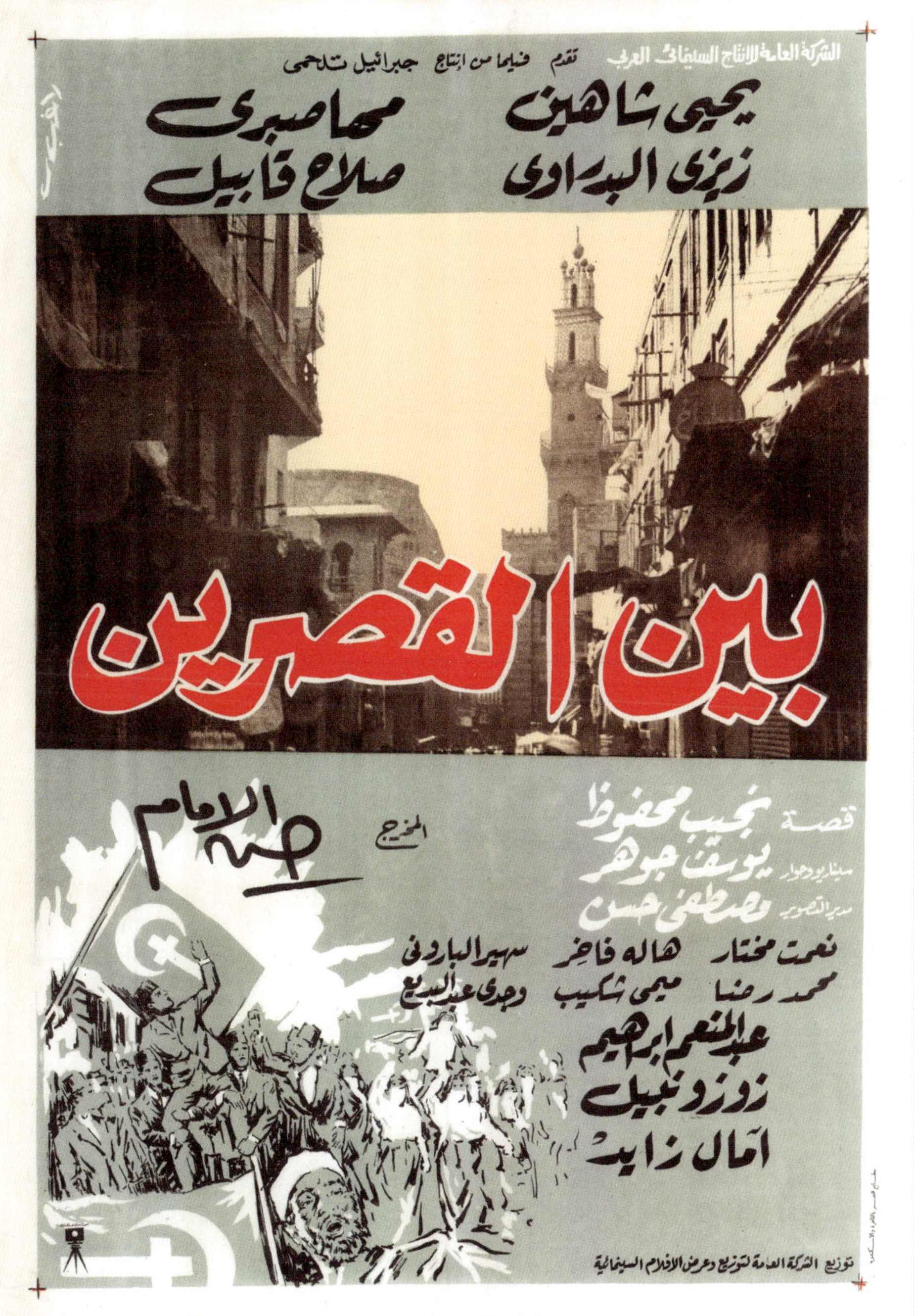

الشركة العامة للإنتاج السينمائي العربي
تقدم فيلما من إنتاج جبرائيل تلحمي
يحيى شاهين
مها صبري
زيزي البدراوي
صلاح قابيل
بين القصرين
قصة نجيب محفوظ
سيناريو وحوار يوسف جوهر
مدير التصوير مصطفى حسن
المخرج حسن الإمام
نعمت مختار
هاله فاخر
سهير البارودي
محمد رضا
ميمي شكيب
وجدي عبد البديع
عبد المنعم ابراهيم
زوزو نبيل
آمال زايد
توزيع الشركة العامة لتوزيع وعرض الأفلام السينمائية

RIGHT Abd al-Gawad (Yahya Shahin, *left-center*), Zubayda (Maha Sabri, *right-center)*, (Mohamed Rida, *right*)

store by a flirtatious dancer who gets her goods for free as the store owner entertains the hope he might receive some of her goods in return. "So how should I enter this payment in the ledger?" asks Abd al-Gawad's assistant. "Write that it was lost to *al-hawa*," is the reply—*al-hawa* meaning both "the air" and "desire."

The Abd al-Gawad of Mahfouz's novel has long since become inseparable in many viewers' minds from Yahya Shahin, the actor who plays him on screen. It now feels as though Shahin's performance came first and Mahfouz merely documented it. He has the perfect foil in Amal Zayid, who plays his wife, Amina, a woman who views her husband as a gift from God and someone who should be revered accordingly. ★

KEY SCENE

Unknown to Abd al-Gawad, his eldest son, Yassin, shares his father's tastes for life's more illicit pleasures. He pays a visit to a house of ill repute to meet the bellydancer Zannuba. She opens the door to the sounds of a party in full swing. "What's this?" asks Yassin. "It looks fun." Zannuba tells him it is an evening in honor of some good friends of her aunt, madam Zubayda. Yassin enters and happily joins in the merriment. Then, through the crowd, he catches a glimpse of his father, who is part of a lurching, drunkenly dancing chain of men led by Zubayda. He is beating a tambourine and singing lustily. Yassin is dumbfounded. He has never seen his father like this. "Dad, you son of a bitch!" he whispers to himself, and then he turns and runs before his father has a chance to spot him.

Al-Tariq

The Road | 1964

A man comes to Cairo in search of his father but instead finds his way into the bed of a married woman and a plot to commit murder

ANOTHER ADAPTATION OF a novel by Naguib Mahfouz (published in English as *The Search*) and another movie widely heralded by critics and audiences alike as one of the best ever made in Egypt. In this case, it is due not so much to the story but to the star turns by the lead actors Rushdi Abaza, Shadya, and Hassan al-Barudi. Abaza is the spoiled son Saber, who, when his mother dies, leaves Alexandria and goes off to Cairo to find the father he never knew. He launches his search with a notice placed in a newspaper, which is where he meets the naive young clerk Elham, who falls in love with him. But Saber lusts after the more mature Karima (Shadya), the sexually unfulfilled wife of his invalid landlord (al-Barudi). As the cuckolded husband, al-Barudi puts in a surprisingly energetic performance, and rather

Director Husam al-Din Mustafa

Screenplay Hussein Hilmi al-Muhandis

Story Naguib Mahfouz

Dialogue Hussein Hilmi al-Muhandis

Produced by Sharikat al-Qahira li-l-Sinima (Cairo Cinema Company)

Music Michel Yusuf

Director of photography Wadid Sirry

Editor Fikri Rustum

Set design Maher Abd al-Nour

Starring Rushdi Abaza, Shadya, Su'ad Husni, Tahiya Carioca, Hassan al-Barudi, Mohamed Tawfiq, Ahmad Luxor, Fayiq Bahgat, Qadriya Kamil, Abd al-Ghani al-Nagdi, Hussein Ismail, Mohamed Atiya, Sayyid Abdullah

Festivals Locarno

Running time 114 minutes

First screening 14 December 1964

Black and white

LEFT Fadl (Rushdi Abaza, *left*), Karima (Shadya, *right*)

شركة القاهرة للسينما
تقدم
قصة نجيب محفوظ
شادية
سعاد حسني
رشدي اباظة
تحية كاريوكا
الطريق
سيناريو وحوار حسين حلمي المهندس
تصوير وحيد سري
المنتج سعيد الدفراوي
اخراج حسام الدين مصطفى
توزيع : الشركة العامة لتوزيع وعرض الأفلام السينمائية (دولار فيلم) ٨٥ شارع رمسيس بالقاهرة

than being irredeemably pathetic, he wins audience sympathy with his trusting nature and the pure delight he takes in his wife. Shadya has her work cut out to avoid alienating viewers as the still relatively young and beautiful wife forced to seek out extramarital sex to fill that particular void in her life. She falls into Rushdi Abaza's bed not out of love but need. Egyptian viewers were never going to condone her behavior, but through her intelligent, nuanced performance, they could at least understand where she was coming from.

Rushdi Abaza, the perennial playboy of the silver screen, has the most conventional role: once again, he is a playboy. There is a bit of a twist, as we are led to believe that his vulnerability to temptation has a cause (his mother is a prostitute) and even a potential solution: he needs to find his long-lost father to rescue him from the stormy seas of emotional instability. And while he is only too eager to jump into bed with a married woman, he remains loyal and loving to the young girl of whom he feels unworthy. Unfortunately, he ultimately squanders whatever sympathy he might have wrung from the audience when he conspires with Karima to murder her husband, take his money, and run. ★

This takes place early on. Saber's mother, Basima, has just been released from jail, where she was serving a sentence for prostitution. As they ride a horse-drawn cart home, the talk is of Basima making a new life for herself. They continue their conversation at home: Basima tells Saber that the only way to make up the money that she would lose from not working is for him to search for his father, who she had falsely told him was dead. Once Saber finds him, the pair can lean on him for money. She gives Saber a photograph of his father, taken at their wedding, and tells him his name, Sayyid al-Reheimi. She reveals she ran away from him and moved to Alexandria because he was unfaithful to her, and then, being alone, she had no choice but to take up prostitution.

فيلمنتاج الشركة العامه للانتاج السينمائى العربى تقدم من اخراج بركات
الحرام
ستوديو مرسيل
بطولة
فاتن حمامة
زكى رستم
عبدالله غيث
قصة
يوسف ادريس
سيناريو وحوار
سعد الدين وهبه
مدير التصوير
ضياء المهدى
انتاج
منير رفلة
مطابع السينما العربية
شارع عرابى بالقاهرة
توزيع : الشركة العامه لتوزيع وعرض الأفلام السينمائية
1965

Al-Haram

Sin | 1965

A poor migrant farmhand is raped by a farmer and becomes pregnant

TO DATE, THIS remains the only movie to portray the lives of the itinerant or migrant workers (*'ommal al-tarahil*) of pre-Revolutionary Egypt. These were lives that were unimaginably harsh, with simple mud-brick dwellings for homes, rags for clothes, and a daily staple fare of mesh, a kind of cheese prepared with food scraps and moldy bread. Medical care was nonexistent, and in case of illness they resorted to folk remedies such as primitive cautery and boiling up herbs and spices. No surprise then that the story told is one of abject misery. It centers around a woman called Aziza (Fatin Hamama), who, while out picking sweet potatoes, is raped. She becomes pregnant but out of shame hides the fact of it from everyone, including her impotent, invalid husband. She carries the pregnancy to term and then strangles the baby after it is born.

Director Henri Barakat

Screenplay Sa'd al-Din Wahba

Story Yusuf Idris

Dialogue Sa'd al-Din Wahba

Produced by al-Sharika al-'Amma li-l-Intag al-Sinima'i al-'Arabi (Arab Public Film Production Company)

Music Suleiman Gamil

Director of photography Diya' al-Mahdi

Editor Rashida Abd al-Salam

Set design Maher Abd al-Nour

Starring Fatin Hamama, Abdullah Ghayth, Zaki Rostom, Hassan al-Barudi, Abd al-Alim Khattab, Kawthar al-Assal, Hassan Mustafa, Abd al-Salam Mohamed, Sami Sarhan, Khairy al-Qalyubi, Lutfi Abd al-Hamid

Festivals Cannes

Running time 99 minutes

First screening 3 May 1965

Black and white

LEFT Aziza (Fatin Hamama, *right*), Abdullah (Abdullah Ghayth, *left*)

Anyone who has seen *Du'a' al-karawan* *(see page 119)* will recognize the director's style immediately. Barakat uses many of the same techniques in both movies, notably frequent flashbacks. *Al-Haram* pitches the audience straight into the story without any exposition and we only gradually piece it together through these flashbacks, which eventually lead us to the cinematic present. After each flashback, Barakat repeats the scene that triggered it, so that the audience has the opportunity to reassess the scene in light of what they have just learned. Heavy with an oppressive air throughout, *al-Haram* is not an easy watch, but there are numerous moments of grace and beauty: the tragic last scene after Aziza has died and the men of the village stand outside their homes in the soft light to bid her farewell ranks as one of the loveliest scenes in Egyptian cinema. Abdullah Ghayth is exceptional as Aziza's wretched husband, but the movie belongs to Fatin Hamama, who delivers a heart-wrenching performance in what may be her finest role. ★

KEY SCENE

Aziza is praying. She begs the saint to make the foreman look kindly upon her sick husband and include him in the party for a well-paid work trip. At the same moment the foreman is calling out the chosen names, and Aziza's prayers seem to have been answered when her name and that of her husband are called out. She comes forward with him, accompanied by their two children. They walk slowly ahead of the silent foreman. Aziza climbs up into the high wagon but her husband cannot manage it, even with the help of Aziza and one of the other women. He falls to the ground and Aziza tells the foreman he slipped. Now she quickly gets him up into the truck with the help of the other workers but the foreman orders him off again. The couple plead but the foreman pulls the husband from the truck. He begs and tries to kiss the foreman's hand. Aziza pleads some more. "I can't take him," says the foreman. "I'm afraid he'll die." Aziza and her two children climb down and the wagon bearing the migrant workers moves off without them.

Al-Mustahil

The Impossible | 1965

Two married lovers find it is impossible to confront society's traditions and values despite their powerful love

HUSSEIN KAMAL MADE his blazing debut as a film director with this very stylized movie. Incredibly, he would follow it with at least three more landmark movies (*al-Bustagi, see page 197; Shay' min al-khawf, see page 203; and Tharthara fawq al-Nil, see page 224*), all delivered in the space of just over five years. *Al-Mustahil* was based on Mustafa Mahmud's 1960 novel of the same name. It is a melodrama about a pair of lovers, Hilmi, a married man with a son, and Fatma, a married

Director Hussein Kamal

Screenplay Mustafa Mahmud and Yusuf Francis

Story Mustafa Mahmud

Dialogue Mustafa Mahmud

Produced by Filmintag

Music Mohamed Abd al-Wahab, with orchestration by Andre Ryder

Director of photography Abd al-Aziz Fahmi

Editor Rashida Abd al-Salam

Set design Hilmi Azab

Starring Nadia Lutfi, Kamal al-Shinnawi, Salah Mansur, Karima Mukhtar, Sana' Gamil, Malak al-Gamal, Fathiya Shahin

Running time 109 minutes

First screening 13 October 1965

Black and white

LEFT Fatma (Sana' Gamil, *right*), Hilmi (Kamal al-Shinnawi, *left*)

woman with a daughter, who discover that, no matter how powerful their love, it cannot survive society's opprobrium.

Kamal manages to imbue a straightforward story with a startlingly new aesthetic. Every element in the film—the lighting, framing, camera angles, set design, props—was planned to reflect the leads' psychological state. Hilmi's bedroom is a product of the breakdown of his marriage: the furniture is mismatched, the lighting is depressing, and when the window is opened it admits a harsh glare that suggests oppressive heat. It evokes the husband's unsettled condition and his desire to flee. Fatma's bedroom is opulent but its largeness leaves a lot of empty space to be filled. Fatma is swallowed up by it. Her liberalism is signaled by several sculptures of black African men around her bed, symbolizing perhaps a raw primitiveness, but it feels hollow. Equal care was taken with the sound design, which is very complex for its day. The sound of Hilmi's footsteps as he walks home is magnified on the soundtrack in a way that suggests heavy tedium. As Hilmi, the husband seeking relief from monotony with a whirlwind affair, Kamal al-Shinnawi successfully plays against type. Nadia Lutfi is also solid as the lost woman tied to a husband for whom she feels nothing, entertaining a fling but ultimately returning to her socially sanctioned role—a conventional Egyptian wife par excellence. ★

KEY SCENE

Hilmi tells Nani that their love has become his whole life. Nani shocks him with her response: "We're living a grand illusion." She wishes she could have been his wife, she says, living with him, cooking for him, waiting on him hand and foot, but it is not so. "It's not too late," he tells her. "We can make it happen." He tells her that he could divorce his wife and marry her. "You can get a divorce too. Nothing can stand in the way of our dreams." She tells him that she could not live with herself if she did that. "I never loved my husband, but I've lived with him. I can never forget my son, or the time we spent together." She has to take responsibility for who she is. "How can you face your wife?" she asks him. "How are you going to say to her, 'I divorce you'? How will you forget your son?" He tells her he is prepared to make an enemy of the whole world for her sake. "You'll only be your own worst enemy," she replies. "You'll be someone else, not the Hilmi I fell in love with." If she is untrue to herself, she says, she will be betraying him. "My love for you has given me a love for the whole world," she says. "It's even given me the strength to put up with living with my husband." She is going back to her family, she tells him, so as not to desecrate their love.

فيلمنتاج
الشركة العامة للإنتاج السينمائى العربى
تقدم
قصة وحوار
مصطفى محمود
المستحيل
موسيقى
محمد عبد الوهاب
بطولة
نادية لطفى . كمال الشناوى . صلاح منصور . كريمة مختار
وضيفة الشرف
سناء جميل
اخراج
حسين كمال
مدير التصوير عبد العزيز فهمى
إدارة الإنتاج كامل حفناوى
توزيع الشركة العامة لتوزيع وعرض الأفلام السينمائية

شركة القاهرة للسينما تقدم
فريد شوقي
سميرة أحمد
محمود المليجي
صلاح قابيل
صلاح منصور
هارب من الأيام
اخراج
حسام الدين مصطفى
قصة ثروت اباظة
سيناريو فايز اسماعيل
تصوير وديد سري
المنتج صبحي فرحات
توزيع : الشركة العامة لتوزيع وعرض الأفلام السينمائية "دولارفيلم" ٨٥ شارع رمسيس بالقاهرة

Harib min al-ayyam

Fugitive from the Days | 1965

A countryside gang leader falls in love with the kidnapped daughter of the village chief

WHEN NOVELIST Tharwat Abaza scored a big hit in 1965, his best-selling book was rushed onto the big screen later that same year. In *Harib min al-ayyam*, the village simpleton, Kamal, finds the only way to earn respect is outside of the law. He commands a gang, whom he instructs to kidnap Durriya, the headman's daughter and the woman with whom he is in love. Shocked to discover the identity of her captor, she rejects his love. She is shot in the leg by one of the gang members, played by Mahmud al-Miligi, as she tries to escape. Kamal brings her a doctor and is killed afterward, by his own wife who is seeking revenge.

Farid Shawqi is excellent in the twin-faceted role of the protagonist, Kamal. On the one hand, he is a figure of ridicule, the village idiot constantly swarmed by children who mock him by repeating

Director Husam al-Din Mustafa

Screenplay Fayiq Ismail

Story Tharwat Abaza

Dialogue Fayiq Ismail

Produced by Sharikat al-Qahira li-l-Sinima (Cairo Cinema Company)

Music Fu'ad al-Zahiri

Director of photography Wadid Sirry

Editor Hussein Ahmad

Set design Maher Abd al-Nour

Starring Farid Shawqi, Samira Ahmad, Mahmud al-Miligi, Salah Qabil, Salah Mansur, Mohamed Shawqi, Widad Hamdi, Raga' Yusuf, Ihsan al-Qal'awi, Hussein Assar, Mohamed Subeih

Running time 88 minutes

First screening 22 November 1965

Black and white

LEFT Kamal (Farid Shawqi)

the gibberish he hurls at them. However, he also possesses an unrecognized cunning and he is smart enough to plot and execute criminal escapades with the help of his gang. Samira Ahmad is also superb as Durriya, whose sympathetic nature fools Kamal into thinking she might return his affections. The cinematography makes inventive use of the simple village in which events unfold: sometimes the camera offers a bird's-eye view, at other times it crouches in narrow alleys, squeezed tight between buildings, a visual expression of how the characters are hemmed in by poverty. This is aided by skillful set design: the headman's house is large and spacious, filled with luxurious pieces of furniture, and overlooking a scene of natural beauty; by contrast, the home of Kamal's girlfriend is a simple mud-brick affair with no furniture and only a half-destroyed brick oven. ★

KEY SCENE

Kamal enters the cave in which Durriya is being held captive bearing a tray of food. He is masked and she draws back in fear. He urges her to eat. She refuses. "Don't you recognize me?" he asks with tenderness. "I know you well," she says, to his great shock. However, her meaning is different: "I know you're a killer and a criminal, and you must ask God to pardon you." Kamal tells her he knows her very well, and that the two of them have a long history. "I used to watch you playing when we were little," he says before unmasking himself. "But why," she asks in astonishment, "did you commit all those crimes?" He tells her he wanted to be respected instead of being cursed and mocked. Nobody has ever treated him as a human being with feelings and emotions, he says. "Was it worth stealing and killing?" she asks. "Now I am the authority!" he says. "Everyone obeys my commands. Can you deny that I'm the most powerful man in the village?" She tells him, "You were far stronger at the start." He asks what she means. "You were content," she answers. No, says Kamal, he was never content with anything, not on the inside. "You're trying to run from the truth," says Durriya. "You're trying to escape from the days, but no one can do that." She asks why he kidnapped her. He confesses his love for her. She recoils: "Get away from me! You're nothing but a murderer!"

Mirati mudir 'amm

My Wife the Director General | 1966

A civil servant discovers that his wife has been appointed as his new boss, and they attempt to hide the fact

THE PREMISE ALONE is the stuff of comedy gold: a husband and their friends are gathered to celebrate the promotion of his wife. He could not be more proud and supportive—until, that is, the wife is transferred to his office and becomes his direct boss. It is the mid-1960s; the first woman to hold a ministerial post in Egypt had only recently been appointed. The new Egypt promised more gender equality, but how far should this go? Installing a wife as her husband's boss was certainly a step too far. Naturally, the husband asks his wife to keep their marriage a secret in the workplace and she agrees.

The scenario offered director Fatin Abd al-Wahab the perfect opportunity to flex his comic talents and the result is a movie that has firmly established its place in the pantheon of Egyptian comedy classics. It demonstrates all the tricks and mannerisms for which Abd

Director Fatin Abd al-Wahab

Screenplay Sa'd al-Din Wahba

Story Abd al-Hamid Gouda al-Sahhar

Dialogue Sa'd al-Din Wahba

Produced by Filmintag

Music Ali Ismail

Director of photography Mahmud Fahmi

Editor Rashida Abd al-Salam

Set design Maher Abd al-Nour

Starring Shadya, Salah zu-l-Fiqar, Yusuf Sha'ban, Adil Imam, Tawfiq al-Diqin, Shafiq Nur al-Din, Kariman, Nabila al-Sayyid, Hussein Ismail, al-Deif Ahmad

Festivals Best Picture Award from the Egyptian Catholic Center

Running time 99 minutes

First screening 20 January 1966

Black and white

LEFT Esmat (Shadya, *left*), Hussein (Salah zu-l-Fiqar, *right*)

al-Wahab's work is now famed, such as the Keatonesque camera gags in which an inanimate object seems determined to thwart a human being. For instance, the wife tries out a boardroom speech on her husband and he flees to the bedroom, so instead she directs the speech at the statue of a cat on the table and the cat turns its back on her. Startled, she goes to find her husband, and when the camera cuts back to the statue it has resumed its original position.

The physical comedy comes out again when the husband is listening with barely suppressed rage to his co-worker, Abu al-Kheir, pontificating on the director's love life and her "feeble husband." As Abu al-Kheir leans back in his chair, the husband reaches out to throttle him, but just as he is about to make contact with his neck, Abu al-Kheir bounds up and the husband's hands close on thin air. Sa'd al-Din Wahba's dialogue is the equal of Abd al-Wahab's visual virtuosity. In one scene, Abu al-Kheir is conversing with the husband and his wife the director general, still unaware, of course, that they are married. She tells her husband, "You need to finish your project on time. Family matters shouldn't interfere with work." Abu al-Kheir concurs: "We never let personal life interfere, do we?" The director general then hurries away, saying she must make dinner for her husband, whereupon Abu al-Kheir obsequiously calls after her, "Of course, ma'am! We positively *revere* family life!"

It goes without saying that the wife's struggle to balance work and relationship is resolved by her resigning from the former. ★

KEY SCENE

The wife, Esmat (Shadya), fixes her hair in the mirror before a meeting with the deputy manager and department heads. At the meeting, the deputy manager introduces Esmat to Abu al-Kheir, head of human resources, as well as to several other mid-level managers. Esmat declares that she is pleased to meet them all. Abu al-Kheir is full of flattery, which riles Hussein (the husband, played by Salah zu-l-Fiqar) since he was trash-talking the new boss not half an hour earlier, saying, "I know the guy! [Esmat is a unisex name] He's a piece of garbage, I can tell you that!" Everyone leaves but Esmat asks Hussein to stay on the pretext of querying him on some detail of business. Once the door is closed, she tells her husband how happy she is to be working with him: "Partners at home and at work!" Hussein then tells her that he wants to keep it a secret that they're married. "You are my husband before God and the law. I'm proud of being your wife," she says. They are interrupted by an employee, whereupon Esmat looks at Hussein sternly and says, "I need that report as soon as possible," every inch the boss. "You're dismissed," she adds curtly.

الشركة العامة للإنتاج السينمائي العربي تقدم
شادية
صلاح ذو الفقار
مراتي مدير عام
اخراج فطين عبد الوهاب
توفيق الدقن
كريمان
شفيق نور الدين
عادل امام
الضيف احمد
عبد المحسن سليم
بالاشتراك مع يوسف شعبان
قصة عبد الحميد جوده السحار
سيناريو وحوار سعد الدين وهبه
مدير التصوير محمود فهمي
المنتج صلاح ذو الفقار
مطابع السينما العربية
توزيع الشركة العامة للتوزيع وعرض الأفلام السينمائية
1966

Al-Qahira 30

Cairo 30 | 1966

A young college graduate enters into a sham marriage to assist a corrupt official in his clandestine affair

Director Salah Abu Seif

Screenplay Salah Abu Seif, Ali al-Zurqani, and Wafiya Khairy

Story Naguib Mahfouz

Dialogue Lutfi al-Kholi

Produced by Sharikat al-Qahira li-l-Sinima (Cairo Cinema Company)

Music Fu'ad al-Zahiri

Director of photography Wahid Farid

Editor Muhyi al-Din Abd al-Gawad

Set design Maher Abd al-Nour

Starring Su'ad Husni, Ahmad Mazhar, Hamdi Ahmad, Yusuf Wahbi, Aquila Ratib, Abd al-Mun'im Ibrahim, Bahiga Hafiz, Shafiq Nur al-Din, Tawfiq al-Diqin, Suhair al-Murshidi, Na'ima al-Sughayar, Ahmad al-Hamaki, Khairiya Khairy, Abd al-Aziz Mekkawi, Ahmad Tawfiq, Ashraf Abd al-Ghafur

Running time 132 minutes

First screening 3 October 1966

Black and white

BASED ON NAGUIB MAHFOUZ'S novel *al-Qahira al-Jadida (Cairo Modern)*, the film follows the stories of a group of students through the 1930s and 1940s, and the different directions they follow in life. Central to the tale are Ali Taha, a young socialist looking to abolish class and build a new society, and his friend the poverty-stricken but opportunistic Mahgub Abd al-Dayim, who agrees to marry a government official's mistress in return for an apartment and a job.

What is fascinating in this film is the way director Salah Abu Seif uses the background scenery to comment on his characters and events. Mahgub willingly allows his "wife" to sleep with another man and in one scene Abu Seif places him against a wall on which there is

ABOVE Ihsan (Su'ad Husni, *left*), Qasim Bey (Ahmad Mazhar, *right*)

شركة القاهرة للسينما تقدم
القاهرة ٣٠
قصة: نجيب محفوظ
سعاد حسني
احمد مظهر
يوسف وهبي
عقيلة راتب
بهيجة حافظ
حمدي احمد
عبد العزيز مكيوي
احمد توفيق
عبد المنعم ابراهيم
شفيق نور الدين
توفيق الدقن
اخراج
صلاح ابوسيف
المنتج
جمال الليثي
مدير التصوير
وحيد فريد
سيناريو
صلاح ابوسيف
علي الزرقاني
وفيه خيري
حوار
لطفي الخولي
توزيع : الشركة العامة لتوزيع وعرض الأفلام السينمائية «فنون دولار فيلم»
مطابع النصر بالقاهرة

Festivals Carlo Vivari Festival. The Academy Awards, where it was nominated for Best Foreign Film. The movie also won the national awards from the Arab League for Best Production, Best Director, Best Story, Best Screenplay, Best Cinematography, Best Scene Design, and Best Actors.

a picture of a ram, making its horns appear to sprout out of Mahgub's head—horns being a symbol in Egyptian culture of cuckolding. When Ali Taha is out with his girlfriend Ihsan, she is complaining about her miserable financial situation, and as they talk, advertisements for a grand lottery prize of thirty pounds—a princely sum at the time—fill the background. At one point we also see a poster for the (actual 1930s) film *The Blue Angel*, whose decadent stylings are totally at odds with the world that the young Egyptian lovers inhabit.

The film has a rare quality in that each of its scenes is filmed in one shot: there are only 230 shots in total in a drama that lasts over two hours. For comparison, the dancer's scene in *Raya wa Sakina* *(see page 26)*, made by the same director, contains over one hundred shots and lasts only three minutes. Abu Seif was not afraid to take a chance on new faces, infusing Egyptian cinema with new stars in the process. Foremost among them is the then-unknown Hamdi Ahmad, who is brilliant as Mahgub, the man who is quite willing to jettison principles and honor in exchange for money and power, yet audiences took him to their hearts anyway. Also arresting is Abd al-Aziz Mekkawi as Ali Taha, another new actor who would go on to become a mainstay of the big screen. This was a fine launchpad in a role that saw him as the personification of the hopes and dreams of the future Egypt, encapsulated in the final scene of the film, in which the young revolutionary circulates among the men exiting the mosques after Friday prayer, flinging his socialism-espousing pamphlets into the air like a flock of white doves. ★

KEY SCENE

Mahgub is expressing his heartfelt gratitude to the government official Qasim Bey, who has just agreed to give him a job in his office. Qasim wishes him a successful career. As Mahgub stands there, he considers all the injustices rampant in Egypt. "What a world this is," he thinks to himself, "made only for the likes of Qasim Bey, with their money, power, and influence." The girl Ihsan, to whom Maghub has just been "married" in order to disguise her true status as Qasim's mistress, is a poor unfortunate, he thinks, obliged to allow the bey to have his way. "This is what the corrupt rich have done to Egypt," he thinks. What chance has his idealistic, hardworking friend Ali Taha got against the likes of Qasim Bey? Truly, Ihsan—whom in his mind Mahgub conflates with Egypt—should be betrothed to Ali Taha, but instead she remains chained to the old order.

Al-Simman wa-l-kharif

Autumn Quail | 1967

A bureaucrat on the make is dumped out of office after the Revolution triggering a downward spiral into despondency and debauchery

AL-SIMMAN WA-L-KHARIF cannot have been the easiest of Naguib Mahfouz's novels to translate to film. It has little plot, a disagreeable main character, and forgettable secondary characters who exist only to engage in stilted political dialogues. It is greatly to the credit of Husam al-Din Mustafa that he managed to fashion such an excellent film from such unpromising material. The story, such as it is, revolves around Issa al-Dabbagh, a bureaucrat who loses his position following the 1952 Revolution. He spends the subsequent years in a fug of indolence, trapped in a loveless marriage, haunting cafés and clubs, drinking, gambling, and consorting with prostitutes—at one point he discovers he fathered a child with one—until, in the end, he eventually comes to terms with the new political reality. Al-Din Mustafa disguises the lack of momentum in the story with a flurry of

Director Husam al-Din Mustafa

Screenplay Ahmad Abbas Salih

Story Naguib Mahfouz

Dialogue Ahmad Abbas Salih

Produced by Filmintag

Music Andre Ryder

Director of photography Cello Cicivelli

Editor Fikri Rustum

Set design Shadi Abd al-Salam

Starring Mahmud Mursi, Nadia Lutfi, Abdullah Gheith, Layla Shu'air, Ihsan al-Qal'awi, Naima Wasfi, Adil Adham, Abd al-Azim Abd al-Haqq, Mimi Shekib

Festivals Nadia Lutfi was awarded Best Actress from the Catholic Center

Running time 131 minutes

First screening 13 February 1967

Black and white

LEFT Issa (Mahmud Mursi, *left*), Hassan (Abdullah Ghayth, *right*)

فيلمنتاج
الشركة العامة للانتاج السينمائى العربى
تقدم
نادية لطفى
محمود مرسى
عبد الله غيث
قصة
نجيب محفوظ
عادل أدهم
احسان القلعاوى
ليلى شعير
السمان والخريف
اخراج
حسام الدين مصطفى
سيناريو وحوار احمد عباس صالح
مدير التصوير كليليو
الموسيقى التصويرية اندريا رايدر
توزيع : الشركة العامة لتوزيع وعرض الافلام السينمائية
جسور

different locations: the office; the house; the beach; the nightclub; the cabaret; the villa; the street; the living room; the bedroom. The scenery is worked hard to add emotional heft to the film: when Issa goes to Alexandria, the change in the weather from bright sun to a sudden storm mirrors the changeable world of politics, in which Issa was lifted up to the ministerial office, then peremptorily dumped. Alexandria is also the site of a statue of Sa'd Zaghlul, leader of the Wafd Party, of which Issa is a member, and the film has him seated beneath the statue to underscore his commitment to his past allegiances.

Mahmud Mursi is perfect as Issa. His overbearing physical presence and arrogant demeanor place him firmly as a man out of time, with attitudes that no longer chime with a refashioned Egypt. Even better is Nadia Lutfi as Riri, the prostitute, who, like Mursi, manages to locate the humanity beneath a hardened exterior. The scene in which she recounts her past life to Issa, finding common ground with him in the contempt society shows them both, is particularly touching. Lutfi's performance was acclaimed not only by audiences but by Naguib Mahfouz himself, who told her that he could not have imagined a better Riri. ★

Issa al-Dabbagh storms into his house after a Revolutionary committee has purged him from office on a charge of accepting bribes to appoint or dismiss village chiefs. He looks over at all the gifts he did, in fact, receive as bribes. He is overwhelmed by the gravity of his situation. His cousin Hassan appears. Hassan works for the Revolution, which inspires Issa's rage. He is rude and insulting to Hassan, whereupon the latter lashes out: "You think the entire world revolves around you! You think people are jealous of your good fortune!" The committee that dismissed him is entirely justified, says Hassan. Issa flies into a rage and calls his mother into the room, insulting Hassan in front of her. She apologizes to Hassan, who storms out. She reproaches Issa for his harsh words, whereupon he sinks into a chair. He tells his mother that he has been fired and he does not know what he did. "Everything's come down around our ears," he says. "Did Hassan have something to do with it?" she asks. "I don't know anything," he replies.

Al-Zawja al-thaniya

The Second Wife | 1967

The head of a village forces a man to divorce his wife so that he can marry her himself

Director Salah Abu Seif

Screenplay Mohamed Mustafa Sami, Sa'd al-Din Wahba, and Salah Abu Seif

Story Ahmad Rushdi Salih

Dialogue Mohamed Mustafa Sami

Produced by Sharikat al-Qahira li-l-Sinima (Cairo Film Production Company)

Music Fu'ad al-Zahiri

Director of photography Abd al-Halim Nasr

Editor Said al-Sheikh

Set design Hilmi Azab

Starring Su'ad Husni, Shukri Sarhan, Sana' Gamil, Salah Mansur, Abd al-Mun'im Ibrahim, Hassan al-Barudi, Suhair al-Murshidi, Mohamed Nouh, Na'ima al-Sughayar, Ibrahim al-Shami, Alexander Mansi, Abd al-Ghani al-Nagdi, Mohamed Idris, Husam al-Din Salih

Running time 112 minutes

First screening 16 October 1967

Black and white

FOR ANYONE WHO thought life was hard in the city, *al-Zawja al-thaniya* existed to show that it was immeasurably worse in the country. Or at least it was in the past, because all the misery, poverty, and suffering experienced by rural villages is shown to have taken place in the darkest days of ignorance and injustice—in other words, before the 1952 Revolution. But despite the blatant propagandizing, Salah Abu Seif's film does transport audiences—especially those who had not lived in the countryside—back to the days when the word of the *umda*, the village chief, was law. Law, but not necessarily just. The *umda* is the best-delineated figure in the screenplay and finely cast, too, in the form of Salah Mansur, who should have won every award going for his performance. Anyone who has never encountered an *umda* of that era only need watch Mansur. His gestures and

RIGHT Atman (Salah Mansur, *left*), Abul 'Ila (Shukri Sarhan, *right*), Fatma (Su'ad Husni, *left-center*)

شركة القاهرة للإنتاج السينمائي قدم
سعاد حسني شكري سرحان
سناء جميل صلاح منصور
سهير المرشدي
عبد المنعم ابراهيم
محمد نوح
حسن البارودي
نعيمة الصغير
الزوجة الثانية
قصة : احمد رشدي صالح
سيناريو :
محمد مصطفى سامي
سعد الدين وهبه
صلاح ابو سيف
اخراج : صلاح ابو سيف
مدير التصوير : عبد الحليم نصر
المنتج رمسيس نجيب
توزيع : شركة القاهرة للتوزيع السينمائي

Festivals Salah Abu Seif was awarded Best Director from the Egyptian Cinema Foundation. Shukri Sarhan won Best Actor and Su'ad Husni Best Actress.

movements, ponderous steps, and the imperious way he looks at others make him the *umda par excellence* of the Egyptian screen. Conversely, Shukri Sarhan, as Abu al-Ila, perfectly embodies the Egyptian populace groaning under the weight of tyrannical leadership, unable to defend himself or his family from injustice, and only too aware that a single misstep can bring down devastating punishment. In this case, the injustice being done to his family is particularly grievous: by threatening him with made-up accusations, the *umda* is forcing Abu al-Ila to divorce his wife, Fatma, so that he can marry her himself and have a child with her. What makes it even more terrible is that the wife is the lovely Su'ad Husni.

The rural visuals are pleasing, as is the music, which nicely conveys the impression of a simpler, slower time. The screenplay is also witty: a good example is when the corrupt police chief (a small role but beautifully filled by Ibrahim al-Shami) is eating at the *umda*'s table, chatting to Mabruk, the spice trader, about "Abu al-Ila and his ilk, the dregs of society, who think nothing of stealing what's not rightfully theirs." He continues on his theme: "They're nothing but cattle! They'd eat the food out of the mouth of the Prophet himself!" As he speaks the director gives us a close-up of him shoveling food into his mouth with gusto. We note also that the meal itself is a bribe from the *umda* designed to persuade the police chief to throw Abu al-Ila in prison for refusing to give up his wife. ★

KEY SCENE

Abu al-Ila sits a broken man in the presence of the *ma'zun* (Islamic marriage clerk), the *umda*, Mabruk the spice seller, and some of the night watchmen of the village. The clerk instructs Abu al-Ila to speak the words "I hereby divorce you" to his wife, Fatma. Abu al-Ila asks, "What kind of religion allows for a divorce like this?" The *umda* flies into a rage, threatening Abu al-Ila. He mumbles the words and then, unable to hold back any longer, he bursts into tears of humiliation. The *umda* offers him money, which he rejects in disgust, and leaves. The *umda* then instructs the clerk to marry him to Fatma. The clerk explains that according to religious law, three lunar months must be allowed to pass between a woman's divorce and her remarriage to make sure she is not pregnant. "The three months are already up!" the *umda* roars. "Set that down in your ledger! The ledgers are mine! The documents are mine! I have the power and no one is going to judge me!" Mabruk then intervenes, twisting a verse of the Qur'an and corrupting its original meaning to favor the *umda*.

Al-Bustagi

The Postman | 1968

A postman from Cairo is transferred to a small village where he reads the locals' letters to relieve his boredom, with tragic results

IT IS HARD to believe that this was only director Hussein Kamal's second film. His first, *al-Mustahil* *(see page 179)*, was an impressive debut but *al-Bustagi* is something else. Its exceptional nature was recognized as such at the time, screened at the Cannes Film Festival and garnering Kamal the State Award for Best Director. Working from a story by Yahya Hakki, the film is centered on Abbas, a postman from Cairo who has been sent to work in the countryside. Appalled by the provinciality of the village and the vulgarity of its people, he first turns to drink then to reading the letters that pass into his care. One exchange in particular seizes his attention, between Gamila, a village girl, and her lover, Khalil, from a neighboring village. But this is no sugar-coated love story. The tiny hamlet of Kom al-Nahl that is

ABOVE Abbas Hussein (Shukri Sarhan)

Director Hussein Kamal

Screenplay Sabri Musa, Donia al-Baba

Story Yahya Hakki

Dialogue Sabri Musa

Produced by Sharikat al-Qahira li-l-Sinima (Cairo Film Production Company)

Music Ibrahim Haggag

Director of photography Ahmad Khurshid

Editor Rashida Abd al-Salam

Set design Hilmi Azab

Starring Shukri Sarhan, Zizi Mustafa, Salah Mansur, Seif al-Din Abd al-Rahman, Suhair al-Murshidi, Mushira Ismail, Abd al-Ghani Qamar, Nahid Samir, Hassan Mustafa, Abd al-Alim Khattab, Ihsan Sharif, Ahmad al-Gezeiri, Alexander Mansi

Festivals Carthage, Tashkent, Cannes. Shukri Sarhan was named Best Actor by the Cinema Foundation. Hussein Kamal won Best Director.

Running time 116 minutes

First screening 15 April 1968

Black and white

شركة القاهرة للانتاج السينمائى تقدم
شكرى سرحان
زيزى مصطفى
صلاح منصور
سيف الدين
قصة يحيى حقى
البوسطجى
اخراج حسين كمال
بالاشتراك مع
سهير المرشدى
والوجه الجديد
مشيره
عبد الغنى قمر
ناهد سمير
حسن مصطفى
عبد العليم خطاب
سيناريو دنيا البابا/صبرى موسى
حوار صبرى موسى
مدير التصوير احمد خورشيد
المنتج المنفذ محمد عبد الجواد
الموسيقى التصويرية ابراهيم حجاج
توزيع : شركة القاهرة للتوزيع السينمائى

Abbas's prison is closed and insular, and an incubator for all manner of social ills, including honor killing and blood feuds.

It is a compelling story and one that Kamal and his team enhance brilliantly with technical and artistic skill. The setting of the decrepit house, for instance, that the postman ends up renting from the *umda*, while large, is crumbling and permeated with damp to such an extent that the postman is forced to live in just a tiny corner of it. The shooting of certain scenes is masterful. Take the scene in which Maryam, the servant girl, is raped in a dovecote by Salama, Gamila's father and *mi'allim* of a country village. The drums beat as the girl and Salama are shown from three different angles, acquainting the viewer with the location, which is filled with white doves, a symbol of innocence and purity, from top to bottom. There is a cut to Salama and the girl at the base of the tower, then there is a shift to a worm's-eye view as the girl screams, and then, suddenly, all is still, in accusation of the entire scene. As Abbas, Shukri Sarhan utilizes all his talents in what is arguably his finest performance: the snobbish city boy, disgusted by the ignorance and backwardness he sees all around him. Zizi Mustafa is similarly superb as Gamila, the naive village girl crushed and ultimately murdered by a regressive society (*see* the Key Scene box). ★

Abbas, the postman, has returned to the post office following a long illness, sickened by the catastrophe he has caused the village girl Gamila. He set in motion a chain of events that led to her being taken by force by her would-be suitor Khalil. Abbas knows Gamila's family will kill her for this perceived loss of honor. As he broods at the post office, the scenes of Abbas are intercut with scenes of Gamila's father pursuing her through the village and down toward the river. Suddenly he catches her and in a scene that is violent, graphic, and shocking, he kills her. As he carries her lifeless body back home, the villagers gather on the hard-earth slopes on which their houses are built and look down impassively. Some of them form a procession behind the father and his dead daughter. Gamila's mother heaps dust on her own head. Abbas joins the villagers and stares at the girl whose death he has unwittingly caused. He rips up the letter he meant to give her and throws it away. He takes handfuls of other letters from his satchel and shreds those, tossing the scraps into the air. The postman walks away, passing out of the frame, which is filled by a rain of white paper blown by the wind. The movie ends with Gamila's wistful voice mingling with that of her sweetheart, telling the final lines of a story: "And the prince took his princess to another kingdom, to live happily ever after far, far away."

Al-Ragul al-laladhi faqada zilluh

The Man Who Lost His Shadow | 1968

An opportunist journalist disowns his stepmother and brother, and abandons his beloved for position and power

Director Kamal El-Cheikh

Screenplay Ali al-Zurqani

Story Fathi Ghanim

Dialogue Ali al-Zurqani

Produced by al-Mu'assasa al-Misriya al-'Amma li-l-Sinima (The Egyptian Public Foundation for Cinema)

Music Andre Ryder

Director of photography Mahmud Nasr

Editor Said al-Sheikh

Set design Maher Abd al-Nour

Starring Kamal al-Shinnawi, Magda, Salah zu-l-Fiqar, Nelly, Yusuf Sha'ban, Imad Hamdi, Nazim Sha'rawi, Suhair Fakhri, Ali Guhar, Fathiya Shahin, Mohamed Sultan, Mahmud al-Rashad, Wagih Sharif

Festivals Tashkent. State Award for Best Director

Running time 127 minutes

First screening 28 October 1968

Black and white

THE SOURCE NOVEL on which this film is based is written from the points of view of four characters, each of whom has their own segment in the book. It tells the story of Yusuf Abdul Hamid, an ambitious Cairo journalist, firstly through the eyes of Mabruka, the young peasant girl who marries Yusuf's aging father despite being attracted to Yusuf; then through the eyes of Samya, a minor actress, whom Yusuf lives with and almost marries but later rejects; then Mohamed Nagi, whom Yusuf pushes out of his job as newspaper editor after Mohamed marries Samya; and finally we have the account of Yusuf himself, editor-in-chief of the newspaper *al-Ayyam*. In his transfer to the screen, director Kamal El-Cheikh retains the balance, not focusing on any one character to the exclusion of the others. He does a fine job in portraying the four quite different voices

RIGHT Yusuf (Kamal al-Shinnawi, *right*), Bahiya (Nelly, *left*)

المؤسسة المصرية العامة للسينما تقدم
الرجل
الذى
فقد
ظله
قصة
فتحى غانم
سيناريو وحوار
على الزرقانى
مدير التصوير
محمود نصر
المنتج المنفذ
سامى سوكه
اخراج
كمال الشيخ
ماجده
كمال الشناوى
صلاح ذو الفقار
نيللى
عماد حمدى
يوسف شعبان
انتاج وتوزيع المؤسسة المصرية العامة للسينما
دار الكاتب العربي (مصر)

of four characters from very different backgrounds. Mabruka speaks the language of a simple country girl, in contrast to Yusuf's educated and intellectual speech. In the novel, Yusuf is often in the background as the other three characters relate their stories, but in the film he is much more to the fore. It falls on Kamal al-Shinnawi, who plays the opportunistic journalist, to illuminate the various facets of his character. When dealing with his superiors his words are oily and glib—he is the Uriah Heep of journalists. But he is far less respectful to the three other main protagonists: to his stepmother Mabruka he is violent and cruel; to Samya he is indifferent and callous. It is to al-Shinnawi's credit that he is able to retain the audience's sympathy for Yusuf. Imad Hamdi is excellent as Yusuf's elderly father, a man in his second childhood attracted to a girl young enough to be his granddaughter. ★

KEY SCENE

In a scene that occurs right at the end of the film, an underling presents Yusuf, the current editor of the newspaper, with the wedding photo of former editor Mohamed Nagi and Samya, who is Yusuf's ex-girlfriend. The fact of the wedding comes as a surprise to Yusuf and prompts him to think deeply about the nature of things. Mohamed Nagi and Samya, he believes, have only married in order to destroy him. As he contemplates he undergoes something of an awakening, coming to a realization of his own true nature and his insignificance in the grand scheme of things. He is, he realizes, nothing but a hanger-on, a sycophant to those with money and power. He is a man without substance, a man "who has lost his shadow." He considers that if the Revolution takes place his orientation will shift to the common people and, as somebody who came up from humble beginnings, he might even emerge as a fighter and revolutionary. Maybe the naive populace will give credibility to his struggle and carry him aloft. Now that Yusuf has realized his true nature—that he is a mere hypocrite and a tool of those in power—he smiles in relief.

Shay' min al-khawf

A Touch of Fear | 1969

A young man becomes a gang leader in a rural village and imposes a reign of fear until the woman he loves stands up to him

LOVE IT OR HATE IT, there has never been another Egyptian film quite like *Shay' min al-khawf*. It takes the form of an epic. This was a deliberate treatment choice by director Hussein Kamal. He diverged slightly from Tharwat Abaza's novel, enlisting scriptwriter Sabri Izzat to co-author the dialogue with another great man of letters, the poet Abd al-Rahman al-Abnudi.

Director Hussein Kamal

Screenplay Sabri Izzat

Story Tharwat Abaza

Dialogue Sabri Izzat and Abd al-Rahman al-Abnudi

Produced by al-Mu'assasa al-Misriya al-'Amma li-l-Sinima (The Egyptian Public Foundation for Cinema)

Music Baligh Hamdi

Director of photography Ahmad Khurshid

Editor Rashida Abd al-Salam

Set design Hilmi Azab

Starring Shadya, Mahmud Mursi, Yahya Shahin, Mohamed Tawfiq, Ahmad Tawfiq, Salah Nazmi, Samira Muhsin, Amal Zayid, Wafik Fahmi, Safinaz, Mahmud Yassin, Hassan al-Subki, Hussein Ismail

Festivals Moscow. Awarded Best Picture by the Egyptian Catholic Center.

Running time 108 minutes

First screening 2 February 1969

Black and white

LEFT Atris (Mahmud Mursi, *left*), Fu'ada (Shadya, *right*)

المؤسسة المصرية العامة للسينما تقدم
شادية
محمود مرسى
والممثل الكبير
يحيى شاهين
شىء من الخوف
قصة ثروت اباظه
اخراج
حسين كمال
مدير التصوير
احمد خورشيد
تأليف الأغانى
عبدالرحمن الأبنودى
سيناريو
صبرى عزت
حوار
صبرى عزت / عبدالرحمن الأبنودى
موسيقى
بليغ حمدى
المنتج
صلاح ذو الفقار
انتاج وتوزيع : المؤسسة المصرية العامة للسينما

The story is simple: the inhabitants of a rural Egyptian village live under the iron fist of strongman Atris. His tyranny is challenged when Fu'ada, the object of his affection, defiantly reopens the water spigot that had been shut off by Atris in an act of collective punishment. Kamal presented this as a tale for the ages, untethered from any specific time or place, peddling the eternal message that injustice and oppression are caused not by the wickedness of evil individuals but by the failure of the masses to speak out. The epic presentation begins with the opening credits, lettered in old-fashioned script and set among folk paintings of the type that commonly decorate old editions of collections like *The Thousand and One Nights*.

The backgrounds and actions of the leading characters are commented on by a chorus, pronouncing lines penned by al-Abnudi set to music by the legendary Baligh Hamdi. The film is tangible proof that a director's inspired touch can lend art to a novel that it did not possess as a literary text. The screenplay added several now iconic scenes, such as the memorable one in which Fu'ada turns on the spigot and the scene in which the village chants en masse that Fu'ada's marriage to Atris is void (*see* the Key Scene box). Kamal chose to shoot in black and white in order to achieve chiaroscuro effects that would have been impossible in color. The score was of a piece with the choral pieces, making this film musically exceptional. Mahmud Mursi is a towering presence as the tyrannical Atris, while Shadya, as Fu'ada, plays one of her finest roles as the only person in the entire village with the courage to stand up to the bully. ★

The revolt begins with a few people walking behind the coffin of Mahmud, a man who always spoke the truth without fear. He had claimed that Atris's marriage to Fu'ada was not legal because the bride had never said the words "I do" as religious law requires. For speaking out in this manner, Atris murdered him. Now as he walks behind his son's coffin, Sheikh Ibrahim takes up a chant: "Atris's marriage to Fu'ada is null and void!" ("Gawaz Atris min Fu'ada batil!"). The chant is taken up by first a few voices, then by more, as the procession winds through the village. What started out as a fearful whisper swells into a chorus and in doing so becomes one of the most powerful sequences in the history of Egyptian cinema. The message of *Shay' min al-khawf* would even find its echoes in the events of January 2011 as feminist activists painted graffiti of Fu'ada/Shadya's image along with the words "I am the one who opened the spigot," while in an echo of the emboldened villagers, protestors on Tahrir Square chanted the slogan "Husni Mubarak batil!"

Miramar

Miramar | 1969

The guests of an Alexandrian boarding house compete for the attentions of a young servant girl, with tragic consequences

Director Kamal El-Cheikh

Screenplay Mamduh al-Leithi

Story Naguib Mahfouz

Dialogue Mamduh al-Leithi

Produced by al-Mu'assasa al-Misriya al-'Amma li-l-Sinima (The Egyptian Public Foundation for Cinema)

Music Michel Yusuf

Director of photography Abd al-Halim Nasr

Editor Said al-Sheikh

Set design Maher Abd al-Nour

Starring Shadya, Yusuf Wahbi, Yusuf Sha'ban, Imad Hamdi, Abd al-Mun'im Ibrahim, Abu Bakr Izzat, Abd al-Rahman Ali, Nadia al-Gindi, Nazim Sha'rawi, Esmat Ra'fat, Suhair Ramzi, Ahmad Tawfiq

Running time 120 minutes

First screening 13 October 1969

Black and white

IN ADAPTING NAGUIB MAHFOUZ'S much-loved 1967 novel for cinema, screenwriter Mamduh al-Leithi did as little tinkering as possible, making changes only "insofar as cinematic necessity dictated." Book and film both bring together an ill-suited assortment of characters with contrasting worldviews and lodge them together at the Pension Miramar in Alexandria, where they compete for the attention of the young serving girl Zuhra. The jealousies she inspires ultimately result in a tragic ending. In the book the sequence of events is retold multiple times from the viewpoints of four different protagonists (as in *al-Ragul al-laladhi faqada zilluh*, *see page 200*), but for the purposes of the film al-Leithi breaks with this structure in favor of a more traditionally linear method of storytelling. The movie has a clear beginning, middle, and end but, at the same time, it loses none of the subtleties of Mahfouz's story.

RIGHT The residents of the Miramar, including Tulba (Yusuf Wahbi, *center*) and Amr Wagdi (Imad Hamdi, *far-right*)

المؤسسة المصرية العامة للسينما
تقدم
ميرامار
قصة نجيب محفوظ
شاديه
يوسف وهبى
يوسف شعبان
عماد حمدى
عبدالمنعم ابراهيم
ابوبكر عزت
ناديه الجندى
سهير سامى
سهير رمزى
احمد توفيق
عصمت رأفت
ولأول مرة نجم التليفزيون
عبدالرحمن على
انتاج جمال الليثى
مدير التصوير عبدالحليم نصر
سيناريو وحوار ممدوح الليثى
اخراج كمال الشيخ
توزيع : المؤسسة المصرية العامة للسينما

Another tweak is in the character of Tulba Marzuk, a Miramar resident, who is not one of the four narrators of the novel. Mahfouz made him a thoroughly disagreeable character in the book. In al-Leithi's script he remains curmudgeonly yet likable, thanks largely to some wonderfully wry lines of dialogue and Yusuf Wahbi's sympathetic performance. The central figure in book and film is Amr Wagdi (Imad Hamdi), an elderly, retired journalist and long-time friend of the pension's owner Madame Mariana; the story starts and ends with him, a nod to the cyclical nature of history. Wagdi almost takes on the role of grandfather to Zuhra (Shadya), the young country girl desperate to become educated and modern. Standing in her way are a trio of other residents (the book's three other narrators), Husni 'Allam (Abu Bakr Izzat), a rich, womanizing playboy, Mansur Bahi (Abd al-Rahman Ali), an indecisive radio host, and Sarhan al-Beheiri (Yusuf Sha'ban), a larcenous party official. All three are venal and out for what they can get—which includes Zuhra. Happily, the tragic end alluded to earlier does not befall Zuhra; instead, it is one of the unsavory gentlemen who is found murdered. Who it is and who did it is not the point—*Miramar* is not a thriller but an enthralling portrait of the hopes and fears of post-Revolutionary Egypt. ★

KEY SCENE

We are at the dining table at the Pension Miramar, where the boarders are gathered to eat. They are introduced to a new arrival, Mansur Bahi. The ever-pompous Tulba Marzuk asks what he does for a living. "I'm an announcer at Alexandria Radio Station," replies Mansur, adding that he graduated from college four years ago. Tulba is surprised that it took four whole years for him to receive a government appointment. Mansur tells him he used to work at the Sawt al-Arab radio station and has only recently moved to Alexandria. Tulba introduces himself as a former deputy minister and his colleague Amr Wagdi as a "very old journalist." He introduces Sarhan al-Beheiri as a manager at the government-owned Textile Weaving Company and a member of the Revolution's ruling junta. Finally, he introduces Husni 'Allam as a rich fellow with "only a hundred feddans to his name!" They all say hello to Mansur. Sarhan asks Husni how he managed to avoid having all his family lands confiscated by the new Revolutionary government—as was the case with his own family. Husni deflects the question and leaves to attend a meeting, the resentment between these two young men already established. "I don't know what all these meetings are in aid of," Tulba says. "The Lord has seen fit to bestow wealth upon the undeserving, indeed."

Bi'r al-hirman

The Well of Privation | 1969

A modern-day Jekyll and Hyde story, in which a severe personality disorder causes a good girl to periodically turn bad

KAMAL EL-CHEIKH'S penchant for making movies about disturbed or unstable characters is to the fore here, with a drama tailored for audiences that are titillated by deviant sexual behavior and salacious psychobabble. For maximum effect, such psychological issues would ideally be manifested in someone who appears to be the epitome of normality, which in this case is girl-next-door Su'ad Husni. She suffers from a simplistic Jekyll-and-Hyde personality disorder in which most of the time she is plain old Nahid, but every now and again she flips and becomes the ultra-promiscuous and slutty Mervat. Appropriately for a film in which the lead character exhibits such a severe personality split that she goes by two different names, Kamal El-Cheikh shot two different endings. He and the producer, Ramsis Naguib, then held a private screening for journalists and critics

Released internationally as *Insatiable*

Director Kamal El-Cheikh

Screenplay Yusuf Francis

Story Ihsan Abd al-Quddus, adapted for the screen by Naguib Mahfouz

Dialogue Yusuf Francis

Produced by Ramsis Naguib

Music Tarek Sharara

Director of photography Wahid Farid

Editor Muhyi Abd al-Gawad

Set design Hilmi Azab

Starring Su'ad Husni, Maryam Fakhr al-Din, Mahmud al-Miligi, Nur al-Sharif, Salah Nazmi, Abd al-Rahman Abu Zahra, Muhyi Ismail, Hamdi Yusuf, Hamza al-Shimi, Thuraya Izz al-Din, Aquila Rif'at

Running time 91 minutes

First screening 29 December 1969

Color

LEFT Nahid (Su'ad Husni, *right*), (Abd al-Rahman Abu Zahra, *left*)

لا تسألوا الناس.. اسألوا الظروف!
احسان
سعاد حسني
مريم فخر الدين
محمود المليجي
نورا الشريف
صلاح نظمي
عبدالرحمن أبوزهره
محيي اسماعيل
حمزه الشيمي
حمدى يوسف
بئر الحرمان
قصة احسان عبد القدوس
نجيب محفوظ
يوسف فرنسيس
وحيد فريد
إخراج كمال الشيخ
بالألوان الطبيعية
الشركة العربية للسينما
وكالة الجاعوني

and invited them to choose between the two. In one version, when Nahid learns about her disorder she goes to her fiancé and tells him everything. He makes no answer, so she removes her engagement ring and goes off to commit suicide. He stops her at the last moment and there is a happy ending. The alternative has Nahid again spill the beans to her fiancé, who again is too shocked to respond, whereupon she goes away but he does not follow. However, her parents, who have learned the truth from her doctor (what happened to doctor-patient confidentiality?), intercept her and lead her away. The latter, slightly ambiguous ending was the one favored by the critics, so this is the one audiences saw.

Husni was at the height of her career at this time and threw herself into the character of the sick seductress with relish. Mahmud al-Miligi was her psychiatrist. El-Cheikh's talent in directing this type of movie was attested to by fellow director Husam al-Din Mustafa, who enthused that "the best thing about Kamal El-Cheikh's work is that I don't feel I'm watching a film because he's so great at making it look natural. I was no longer a director watching a colleague's work: I was so engrossed in the movie that I forgot myself. Kamal is a master at putting you on the edge of your seat." ★

Nahid is at the doctor's office, only she is not Nahid but Mervat and she attempts to seduce the doctor. Luckily he understands what is going on. He tranquilizes Mervat, which allows Nahid to regain control. She is shocked to find herself dressed in the manner of Mervat. The doctor explains all: Nahid, he says, created Mervat because she was afraid of being deprived of love in the way that her mother was by her husband's absences. When Nahid's former fiancé died, says the doctor, her subconscious then created Mervat, who launched herself into a life of wild sex to avoid being alone. (This is pre-Facebook, obviously.) "There will be no more Mervat," he reassures her. "She's finished for good." Then he leaves her to sleep and calls her father on the telephone, telling him to come right away. Meanwhile, Nahid wakes and slips out to see her current fiancé, to whom she tells all and offers to give back his engagement ring. She leaves to find her parents waiting outside. Her mother wraps a coat around her shoulders and leads her to the car. The fiancé stays where he is, as decided by the unsympathetic and unromantic film critics of Egypt.

Al-Ard

The Land | 1970

The inhabitants of a village make a stand against the authorities who try to loosen their hold on the land

Director Youssef Chahine

Screenplay Hassan Fu'ad

Story Abd al-Rahman al-Sharqawi

Dialogue Hassan Fu'ad

Produced by al-Mu'assasa al-Misriya al-'Amma li-l-Sinima (The Egyptian Public Foundation for Cinema)

Music Ali Ismail

Director of photography Abd al-Halim Nasr

Editor Rashida Abd al-Salam

Set design Salah Gaber

Starring Nagwa Ibrahim, Mahmud al-Miligi, Izzat al-Alayli, Yahya Shahin, Hamdi Ahmad, Abd al-Rahman al-Khamisi, Salah al-Sa'dani, Ali al-Sharif, Tawfiq al-Diqin, Abd al-Warith Assar, Abd al-Muhsin Selim, Ibrahim al-Shami, Hussein Assar

Festivals Cannes; Moscow, where it won an Award of Merit. Awarded Best Film by the Catholic Center. Won State Award for Best Picture. Al-Miligi won State Award for Best Actor.

Running time 130 minutes

First screening 26 January 1970

Color

AS THE TITLE SUGGESTS, *al-Ard* is at heart a homage to the physical and emotional attachment that Egyptian *fallahin* feel for the land. It is also a drama about greed, selfishness, and exploitation of the working classes. The setting is a small village in the Nile Delta that subsists on growing crops. That existence is threatened when the authorities halve the village's water ration. The villagers have to organize themselves to mount a protest. However, those who should represent the village against the authorities are more concerned with looking after their own interests. The bey, for example, while pretending to help the villagers, is using the dispute to build himself a new road on land taken from the peasants. The

ABOVE Abu Sweilem (Mahmud al-Miligi)

المؤسسة المصرية العامة للسينما تقدم
نجوى ابراهيم
عزت العلايلى
والممثل الكبير
محمود المليجى
بطولة
يحيى شاهين
حمدى احمد
توفيق الدقن
عبد الوارث عسر
حسين اسماعيل
فاطمة عمارة
عبد المحسن سليم
صلاح السعدنى
على الشريف
ابراهيم الشامى
حسين عسر
مع الفنان
عبد الرحمن الخميسى
إخراج
يوسف شاهين
الأرض
بالألوان الطبيعية
مدير التصوير : عبد الحليم نصر
سيناريو وحوار : حسن فؤاد
موسيقى : على اسماعيل
عن قصة عبد الرحمن الشرقاوى
الإعلان بريشة الفنان جمال كامل
توزيع: المؤسسة المصرية العامة للسينما

film's main protagonist and personification of the honorable *fallahin* is Mohamed Abu Sweilem (Mahmud al-Miligi), who leads his fellow landworkers—a cast considerably slimmed down from the novel, condensed and merged for the dramatic purposes of the film.

Chahine's depiction of the struggle is more nuanced than simply bad overlords versus good *fallahin*. When the water truck arrives the lined-up villagers begin to squabble, which quickly turns into a brawl—although this is immediately halted when a woman appears with the news that a cow has fallen into a waterhole and everyone unites in the rescue. There is a romantic subplot in which Abu Sweilem's daughter, Wasifa (a dedicated performance by Nagwa Ibrahim), is faced with a choice between two suitors, a simple fellow *fallah* or the educated son of a sheikh with good economic prospects, but the standout scenes revolve around al-Miligi. Chief of these is a barnstorming speech castigating the self-centered village officials and the film's powerful denouement (*see* the Key Scene box), which lends poignancy to the words of the film's main theme: "If the land is thirst we would irrigate it with our blood." ★

KEY SCENE

Two *fallahin* are talking during their break from harvesting cotton on Mohamed Abu Sweilem's land: Ilwani proposes a business venture to Abd al-Hadi, namely that the latter sell his land and buy some sheep, then hire Ilwani to take them out to pasture. Ilwani refuses: "Your land is like the clothes on your back," he says. As they speak we see the police arrive and storm in, beating up Ilwani and everyone else who is working the land. Abd al-Hadi tries to resist, but is struck down by a violent punch. Everyone runs away. The last man standing is Mohamed Abu Sweilem, who is clubbed with rifle butts until he bleeds. The chief of police commands that a rope be tied to his feet and attached to the chief's horse. The stricken Abd al-Hadi and Wasifa watch as Abu Sweilem is forcibly removed from his land, dragged along, face-down. The close-up of Abu Sweilem's bleeding hands clutching at the earth remains one of the most iconic scenes in the history of Egyptian cinema.

Ghurub wa shuruq

A Sunset and a Sunrise | 1970

A husband discovers that finding your wife in the bed of your best friend is not the worst that can happen

THERE HAVE BEEN many films set in the years immediately prior to the 1952 Revolution, but *Ghurub wa shuruq* is distinguished by being based on a story by Gamal Hammad, who as a military officer actually played a major role in the Free Officers' coup. His most significant piece of writing prior to drafting this story was the first Revolution Proclamation that was read over the radio by Anwar Sadat. In this tale the politics take a back seat to affairs of the heart. Azmi Pasha is the head of the political crimes department. He is callous and unfeeling toward everyone, including his daughter Madiha. While withholding his love from her, he is happy enough to find her husbands. That is husbands, plural, as Madiha easily tires of her partners, and when she does, Azmi uses his office to get rid of them, and then finds her someone else. Of course, sooner or

Director Kamal El-Cheikh

Screenplay Ra'fat al-Mihi

Story Gamal Hammad

Dialogue Ra'fat al-Mihi

Produced by al-Mu'assasa al-Misriya al-'Amma li-l-Sinima (The Egyptian Public Foundation for Cinema)

Music Andre Ryder

Director of photography Kamal Karim

Editor Said al-Sheikh

Set design Maher Abd al-Nour

Starring Su'ad Husni, Rushdi Abaza, Salah zu-l-Fiqar, Mahmud al-Miligi, Ibrahim Khan, Mohamed al-Dafrawi, Kamal Yassin, Nadia Seif al-Nasr, Salah Nazmi, Mimi Gamal, Zizi Mustafa, Adawi Ghayth

Festivals Carlo Vivari. Su'ad Husni was awarded the State Award for Best Actress, and Ra'fat al-Mihi for Best Screenplay.

Running time 119 minutes

First screening 19 March 1970

Black and white

LEFT Madiha (Su'ad Husni, *left*), Essam (Rushdi Abaza, *right*)

المؤسسة المصرية العامة للسينما تقدم
سعاد حسني • رشدي اباظه
صلاح ذو الفقار
مع
محمود المليجي
ابراهيم خان
محمد الدفراوي
صلاح نظمي
كمال يس
نادية سيف النصر
كمال كريم
رأفت الميهي
غروب وشروق
انتاج
حسن رمزي
قصة جمال حماد
اخراج
كمال الشيخ
توزيع : المؤسسة المصرية العامة للسينما

later she runs up against a husband who is not so accepting of her disposable attitude to men. When husband Samir finds her in the bed of one of his friends he decides to pay her back, but this is something Azmi cannot allow and so he disposes of Samir in a very permanent fashion.

Ra'fat al-Mihi (who would go on to become a noted director in his own right) had the job of turning the story into a screenplay. He worked closely with director Kamal El-Cheikh and the script went through six full revisions before all parties were satisfied. The social and political setting of Cairo at the turn of the 1950s permeates the film. The royal palace controls the populace; the British control the king. For maximum historical credibility, El-Cheikh filmed most of the events in the villa of Nahhas Pasha, one of the most prominent politicians prior to 1952, and one of the worst treated after the Revolution. The authenticity this lent the film cannot be overestimated. Mention must also be made of the actors' commitment to this particular project. Ibrahim Khan, who played Samir, was nearly killed shooting a scene in which he is run down by a car driven by the political police: the driver, misjudging his speed, hit Khan for real. Forgoing the services of a stuntwoman, Su'ad Husni insisted on allowing herself to be dragged downstairs in the scene in which Samir discovers her betrayal; she ended up covered with cuts and bruises for her art. ★

This is the scene in which Samir discovers that his wife is unfaithful. It sets in motion a chain of events that leads to Samir's killing and his friends abandoning their lives of pleasure to engage in the struggle to liberate their country from corruption. It begins with Samir arriving at the apartment belonging to his friend Essam. The audience is way ahead of him and already knows what he is going to find there. El-Cheikh masterfully ratchets up the tension, focusing on Samir's footsteps as he heads toward the apartment. He opens the apartment door and enters. He is there as a favor to see a woman out of the apartment—Essam has no idea that his conquest is actually his friend's wife. Tutting at Essam's Lothario-like behavior, Samir knocks on the bedroom door to wake the woman inside. He looks in and is stunned to see the person emerging from the sheets is his wife. Shock quickly turns to rage and he beats her savagely. She tries to tell him that nothing happened between her and Essam, but he drags her out of the apartment in her nightdress, to her intense humiliation.

Al-Sarab

The Mirage | 1970

A man with an Oedipus complex seeks help from a psychiatrist who ends up having an affair with his wife

Director Anwar al-Shinnawi

Screenplay Ali al-Zurqani

Story Naguib Mahfouz

Dialogue Ali al-Zurqani

Produced by al-Mu'assasa al-Misriya al-'Amma li-l-Sinima (The Egyptian Public Foundation for Cinema)

Music Andre Ryder

Director of photography Mahmud Nasr

Editor Kamal Abu al-Ila

Set design Nihad Bahgat

Starring Magda, Nur al-Sharif, Rushdi Abaza, Aquila Ratib, Tahiya Carioca, Abbas Fares, Aziza Hilmi, Zinnat Sidqi, Mimi Gamal, Mohamed Abaza, Zinnat Ilwi

Running time 140 minutes

First screening 28 December 1970

Black and white

THIS MOVIE WAS the directorial debut of Anwar al-Shinnawi, who was an assistant director before he stepped up to the helm. His choice of subject matter suggests he was not lacking in confidence. Based on an early (1948) short novel by Naguib Mahfouz, it is the story of Kamil, who is raised under the loving but domineering thumb of his mother. As a result he is chronically introverted, struggles to interact with others, and when, wonder of wonders, he does finally marry, he is discovered to be impotent. He consults a psychiatrist who, while he makes little headway with Kamil, does considerably better with the wife, having an affair with her and getting her pregnant. This cannot end well and it does not. In the wrong hands this could have been a lurid affair, but al-Shinnawi manages to craft an unusual movie of the first order. Rather than playing up the melodrama, he leans toward the psychological. He employs some clever directorial flourishes to achieve this: for instance, when the student Kamil is called to the front of the auditorium we see the scene from his point of view, eyes firmly fixed downward on his feet as he hesitantly proceeds down the steps of the lecture hall, desperate not to catch anybody's eye. It is an extremely skillful evocation of social anxiety. Another example of al-Shinnawi's smarts is how he manages to suggest Kamil's masturbatory habits without falling foul of the censor. He shows him peeking through the blinds at the maid smoothing her stockings up to her thighs and then cuts to a rocking chair shaking violently as the maid pumps a plunger to unblock the sink.

The cinematography was groundbreaking in other ways. It ventures to places that had not been seen at the cinema before, notably the Heliopolis tramway, which runs by the heroine's house. The shots of the tram were not gratuitous: its carriages play a role in events, including Kamil's first encounter with his future wife Rabab. The tram is where he falls in love with her, where he holds her hand for

المؤسسة المصرية العامة للسينما
تقدم
ماجده
نور الشريف
عقيله راتب
تحيه كاريوكا
عباس فارس
ضيف الشرف
رشدى أباظه
قصة
نجيب محفوظ
السراب
سيناريو وحوار علي الزرقاني
مدير التصوير محمود نصر
موسيقى أندريا رايدر
إنتاج
ماجده
إخراج
أنور الشناوى
توزيع : المؤسسة المصرية العامة للسينما
مطابع النصر بالقاهرة

RIGHT Kamil (Nur al-Sharif, *left*), Rabab (Magda, *right*)

the first time. They pine for each other while gazing out of the tram's windows. After the final tragedy in which Kamil loses Rabab, the film ends with a shot of the tram motionless at the station. No matter how skilled the director, the film could never have worked if the character of Kamil was not one hundred per cent believable, and it is all credit to a baby-faced Nur al-Sharif, who turns in a superbly neurotic performance. His bewilderment bordering on terror in the scene in which he is subjected to crude sexual advances by a working-class woman helped launch his career. ★

KEY SCENE

The movie's first scene is key to introducing audiences to Kamil's social anxiety disorder. He is in a large hall in the Faculty of Law, sitting by himself at the rear, waiting for the lecture to begin. All the other students are outside chattering and laughing. When they come in to take their seats, clustering in friendly nodes, Kamil's isolation, especially from the girls, is made clear. The lecture begins. The professor throws out questions to the students, asking how they would handle a given criminal case. He singles out Kamil and asks him to introduce himself: "I don't know you, after all. You always sit all by yourself at the back." Kamil gives his name, visibly embarrassed at having to do so, particularly because he has an unusual surname. The students titter. The professor tells them to be quiet and asks Kamil to come to the front. Kamil makes his way down the stairs of the hall, dragging his feet, painfully aware that everybody is watching him. He reaches the professor, who asks, "Did you hear that last question or not?" Kamil remains silent. The professor urges him to reply. He answers, "No," whereupon all the students laugh. It is more than Kamil can bear and he runs from the lecture hall.

Imra'a wa ragul

A Woman and a Man | 1971

A gritty tale of lust, infidelity, and ultimately murder set in and around a stone quarry

THIS FILM IS ADAPTED from a short story entitled "Abu Fuda," from a collection by Yahya Hakki entitled *The Blood of Lowlifes*. Despite his limited output, many critics consider Hakki the father of the Egyptian short story and someone who greatly contributed to the popularity of the genre, as well as generously supporting the work of subsequent generations of writers. He repeatedly wrote about the deprived, and the physically and mentally disabled, and this particular story also deals with a marginalized element of society. In this case it is a community whose lives revolve around the stone quarries that are found on the outskirts of some governorates in Egypt. This inhospitable setting had rarely been used in Egyptian cinema before. The screenplay made the landscape integral to the plot, while the cinematography played up the inhospitality and giddy elevations of the quarry, with strange camera angles that accentuated the drama. When the point of the scene is to show the harsh working conditions of the stonecutters, the camera shoots from the bottom of the cliffs to exaggerate the quarry's dizzying height. The camera pans down to follow a workman suspended by ropes down the rock face. A bird's-eye view captures another quarry worker enlarging a hole in the rockface to make it big enough to stick in some dynamite. A long shot makes the workmen appear like scurrying ants as they run for cover on the quarry floor before the explosion blows out the rock. There are other examples of inventive camerawork away from the quarry, such as the close-ups of the feet of peasant women walking by when Gasser is in his wood lean-to waiting for Nargis to pass by.

Gasser and Nargis are two of the three that make a taut love triangle of husband, wife, and lover. The husband is Ismail (Tawfiq al-Diqin). He is innocent and trusting, which is unfortunate for him, with a slowness in the way he looks at others, and a simpleton's speech that suggests some undiagnosed mental disability. As a guest at Gasser's

Director Husam al-Din Mustafa

Screenplay Sabri Izzat and Faysal Nada

Story Yahya Hakki

Dialogue Sabri Izzat and Faysal Nada

Produced by Ihab al-Laythi

Music Mursi al-Hattab

Director of photography Ali Khairallah

Editor Hussein Ahmad

Set design Hilmi Azab

Starring Rushdi Abaza, Nahid Sharif, Tawfiq al-Diqin, Ibrahim al-Shami, Zizi Mustafa, Hussein Ismail, Farouk Falawkas

Running time 96 minutes

First screening 28 June 1971

Black and white

engagement to the foreman's daughter, Ismail watches his wife Nargis dance and sing in front of the rest of the men. He thinks she is singing to him alone and sits there smiling, looking around shyly at the assembled men who, he believes, are witnessing an intimate moment of his wife wooing him in public. Egyptian audiences would of course consider it "unmanly" to allow one's womenfolk to sing and dance in public. Besides, everyone can see she is flirting with Gasser. Nahid Sharif was already established in Egyptian cinema as a sex symbol and so she was perfect as a cheating she-devil of a wife. Rushdi Abaza, as her lover Gasser, is torn up with anguish at his betrayal of Ismail and abandonment of his fiancée, but faced with the seductive power of Nahid Sharif, what is a man to do? ★

KEY SCENE

The most tragic scene in the film has Ismail, the cuckolded husband, praising his wife in front of her barely-secret lover. It begins with Ismail turning on the lamp for an evening of smoking and conversation with Gasser, who fires up his waterpipe. Ismail starts pouring out his life story to Gasser: when his father died, Ismail says, he left him a wealthy man. He married Nargis, a pretty girl from Beheira, then spent all his fortune on her. But even though the money was all gone they managed: "Nargis did it all," says Ismail with amazement. "She goes to market and takes care of everything. Thanks to her, I want for nothing." He tells Gasser how Nargis raises chickens, and sells eggs, live chicks, cheese, butter, and milk. At this point Nargis enters. "Such a good girl, the best woman in the world," says proud Ismail. "An honest woman and no mistake!" She then offers them meat for dinner. "Bless you!" says her husband, completely unaware that it is all lies and that she makes money by selling her body. Gasser refuses to eat with them, considering that a meal bought with a whore's earnings is tainted. He has no problem falling into her bed, though.

ABOVE Gasser (Rushdi Abaza, *right*), Nargis (Nahid Sharif, *left*)

Tharthara fawq al-Nil

Adrift on the Nile | 1971

On a houseboat on the Nile a gang of artists and intellectuals gathers to drink, get stoned, and despair at the lost promise of the Revolution

Released internationally as *Chattering on the Nile*

Director Hussein Kamal

Screenplay Mamduh al-Leithi

Story Naguib Mahfouz

Dialogue Mamduh al-Leithi

Produced by Gamal al-Leithi

Music Ali Ismail

Director of photography Mustafa Imam

Editor Rashida Abd al-Salam

Set design Maher Abd al-Nur

Starring Ahmad Ramzi, Imad Hamdi, Suhair Ramzi, Adil Adham, Ahmad Tawfiq, Salah Nazmi, Mervat Amin, Magda al-Khatib, Ahmad al-Gezeiri, Ni'mat Mukhtar, Anwar Madkur, Mohamed Sultan, Hamdi Yusuf, Mahmud Farid, Aida al-Sha'ir, Qadriya Kamil, Fathiya Ali

Running time 121 minutes

First screening 15 November 1971

Black and white

THE IMPORTANCE OF this work lies in its portrayal of a specific and traumatic era in Egyptian history: the years immediately following the military defeat of 1967 and before the redemption that came in 1973. The source was a novel by Naguib Mahfouz in which the main theme is the author's/characters' disappointment with the aftermath of the 1952 Revolution. Mahfouz believed the revolutionary leaders had strayed from their goals and become no better than the regime they had ousted, replacing the aristocracy of old with military officers who were equally susceptible to blatant abuses of power. The Revolution, contended Mahfouz, had failed in achieving anything resembling democracy, in respecting differences of opinion, in offering meaningful progress, and in abolishing the cruelties of the state security apparatuses.

RIGHT Nargis (Mervat Amin, *left*), Ragab (Ahmad Ramzi, *center*)

افلام جمال الليثى تقدم
قصة الكاتب الكبير
نجيب محفوظ
احمد رمزى • ماجده الخطيب
فى
ثرثره فوق النيل
مع
ميرفت أمين
عماد حمدى
عادل أدهم
سهير رمزى
نعمت مختار
أحمد توفيق
صلاح نظمى
سيناريو وحوار
ممدوح الليثى
مدير التصوير: مصطفى إمام
الموسيقى التصويرية: على اسماعيل
إخراج:
حسين كمال
توزيع أفركو

All of this comes through clearly in the movie, even if screenwriter Mamduh al-Leithi had to jettison much of the detail of the novel to make it work for the screen. The protagonist remains Anis (Imad Hamdi), a civil servant working at the Ministry of Health and our narrator. He is part of a group of friends that include an actor named Ragab (Ahmad Ramzi), a lawyer, a journalist, and a writer. They were all once revolutionaries, fighting for their country's future, but when the Revolution was over they were cast aside. Now they spend their time on Ragab's Nile houseboat smoking hash and drinking, as one of the characters explains, maintaining a self-induced coma to insulate themselves from reality. The state of affairs is broken when a car in which the gang is joyriding is involved in a hit-and-run incident in which a peasant woman is killed, an event that brings Anis to his senses. He attempts to awaken the others to the fact that they need to re-engage and make a difference. Failing to rouse them, he sinks back into the stoned stupor from which he briefly emerged. It is a highly subversive film and even today remains banned in some Arab countries. ★

KEY SCENE

We are on a houseboat on the Nile. Among those gathered on this particular evening is an occasional visitor, the journalist Samara. She invites everyone to come with her at six the next morning to Tahrir Square, where a bus is set to leave for the front, where Egyptian forces are dug in, facing off against the Israelis. A number of prominent artists and stars will be onboard. Everybody declines and continues dancing, smoking, and talking, much to Anis's disgust. "Nobody here deserves to visit the front!" he shouts. The others start to make fun, which drives him to fury. "You're all shiny and cultured on the outside, but hollow on the inside," he accuses the lawyer. "You are capable of changing nothing." To the journalist: "You're just an illusion. You only write what you've been paid to." To Saniya: "All you care about is finding reasons to cheat on your husband." To the novelist: "Nothing you do is any use. What can you believe in when you're this debauched?" To the student: "Your generation is lost. You've no culture or morals." Finally he turns his anger on himself: "I am nothing. I'm half-mad and half-dead. I'm a chair with drugs on it." Rather than being insulted, the group finds the outburst amusing: they all laugh and continue partying.

Zawjati wa-l-kalb

My Wife and the Cur | 1971

A newlywed man is forced to leave his wife to work in a remote lighthouse, where he is tortured by memories of his philandering youth

THIS WAS SAID MARZUK'S first feature, the first in what was to be a long line of sexually driven stories he committed to film. Time and again in Marzuk's work, sex drives the plot, sometimes in blatant fashion, other times concealed under a bonnet of religious or social respectability. Apparently, Marzuk was inspired to write *Zawjati wa-l-kalb* by the sight of a solitary lighthouse surrounded by sea. He was intrigued by what he imagined must be the utter isolation experienced by the men who work in such a place. For the purposes of his film, Marzuk casts Mahmud Mursi as Mursi, an older man who has just married the young and beautiful Su'ad and has left her alone to join three colleagues in their stone tower far from civilization. Marzuk makes much of the tedium and repetitiveness of everyday life in the lighthouse; he repeats certain movements and scenes, such as Mursi's

Released internationally as *My Wife and the Dog*

Director Said Marzuk

Screenplay Said Marzuk

Story Said Marzuk

Dialogue Said Marzuk

Produced by al-Mu'assasa al-Misriya al-'Amma li-l-Sinima (The Egyptian Public Foundation for Cinema)

Music Ibrahim Haggag

Director of photography Abd al-Aziz Fahmi

Editors Atiya Abdu and Hussein Afifi

Set design Abd al-Mun'im Shukri

Starring Su'ad Husni, Mahmud Mursi, Nur al-Sharif, Hassan Hussein, Abd al-Mun'im Abu al-Futuh, Zizi Mustafa, Wahid Seif

Festivals Moscow

Running time 95 minutes

First screening 17 November 1971

Black and white

LEFT Su'ad (Su'ad Husni, *right*), Abbas (Nur al-Sharif, *left*)

المؤسسة المصرية العامة للسينما
تقدم
إنتاج
عبد العزيز فهمي
سُعاد حسني
محمود مرسي
نور الشريف
زوجتي والكلب
حسن حسين
عبد المنعم ابو الفتوح
زيزي مصطفى
وحيد سيف
عبد المنعم بسيوني
مدير التصوير
عبد العزيز فهمي
سيناريو وإخراج
سعيد مرزوق
توزيع : المؤسسة المصرية العامة للسينما

footsteps, the young Nur caressing his photos of naked women, Hafiz dropping off to sleep, and Abbas's dull, soporific tones. The exterior of the lighthouse—thanks to Abd al-Aziz Fahmi's cinematography—evokes a similar sense of oppressiveness with a featureless blue sky and an unbroken expanse of water. The editing is brilliant, cutting between scenes to suggest thoughts rapidly tumbling through the agitated Mursi's head, settling to a slower rhythm for the other men in the lighthouse. Ibrahim Haggag's score is intelligent and supremely expressive. Its centerpiece is a choral humming of Sayyid Darwish's traditional song "Zuruni kulli sana marra" ("Visit Me Once a Year"), which is repeated throughout the movie.

There is little in the way of a plot: the men play cards, Nur catches a fish and they eat it, and Mursi becomes increasingly tormented by the possibility of his wife looking for male company while he is so far away. Instead, Marzuk brings a whole new approach to narrative structure, using evocative imagery to take us on a psychological journey around Mursi's inner life and emotions. In one scene in which Mursi reads a letter from his wife, Marzuk not only uses Su'ad's own voice but has her stand next to her husband as she speaks the words she has written. When Mursi eats his fish, the camera reverses to show Su'ad, as if she were sitting across from him watching. In his head, she is always with him. Even the naming of the characters seems to have some deeper meaning. Mursi is played by Mahmud Mursi (who is excellent), Nur by Nur al-Sharif, and Su'ad by Su'ad Husni. This blurring of fiction and reality adds to the unconventionality of the film and sends the audience away with plenty to think about. ★

We are in the lighthouse and Mursi and Abbas are laying down a carpet so that the four men can sit and play cards on the floor. As they play, chat, and laugh, the men—and we the audience—can forget their loneliness. The effect is heightened by the soundtrack of a crowded coffee shop that Marzuk superimposes onto the scene. Eventually, the game ends and the camera pulls back to show the four of them surrounded by cold, empty space. Two of the men retire to bed, leaving just Mursi and Nur. Mursi tells tales of his youth, when he would cheat on his colleagues with their wives. "But they were your friends," says Nur, shocked that anyone could so easily betray such trust. In this way Mursi sows the seeds of his own grief: later, when Nur is returning to land, Mursi gives him a gift to deliver to Su'ad, but almost immediately he remembers the stories he told the boy and he becomes terrified that Nur might follow his example.

Kilmit sharaf

Word of Honor | 1972

A thriller in which a man continually attempts to escape from prison to prove his innocence to his dying wife

Director Husam al-Din Mustafa

Screenplay Farouk Sabri and Farid Shawqi

Story Farouk Sabri

Dialogue Farouk Sabri and Farid Shawqi

Produced by Aflam 'Abir al-Sharq (Perfume of the East Films)

Director of photography Ali Khairallah

Editor Fikri Rustum

Set design Mohamed Bahig

Starring Farid Shawqi, Ahmad Mazhar, Nur al-Sharif, Hind Rustum, Nelly, Rushdi Abaza, Ahmad Luxor, Canaan Wasfi, Aziza Rashid, Magdi Wahba, Sami al-Adl

Festivals Best Picture Award from the Catholic Center

Running time 90 minutes

First screening 27 March 1972

Black and white

A PRISON BREAKOUT movie with a difference, in that the attempt to get out of jail hinges on the efforts of the prison warden. The prisoner Salim has made numerous failed attempts to escape, only succeeding in getting more years added onto his sentence. After the latest foiled scheme he tells the prison warden that the reason he is so keen on his freedom is that he wants to prove his innocence to his wife, who is seriously ill and does not have long to live. The warden decides to help Salim obtain the evidence of his innocence, but they are thwarted by the premature death of the man who most likely committed the crime for which Salim was convicted. Nevertheless, the warden places his trust in the prisoner and takes a huge risk in allowing him out on a promise that he will voluntarily return to his cell. Although the story largely plays out in an extremely limited setting—a prison—the movie is never boring. The director, Husam al-Din Mustafa, wisely employs flashbacks to provide a little visual variety. He also manages to deliver a hefty dose of suspense. Aiding him in keeping the audience enrapt is a star turn by Farid Shawqi as Salim. Rarely has a jailbird possessed such charisma—one look into the pools of sincerity that are his eyes and it is no wonder the warden caved in.

Credit should also be given to Rushdi Abaza; although he is not on screen for long, as the feared prisons inspector he is essential to the film's success. If the warden did not truly fear him, there would be no suspense (*see* the Key Scene box). Hind Rustum is also solid as the suffering—in more than one sense—wife who is distraught that her trust in her husband has been betrayed. Even if he can do nothing to prevent her terminal illness, Salim must at least bring some relief to his dear wife by establishing his innocence of the crime for which he was imprisoned. His efforts would have been meaningless had Rustum been unconvincing.

ABOVE Salim Abu al-Naga (Farid Shawqi, *left*), Lieutenant (Rushdi Abaza, *center*), Ahmad (Ahmad Mazhar, *right*)

In addition to being a thoroughly entertaining movie, *Kilmit sharaf* also had an important social impact. In response to the film's message the Ministry of the Interior passed a new law to allow temporary compassionate furloughs from prison in compelling cases for individuals serving long sentences. ★

KEY SCENE

This begins with the arrival of the prisons inspector at the maximum-security wing. He requests to see the prisoner Salim Abu al-Naga. The warden tells him that Abu al-Naga is in the prison hospital, only to be contradicted by a warder who says, no, he's in his cell. The inspector then rebukes the warden for being unaware of the exact whereabouts of a dangerous criminal. He demands to be taken straight to the cell. The warden knows, of course, that Salim is not in his cell because he has allowed him out of the prison to visit his wife. He was acting on his own authority and should this be discovered he might even end up in a cell himself. The inspector enters the wing and orders a guard to open Abu al-Naga's cell. A warder places a key in the door, unlocks it, and swings open the door. The warden is so nervous he can hardly stand. As he steels himself for the wrath of the inspector he hears voices: it is the inspector speaking and the voice answering in reply is Salim Abu al-Naga's. The warden pulls the warder out. "When did he get back?" he asks. "Just a few moments ago," says the warder. "He said he was allowed to come back from the prison hospital unescorted, sir." The warden staggers into the cell in time to hear Salim promise the inspector that he will not make another escape attempt—he meets the warden's eyes—"My word of honor." When the inspector leaves, the warden takes Salim into his arms in an embrace of mutual gratitude.

Qa' al-madina

Dregs of the City | 1974

A drama in which a high-class judge desires sex only with lower-class women

IN THIS PSYCHOLOGICAL drama, the director leads the audience into the dark, seamy underbelly of society. We are led there by Judge Abdullah (Mahmud Yassin), a man of status who, despite approaching middle age, remains unmarried. For female company he visits the brothel run by Madame Shindi. Unfortunately the judge experiences performance issues, which the film suggests arise from status anxiety. At home he has a new servant, an attractive working-class woman, Shuhrat (Nadia Lutfi). She is married with two children, but taking advantage of his position of power Abdullah forces himself upon her. Shuhrat resists but eventually Abdullah prevails, and to his delight manages to perform the sexual act. Resigned to her fate, Shuhrat, who

Director Husam al-Din Mustafa

Screenplay Ahmad Abbas Salih

Story Yusuf Idris

Dialogue Ahmad Abbas Salih

Produced by Hayman Film

Director of photography Ibrahim Salih

Editor Fikri Rustum

Set design Nihad Bahgat

Starring Nadia Lutfi, Mahmud Yassin, Nelly, Tawfiq al-Diqin, Mimi Shekib, George Sidhom, Fayiq Bahgat, Abd al-Ghani al-Nagdi, Canaan Wasfi

Festivals Best Actress Award from the Film Association for Nadia Lutfi

Running time 105 minutes

First screening 28 January 1974

Color

LEFT Abdullah (Mahmud Yassin, *left*), Shuhrat (Nadia Lutfi, *right*)

هيمن فيلم
يقدم
نادية لطفى · محمود ياسين · نيللى
توفيق الدقن
جورج سيدهم
قصة: د. يوسف ادريس
قاع
المدينه
بالالوان الطبيعيه
إخراج
حُسام الدين مصطفى
سيناريو وحوار: احمد عباس صالح
مدير التصوير: ابراهيم صالح
التوزيع بمصر وجميع أنحاء العالم: هيمن فيلم ١٦ شارع عدلى - القاهرة

badly needs the money the job brings, decides that if she is going to be used for sex, then she is going to make sure Abdullah pays. Over time she develops a hold on him. She asks for money and he complies. She begins to dress differently and gains in confidence, to the point where she is no longer docile and subservient. This does not suit Abdullah at all and he dismisses her, refusing any sort of severance pay or the loan she asks for. Not long after, he realizes that his watch is missing. Abdullah is sure that Shuhrat has stolen it and while it is not particularly valuable, he wants it back. With the help of his friend he achieves this (*see* the Key Scene box), but in doing so he manages to ruin the reputation of Shuhrat by letting the whole street where she lives know that she has been unfaithful to her husband, who happens to be sick and bedridden. Branded a fallen woman, the only option for Shuhrat is to continue on the path she has begun and turn to prostitution to support her family. The seamy side of society is not the lower classes and the prostitutes, after all, but the privileged and the powerful who would abuse them. ★

KEY SCENE

Judge Abdullah has enlisted the help of his friend Sharaf the actor who puts on a policeman's uniform and together the pair heads to where Shuhrat lives. They drive through old neighborhoods and slum areas of tumbledown houses until they reach the place they are looking for. Their arrival draws a crowd of the curious. They enter the decrepit building and take the stairs up to the roof, where they are told Shuhrat lives. They find her squatting beside a metal washtub in which she is bathing her son. They enter her miserable hovel, where they see her husband lying sick in bed. Sharaf takes in the scene and is overcome with pity for the woman and her wretched situation. He walks away, washing his hands of the whole affair. Abdullah demands his watch, otherwise he will bring his police friend back to arrest her, and Shuhrat gives it up. He leaves with his worthless watch, having broadcast Shuhrat's role as his whore to the entire alley.

Al-Mumya'

The Mummy | 1975

A somber and highly stylized tale of tomb robbers considered by some to be the *Citizen Kane* of Egyptian cinema

Released internationally as *The Night of Counting the Years*

Director Shadi Abd al-Salam

Screenplay Shadi Abd al-Salam

Story Shadi Abd al-Salam

Dialogue Shadi Abd al-Salam

Produced by al-Mu'assasa al-Misriya al-'Amma li-l-Sinima (The Egyptian Public Foundation for Cinema) with Roberto Rossellini

Music Mario Nascimbene

Director of photography Abd al-Aziz Fahmi

Editor Kamal Abu al-Ila

Set design Shadi Abd al-Salam

Starring Ahmad Mar'i, Nadia Lutfi, Ahmad Higazi, Zuzu Hamdi al-Hakim, Mohamed Khairy, Shafiq Nur al-Din, Mohamed Nabih, Ahmad Anan, Mohamed Murshid, Abd al-Azim Abd al-Haqq, Abd al-Mun'im Abu al-Futuh

Running time 99 minutes

First screening 27 January 1975

Color

***AL-MUMYA'* IS NOT** just one of the most important films in the history of Egyptian cinema, it is a film of world significance—as evidenced by the fact that in 2009 it was selected by Martin Scorsese's World Cinema Foundation to be restored, preserved, and exhibited for a global audience. It is a movie unlike anything ever made before—and arguably since—in Egypt. One might call it epic or even operatic, except there is no grand drama, or booming music, or a cast of thousands. Instead it is a stark and austere movie, with minimal dialogue, full of stern visages and bookended by solemn processions. In the whole movie not one character ever smiles.

The film is loosely based on true events. It is the late 19th century in Upper Egypt. For decades a local clan has kept itself in funds by raiding a cache of mummies hidden in a mountain cave, and drip-feeding pieces onto the black market. But when one of the family elders dies and his sons are initiated into the illicit trade they are appalled to

RIGHT Wanis (Ahmad Mar'i, *right*), Zeina (Nadia Lutfi, *left*)

Festivals Venice; Carthage; London; Berlin; Sydney; Chicago; Belgrade; San Francisco; Carlo Vivari. Award of Merit from the Film Association. Best Actress for Nadia Lutfi from the Egyptian Catholic Center.

witness their uncle beheading a mummy to free a golden necklace and want nothing to do with the desecration of their ancestors. The elder brother is killed to prevent him informing the authorities and it falls to the younger brother to decide whether to preserve the secret or not. All of this plays out at an almost excruciatingly slow pace, with the dialogue entirely in classical Arabic, lending it an almost Shakespearean quality. The photography is simply beautiful, with slow camera movements, unusual angles, and extraordinary filtered lighting. The desert, the Nile, and ancient monuments all take on a symbolic weight, and the whole of the film has a languid, melancholic, and dreamlike air.

Astonishingly, this was Shadi Abd al-Salam's first film as a director, and he also wrote the story and screenplay. All his previous work had been as a set designer, and here the settings—all shot in Upper Egypt—and the costumes are magnificent. The visuals are augmented by suitably haunting music composed by the Italian Mario Nascimbene. Even more astonishing is that Shadi Abd al-Salam never made another feature film. He directed some documentaries but his great project on the pharaoh Akhenaten, for which he worked on the screenplay for ten years, remained unfilmed when he died in 1986. ★

KEY SCENE

We are in the simple home of the wife of Selim, the deceased chief of the clan. Two of the clan elders speak with Selim's eldest son and heir. He tells them that he rejects the village's long-standing livelihood of trading in the contents of tombs. "I will no longer live by stripping corpses." One of those present tells him, "Now your father is dead, you are the only one who knows where the coffins are. Your father's share of the treasure will go to you and your brother." The son rejects the offer of treasure stolen from their ancestors. "They've been dead for thousands of years," says one of the elders, "it's not as if we'd be cheating their parents or children out of their inheritance." They offer Selim's widow their condolences, exchanging ritual words of consolation. Then they present Selim's son with an artifact from the tomb. "This was your father's share," they say, and advise him to sell it to Ayyub the trader. "Don't lend your ears to those fine fellows from Cairo and the archaeologists, who'll lock you up in jail if they find a single artifact in your possession," they warn. "The secret is worth more than the life of any member of the clan. These artifacts are the clan's livelihood. You must be strong." The son remains unmoved and tells them that this life is sinful and is poison to him. He hands back the treasure. The elders let him know that this is not the end of the matter and they leave.

Uridu hallan

I Want a Solution | 1975

A woman seeks to divorce her husband in a family court where she meets women much worse off than herself

Director Said Marzuk

Screenplay Said Marzuk

Story Hassan Shah

Dialogue Sa'd al-Din Wahba

Produced by Salah zu-l-Fiqar Films

Music Gamal Salama

Director of photography Mustafa Imam

Editor Said al-Sheikh

Set design Maher Abd al-Nour

Starring Fatin Hamama, Rushdi Abaza, Layla Tahir, Raga' Hussein, Kamal Yassin, Amina Rizq, Suhair Sami, Sharif Lutfi, Marwan Hamid, Wahid Seif, Sayyid Zayyan, Ibrahim Sa'fan, Usama Abbas, Ali al-Sharif, Mohamed al-Sab', Abd al-Alim Khattab, Kawthar Shafiq, Layla Fahmi, Hisham Selim

Running time 106 minutes

First screening 31 March 1975

Color

IT IS RARE TO FIND an Egyptian movie based on a story written by a woman, but here modern journalistic legend Hassan Shah presents a tale that no man would have written because it deals with an issue with which they would have had no grievance. Most of the events of *Uridu hallan* take place in the family affairs court, where documentary footage of scenes in its hallways and corridors is used to point up everything that was wrong with the Family Affairs Law of 1965. This allowed a husband to verbally divorce his wife without ever having to put anything in writing, thus leaving her in legal limbo. A woman who objected and demanded her rights to an official divorce could be dragged through the mud by means of a variety of laws on the books, for example the *ta'a*, or obedience law, which was so weighted in

LEFT Durriya (Fatin Hamama, *middle*), Fathi (Rushdi Abaza, *right*), (Mohamed al-Sab', *left*)

افلام صلاح ذو الفقار تقدم
فاتن حمامه
رشدى اباظه
اخراج
سعيد مرزوق
أريد حلاً....
بالألوان الطبيعية
ليلى طاهر
امينه رزق
سيد زيان
ابراهيم سعفان
قصة حسن شاه
حوار سعدالدين وهبه
سيناريو سعيد مرزوق
مدير التصوير مصطفى امام
انتاج
صلاح ذو الفقار
التوزيع لجميع انحاء العالم ، افلام ايهاب الليثى ٣٧ شارع قصر النيل - القاهرة

favor of the man that it could lead to a woman being quite literally dragged back into the marital home by the police. This is the fate that befalls Durriya (Fatin Hamama) in her attempts to divorce her philandering and abusive husband, Midhat (a truly chilling performance by Rushdi Abaza).

This movie, arguably the most influential social drama of its generation, sparked endless debate—although matters only really improved with the passage of the *khul'* law, which did not happen until 2000. This allowed a woman to file for divorce based on a *hadith* of the Prophet Mohamed, which is quoted by the protagonist of *Uridu hallan* in a scene in which she makes her plea to the minister of justice. Hassan Shah's title—in English "I Want a Solution"—is supremely eloquent. The woman wanting a solution is every woman who has found herself in Durriya's tragic shoes. Fatin Hamama departed from her usual role of sentimental heroine, showing exceptional spunk as Durriya, the intelligent and cultured woman who not only knows her rights but is well read in Islamic jurisprudence. We discover with delight that she is more than capable of conducting an argument on equal terms with the minister of justice. Amina Rizq scintillates in a small but unforgettable role as a fellow complainant in court. In a rare moment of female bonding in Egyptian cinema, she shares her problem with Durriya and although she has only a few moments of screen time, and although hers is not the primary case in the film, *Uridu hallan* is forever linked in audiences' minds with Amina Rizq. It is not that she upstages her fellow actors, more that the unjust decision imposed on her by the court was so shocking that many believe it was the ultimate impetus for the eventual change in the law. ★

Festivals Awarded Best Picture by the Ministry of Culture. Fatin Hamama was awarded Best Actress at the Cairo International Film Festival and also from the Film Association. Said Marzuk was awarded Best Director by the Film Association. Amina Rizq won an award for Best Actress.

In a scene that captured audiences' hearts, looking to avoid her husband, Durriya takes a seat on a bench under the courthouse stairs. She finds herself next to another plaintiff, Hayat al-Barrani (Amina Rizq). Durriya asks her how her case is going. "I lost," says Hayat, "and the court made me pay the costs." She is here to appeal. "I lived with my husband for thirty years," says Hayat. "I did everything for him that it was a wife's duty to do. Then he divorced me, married a younger woman, and threw me out into the street." He refuses to pay her alimony and now she is advancing in years. "I can't understand why he did this to me. He won't even speak to me."

Al-Karnak

The Karnak | 1976

Three university students have their lives destroyed after they are overheard talking politics in a Cairo café

Director Ali Badrakhan

Screenplay Mamduh al-Leithi

Story Naguib Mahfouz

Dialogue Mamduh al-Leithi

Produced by al-Leithi Films

Music Gamal Salama

Director of photography Muhsin Nasr

Editor Said al-Sheikh

Set design Maher Abd al-Nour

Starring Su'ad Husni, Kamal al-Shinnawi, Nur al-Sharif, Farid Shawqi, Shwikar, Tahiya Carioca, Mohamed Subhi, Salah zu-l-Fiqar, Imad Hamdi, Mohamed Tawfiq, Na'ima al-Sughayar, Fayiz Halawa, Ali al-Sharif, Farouk Yusuf, Yunis Shalaby, Wahid Seif, Usama Abbas, Adli Kasib, Hassan Husni

Running time 143 minutes

First screening 26 January 1976

Color

THE KARNAK of the title is a café in downtown Cairo. Owned by a former bellydancer, it is the gathering place for a bunch of regulars, including several university students and a handful of older patrons. One day, three of the students, who were always engaged in heated political debates, disappear. After some time they return, but as broken versions of their former selves. Gradually what happened to them is

OPPOSITE Zeinab (Su'ad Husni, *left*), Ismail (Nur al-Sharif, *right*)

Festivals Ali Badrakhan was awarded Best Director by the Ministry of Culture. The Film Association awarded it Best Picture, and awarded Nur al-Sharif and Su'ad Husni Best Actor and Best Actress, respectively. Kamal al-Shinnawi was awarded Best Actor by the Film Critics' and Screenwriters' Guild.

revealed. Mamduh al-Leithi broke with Mahfouz's short source novel in his screenplay for *al-Karnak*. Much like *Miramar*, Mahfouz divided his book into four parts, each one bearing the name of one of the four main protagonists: Qurunfila, Ismail al-Sheikh, Zeinab Diyab, and Khalid Safwan. Mahfouz has his narrator relate the stories of the four one after the other with overlapping time frames, showing us each of the characters through the others' eyes. However, al-Leithi chose to structure his screenplay in strict chronological fashion, placing the events in their correct order of occurrence. It is a finely crafted screenplay that establishes him as the film's author just as much as the original novelist. He makes the film more optimistic than the novel, which was written in the wake of the crushing 1967 defeat and is suffused with anger. Al-Leithi updates it to the mid-1970s, when the successes of the October War have gone some way to soothing the pain.

Ali Badrakhan proved to be a fine actors' director, coaxing nuanced performances out of what was a very fine cast including Nur al-Sharif as Ismail, Su'ad Husni as his girlfriend Zeinab, and Kamal al-Shinnawi as intelligence officer Khalid Safwan. Husni, in particular, is the emotional heart of the film, as in a harrowing flashback it is revealed that she was raped in prison by her jailers, an ordeal from which she is never able to recover.

The director skillfully evokes the oppressive atmosphere of the world in which the protagonists are trapped, breaking the tension occasionally with wry touches, for example, underscoring a political argument at the café with the noise of a football match between fierce rivals Ahly and Zamalek. ★

KEY SCENE

In the political prison, the detainees are waiting for Khalid Safwan to come out of the toilet. Safwan is the officer who arrested and tortured them, causing the deaths of many of their number. When he emerges and sees them, he tries to bolt back into the toilet, but he is grabbed. He tells them he was only obeying orders. Some of the detainees try to assault him but they are stopped by some of the others, who want to interrogate Safwan. "Where were you the day after the Revolution?" they ask. "At home," he says, an admission that he never took part in the Revolution he claims to uphold. "You and your kind are the Revolution's biggest mistake," says one prisoner. "Everyone's guilty! Everyone's a victim!" screams Safwan. The prisoners set upon him, beating him until the guards intervene. They announce the release of prisoners of conscience after Thawrat al-Tas-hih (the "Corrective Revolution") of 15 May 1971, in which Khalid was transferred to the Misr Prison.

Al-Mudhnibun

The Culprits | 1976

An investigation into the murder of an actress exposes the dirty little secrets of her friends and acquaintances

A WELCOME CHANGE from all the sex dramas and socially conscious fare prevalent at this time, *al-Mudhnibun* is a satisfying detective movie that delivers excitement and suspense. Oddly, detective tales were relatively uncommon in Egyptian cinema until recently, but director Said Marzuk saw the potential for a good crime thriller in Naguib Mahfouz's novel of the same name. As in the novel, the film begins with a single crime, which, as the police investigate, leads to ever more instances of corruption and profiteering. That initial incident is the murder of an actress, Sana' Kamil (Suhair Ramzi), who is killed at her home after a party to which all her friends and acquaintances had been invited. By the time the film is partway through, the police are investigating no fewer than eleven other crimes and misdemeanors of varying severity. There are political

Director Said Marzuk

Screenplay Naguib Mahfouz

Story Mamduh al-Leithi

Dialogue Mamduh al-Leithi

Produced by Ihab al-Laythi Films

Music Gamal Salama

Director of photography Mustafa Imam

Editor Said al-Sheikh

Set design Maher Abd al-Nour

Starring Suhair Ramzi, Hussein Fahmi, Imad Hamdi, Zubayda Tharwat, Kamal al-Shinnawi, Salah zu-l-Fiqar, Adil Adham, Omar al-Hariri, Tawfiq al-Diqin, Abd al-Warith Assar, Hayat Qandil, Samir Sabri, Samir Ghanim, Abd al-Mun'im Ibrahim, Wahid Seif, Usama Abbas, Layla Fahmi, Na'ima al-Sughayar, Saida Galal, Said Abd al-Ghani

Running time 118 minutes

First screening 23 September 1976

Color

LEFT Sana' Kamil (Suhair Ramzi, *right*), Mamduh (Adil Adham, *left*)

أفلام إيهاب الليثي
تقدم
قصة
نجيب محفوظ
المذنبون
بالألوان الطبيعية
فيلم للمخرج
سعيد مرزوق
حسين فهمي
سهير رمزي
صلاح ذوالفقار
عادل أدهم
يوسف شعبان
عماد حمدي
توفيق الدقن
ابراهيم خان
نبيل بدر
ليلى فهمي
زبيده ثروت
كمال الشناوي
سيناريو وحوار:
ممدوح الليثي
مدير التصوير:
مصطفى إمام
حياه قنديل
سمير صبري
نعيمه الصغير
عمر الحريري
رجاء صادق
عبد المنعم ابراهيم
أسامه عباس
والوجه الجديد
سعيد عبد الغنى
ابراهيم عبد الرازق
سمير غانم
احمد نبيل
عبد الوارث عسر
محمد السبع
وحيد سيف

overtones: Mahfouz and Marzuk suggest that swapping socialism for Sadat's open-door economics has led to a collapse of social mores and an increase in corruption (the film stopped short of revealing, as in the book, that the rot goes all the way to the top).

The cast is terrific, mixing familiar, much-loved faces—some of whom feature in just the briefest of cameos—with young, up-and-coming stars. The photography is playful, but what audiences will possibly remember is the excellent set design. The locations all have distinct characters. For example, when the detectives go to visit the house of the headmaster, Alif al-Bahrawi (Imad Hamdi), the surroundings reflect the man's poverty: the paint is chipped and peeling, the rug is worn, the furniture is cheap and shabby—no wonder he is selling exam papers for money. Contrast this with the home of the murdered actress with groovy wall murals, arty nudes on the walls, a futuristic space helmet–like TV, and everything all in white—all the better to highlight the crimson pools of blood. ★

Festivals Cairo International Film Festival, where Imad Hamdi was awarded the prize for Best Actor, and Best Picture at the Ministry of Culture official competition.

This gathers together most of those arrested as a result of the murder investigation and places them in a prison cell with an assortment of other lawbreakers from lower down the social ladder. Among the white-collar criminals we have the headmaster, a film producer turned gold smuggler, a civil servant who deals in stolen supplies of food and drugs, and a doctor who performs illegal abortions. The headmaster, who has partly lost his mind at this point, laments the state of his school, which he says must be suffering from neglect now he is in jail. "That's what the ministry wants!" he wails. He tells his cellmates that they promised him a promotion, for which he waited long years, "And I'm still running in place! It never came!" The civil servant gives him a cigarette and urges him to forget his sorrows. The doctor starts to lament his own predicament: his wife is cheating on him with his best friend, the director of housing. "If I could only get my hands on him!" Just then, the cell door opens and who should be led in but the very same director of housing. The doctor leaps upon him.

Al-Saqqa mat

The Water Carrier Is Dead | 1977

A water carrier with a pathological fear of death befriends a professional mourner

Director Salah Abu Seif

Screenplay Muhsin Zayid

Story Yusuf al-Siba'i

Dialogue Muhsin Zayid

Produced by Aflam Misr al-'Alamiya (Egypt International Films)

Music Fu'ad al-Zahiri

Director of photography Mahmud Sabu

Editor Rashida Abd al-Salam

Set design Mukhtar Abd al-Gawad

Starring Farid Shawqi, Izzat al-Alayli, Shwikar, Amina Rizq, Tahiya Carioca, Nahid Gabr, Bilqais, Hassan Hussein, Mohamed Abu Hashish, Ibrahim Zaghu, Sharif Salah al-Din

Festivals Awarded Best Picture, Best Director, and Best Actor (for Izzat al-Alayli) by the Film Association

Running time 104 minutes

First screening 28 November 1977

Color

WHEN SCREENWRITER Muhsin Zayid and director Salah Abu Seif collaborated on a film adaptation of Yusuf al-Siba'i's story about death, little did they know that the novelist would himself be unexpectedly snatched from life only the following year. (While serving as Sadat's minister of culture, al-Siba'i was assassinated in Cyprus by a rogue faction of the PLO incensed by Egypt's ongoing peace talks with Israel.) The story concerns a friendship that develops between two men, one a water carrier whose wife died twenty years previously and who spends his days mourning her loss, and the other a professional mourner whose daily exposure to mortality inspires him to seize every opportunity that comes his way—as he puts it, "Death is a coward and fears those who never fear him."

RIGHT Mi'allim Shusha (Izzat al-Alayli, *right*), Shehata (Farid Shawqi, *left*)

افلام مصر العالمية
يوسف شاهين وشركاه
والشركة التونسية السينمائية
يقدمان
قصة
يوسف السباعى
السقامات
بالالوان الطبيعية
فريد شوقى
عزت العلايلى
شويكار
الصبر
أمينه رزق
تحيه كاريوكا
ناهد جبر
بلقيس
حسن حسين
ابراهيم قدرى
ابراهيم زاغو
محمد ابو حشيش
مع الطفل
شريف صلاح الدين
التوزيع الداخلى
مترو جولدوين ماير
القاهره
إخراج
صلاح ابو سيف
التوزيع الخارجى
أفلام مصر العالمية
والساتبك بتونس
أعدها للسينما
محسن زايد
مدير التصوير : محمود سابو ● الموسيقى التصويرية : فؤاد الظاهرى

Abu Seif was an artistic force to be reckoned with and ruthlessly tailored the source work to fit not only the demands of the cinematic medium, but also his own ideas. He rejected the ending of al-Siba'i's novel, in which the water carrier dies and his son, dressed in black, leads the procession at his wake. Abu Seif felt this was just too depressing. To add a lighter touch and infuse some optimism into the proceedings, he added his own flair, which in retrospect seems a wise choice for the novel's adaptation.

Another joy of the movie is in its presentation of old professions that have long ago died out. The prime example is the water carrier, who belongs to a time before all houses had plumbing to deliver potable water, and the *metayyibati* (claqueur), one who dissolves friction between people, both of which are now only historical curiosities, but which were considered cultural professions in the thirties. Similarly, there is much pleasure to be had in the evocation of the old Husseiniya neighborhood of Cairo. Some might say Abu Seif is a little too sentimental in his nostalgia tripping, but he is never schmaltzy and the historical flashbacks add much to the picture. Izzat al-Alayli's performance as the gloomy Shusha is marvelous, especially his dialogue with Death near the graveyard. Equally enjoyable is Farid Shawqi as Shehata, the cheerful and life-loving optimist who embraces life with open arms and an open heart. ★

KEY SCENE

It is early in the would-be friends' relationship, and Shusha is sitting with Shehata at a café. Shusha sees a sign for an undertaker and takes it as a bad omen. He asks Shehata to switch places with him. Shehata asks him why he is always so uncomfortable at any mention of death: "Is it because your wife died?" Shusha shushes him and tells him not to speak of such matters. Shehata persists. He says that Shusha should not be afraid to talk about his fear of death. "People cry at funerals," he says, "not for the one who died, but for their own selves. Some of them cry in fear of death right up till the minute they themselves die!" He cannot understand what he calls the "living dead," those who live in crippling fear of death. "I don't fear death," he says cheerfully. "I decided to enjoy life until death comes for me." Shusha seems to approve of this view, although this might have something to do with the hash in his waterpipe. Shehata advises him to abandon his fear of death: "Take your due from life before you die!" They both laugh.

Wa la yazal al-tahqiq mustamirran

Investigation Still in Progress | 1980

A woman has an affair with her husband's friend, and then it gets messy and ends in multiple murders

ONCE DIRECTOR ASHRAF FAHMI became a regular on the scene, he made it his business to grind out social dramas, handled competently and effectively. For *Wa la yazal al-tahqiq mustamirran*, Fahmi made use of monographs on psychology penned by Dr. Abd al-Mun'im Sa'd to underpin the motivations that drove his characters—not that they behave in a way that hadn't been seen at the Egyptian cinema before. Nabila Ebeid is Zeinab, a gold-digging wife who is weary of her modestly ambitioned schoolteacher husband, Hussein.

Director Ashraf Fahmi

Screenplay Mustafa Muharram and Bashir al-Dik

Story Ihsan Abd al-Quddus

Dialogue Mustafa Muharram and Bashir al-Dik

Produced by Ashraf Fahmi

Music Gamal Salama

Director of photography Essam Farid

Editor Abd al-Aziz Fakhri

Set design Maher Abd al-Nour

Starring Mahmud Yassin, Nabila Ebeid, Mahmud Abd al-Aziz, Layla Hamada, Malak al-Gamal, Tawfiq al-Diqin, Nawal Fahmi, Ali al-Gindi

Running time 94 minutes

First screening 6 October 1980

Color

LEFT Midhat (Mahmud Abd al-Aziz, *right*), Zeinab (Nabila Ebeid, *left*)

وهيب فهمي
محمود ياسين نبيلة عبيد محمود عبد العزيز
ليلى حمادة توفيق الدقن
ولايزال التحقيق مستمرا
قصة إحسان عبد القدوس إخراج أشرف فهمي
تصميم / أبو السعود
سيناريو مصطفى محرم
حوار بشير الديك
مدير التصوير عصام فريد
موسيقى تصويرية جمال سلامه
المنتج جرجس فوزي
التوزيع الداخلي: شركة أفلام النصر (محمد حسن رمزي وشركاه) • التوزيع الخارجي: الشركة اللبنانية للتجارة والاستثمار السينمائي (صباح إخوان) بيروت
مطابع النصر سيد علي ابراهيم
ترخيص /٧٩

He is played by Mahmud Yassin, and the role of a serious man with a strong moral code, prone to slip into idealistic thinking, is one that comes easy to him. The fun comes when he realizes that Zeinab's materialistic desires have steered her passions elsewhere, and he transforms into a man whose desire for vengeance will stop at nothing short of murder. He is good, but then he has to be: if Yassin could not convince us of Hussein's capacity for rage, the movie would have flopped. The other two people in what turns out to be not so much a love triangle as a love parallelogram are Hussein's friend Midhat (Mahmud Abd al-Aziz), whose insecurities lead him to make a play for Zeinab, and Hussein's sweetly winsome sister, Mervat (Layla Hamada). Two of these people will end up dead by the end of the film, but I won't tell you which two.

The film is careful to maintain the suspense, which is helped by a particularly expressive score by Gamal Salama. ★

Festivals Nabila Ebeid was awarded the prize for Best Actress at the Alexandria Film Festival. Ashraf Fahmi was awarded Best Director by the Film Association, which also awarded Mahmud Yassin the prize for Best Actor.

Midhat and Zeinab are seated on the balcony at the home of the latter, awaiting the arrival of her husband, Hussein. Mervat, Hussein's sister, is also around, in the kitchen making lunch. Midhat confesses his attraction for her to Zeinab, and she indicates that it is mutual. She complains about Hussein's way of conducting his life. Midhat tells her, "Let me make your husband an offer." At which point they are interrupted by the arrival of Hussein. He is unusually happy. He tells them he has just come from a celebration at the school where he teaches in honor of his promotion to 'Teacher, First Class.' "How much more are they going to pay you?" says Zeinab. "It's an honorary promotion," says Hussein. Unimpressed, Zeinab stalks off to join Mervat in the kitchen. Hussein tells Midhat that he has never been so happy as when he was at the celebration, surrounded by the schoolchildren he cares for so deeply. "They gave me this pen as a present!" Hussein hands Midhat the pen. The latter turns it over in his hands, lost in memories of his own childhood, when he and Hussein were classmates; we see the teacher berate him for a poor answer in class and how he was made to stand in the corner. The same teacher then launches into praise for Hussein. We see his father spank him for failing his tests, while Hussein passes with flying colors. Back in the present, Hussein belittles the gift Midhat has received from his pupils. "Success isn't anything without money," he says. Hussein disagrees. Midhat makes his offer to Hussein, the chance to make more money by working with him.

Ahl al-qimma

People at the Top | 1980

A former pickpocket falls in love with the niece of the officer who arrested him

Director Ali Badrakhan

Screenplay Mustafa Muharram

Story Naguib Mahfouz

Dialogue Mustafa Muharram

Produced by Aflam 'Abd al-Azim al-Zughbi Films

Music Gamal Salama

Director of photography Muhsin Nasr

Editor Said al-Sheikh

Set design Maher Abd al-Nour

Starring Su'ad Husni, Nur al-Sharif, Izzat al-Alayli, Omar al-Hariri, Aida Riyad, Mahmud al-Qal'awi, Sabri Abd al-Mun'im, Nadia Izzat, Hilmi Abd al-Wahab, Ibrahim Qadri, Hassan Hussein, Salah Rashwan, Nabil Badr al-Din, Nadia Rafiq

Running time 119 minutes

First screening 11 May 1981

Color

THE FILM IS AN ADAPTATION of a short story of the same name taken from a collection by Naguib Mahfouz entitled *Al-hub fawqa hadabat al-haram (Love on the Pyramids Plateau)*—which, incidentally, was also made into a movie. The written story and film both portray the economic gangsterism encouraged by Sadat's open-door policy. Director Ali Badrakhan entrusted Mustafa Muharram with the task of writing the screenplay—and what a terrific job he did. It is rich with the idiomatic language and vocabulary of the world of

RIGHT Mohamed (Izzat al-Alayli, *left*), Za'tar (Nur al-Sharif, *right*)

أفلام عبد العظيم الزغبى تقدم
سعاد حسنى
نور الشريف
عزت العلايلى
عمر الحريرى
عايده رياض
ناديه عزت
ناديه رفيق
صبرى عبد المنعم
حلمى عبد الوهاب
ابراهيم قدرى
حسن حسين
صلاح رشوان
نبيل نور الدين
محمود القلعاوى
أهل القمة
قصة نجيب محفوظ
إخراج على بدرخان
سيناريو وحوار مصطفى محرم
مدير التصوير محسن نصر
مونتاج سعيد الشيخ
ترخيص ٨١/٣١
التوزيع لمصر وجميع أنحاء العالم : شركة شافعى لتوزيع الأفلام شارع جواد حسنى/القاهرة
مطابع السينما العربية

Festivals Torino, Italy, Locarno, the Academy Awards, Poitiers (France), Montreal. Awarded Best Picture and Best Screenplay by the Film Association, and the State Award of Merit for Best Picture. Also awarded a prize by the Egyptian Critics' Association, Best Actress and Actor for Su'ad Husni and Nur al-Sharif, respectively, and the Egyptian Screenwriters' and Film Critics' Guild Gold Award of Merit as part of the proceedings of the Cairo International Film Festival.

pickpockets, full of the jargon and slang that they use to communicate without anybody else having the faintest idea what they are talking about. Muharram also delves deeply into the world of the police. He represents them in a new cinematic light: they are no longer society's knights in shining armor, they are human beings, just as susceptible to doubt, failure, compromise, and wrongdoing as anybody else.

The story brings these two worlds together. Mohamed Fawzi (Izzat al-Alayli) is an officer investigating the hiring of the pickpocket Za'tar al-Nuri (Nur al-Sharif) by Zaghlul (Omar al-Hariri), the owner of an import-export company. He suspects they are dealing in smuggled goods. Meanwhile, al-Nuri then falls in love with a girl, Seham, who turns out to be Mohamed Fawzi's niece. As he profits in his new line of "business," challenging Zaghlul, and becoming extremely wealthy in his own right, al-Nuri ascends the social ladder, becoming part of the Sadat-era nouveau riche. The film is a study in the changes, compromises, and acceptance that eventually bring Fawzi and al-Nuri to an understanding. ★

KEY SCENE

We are in Zaghlul's office, where al-Nuri is already seated. The secretary speaks to Zaghlul about some work-related issues and asks him to sign a check for a donation to various charities. Zaghlul signs as al-Nuri looks on. Zaghlul tells al-Nuri that he is acting strangely. "Are you in love?" he asks. Al-Nuri says he is. But it is complicated. He explains that the girl's uncle is none other than Detective Mohamed Fawzi. "But why would you pick a girl like that?" asks Zaghlul. Al-Nuri says that he never meant to fall in love, but now he has and she is the one his heart desires. "Well, I can't blame you," says Zaghlul. "The girl is worth it; I saw her once." He tells al-Nuri not to be disheartened and that things might not be as difficult as they seem. "But her uncle's a police detective," says al-Nuri. Zaghlul waves that aside: "Money is everything now. The class distinctions that used to keep us apart don't exist any more. A man can only be judged by how much he makes." Al-Nuri's earnings, says Zaghlul, far outstrip even the chairman of the board of a government company. "Girls don't care where you came from, they only care how much you make." It's that girl and her low-income family, says Zaghlul, who should be chasing after al-Nuri. "Work as hard as you can. Put your past behind you. Do that and you can ask a princess for her hand and she'd say yes."

Maw'id 'ala al-'asha'

Dinner Date | 1981

A desperate housewife leaves her husband for her hairstylist, triggering a cycle of violent revenge

MOHAMED KHAN'S BRILLIANCE as a filmmaker shows in small details, which often speak for the whole work. In one scene in *Maw'id 'ala al-'asha'*, the lead character, Nawal (Su'ad Husni), a sad and unhappy housewife, admires a painting of a small girl holding her father's hand as they walk off into the distance, their backs to the viewer. Nawal tries to acquire the painting at an auction because she feels it speaks to her as someone in need of a guiding hand herself. She fails to get the painting and breaks down weeping. Instead, her misery and sense of isolation are symbolized by another painting we see, that of a woman stuck on a balcony.

Director Mohamed Khan

Screenplay Bashir al-Dik

Story Mohamed Khan

Dialogue Bashir al-Dik

Produced by Aflam al-Gawhara (Jewel Films)

Music Kamal Bekir

Director of photography Muhsin Nasr

Editor Nadia Shukri

Set design Maher Abd al-Nour

Starring Su'ad Husni, Hussein Fahmi, Ahmad Zaki, Zuzu Madi, Raga' al-Giddawi, Iglal Zaki, In'am Salusa, Amal Ibrahim, Adawi Gheith, Sami Sarhan, Hafiz Amin, Khairy Beshara, Marwa al-Khatib, Aliya Ali

Running time 105 minutes

First screening 16 November 1981

Color

LEFT Nawal (Su'ad Husni, *left*), Izzat (Hussein Fahmy, *right*)

أفلام الجوهرة
تقدم
سعاد حسني
حسين فهمي
أحمد زكي
موعد على العشاء
زوزو ماضي • رجاء الجداوي • إجلال زكي
قصة
محمد خان
سيناريو وحوار
بشير الديك
مدير التصوير
محسن نصر
فيلما من إخراج
محمد خان
مونتاج
نادية شكري
موسيقى
كمال بكير
إنتاج
أفلام الجوهرة
التوزيع
صوت الحب
٣٢ شارع طلعت حرب - القاهرة
ترخيص رقم ١٠١/٨١

Khan incorporates numerous shots of Nawal behind various types of barrier: bars, car windows, and so on. The message is clear: she is a woman trapped by her expected role in society. At first it is the role of obedient daughter, marrying at a too-young age, against her own wishes, to please and benefit her domineering mother. Then it is the role of the good wife, married to a businessman husband, Izzat (Hussein Fahmi), who is selfish and cold, and cares only for his career. At one point he tells Nawal that the reason he likes having her around is that she reminds him of how he used to be before he became successful. Su'ad Husni is exceptional as Nawal: her eyes, face, and body almost vibrate with her suppressed misery.

Happily, Nawal does find true romance in the shape of hairstylist Shukri (a young Ahmad Zaki). The chemistry between the two actors is electric. Sadly, it does not last. Although Nawal divorces Izzat, when he learns of Shukri he is enraged and from here the film takes a much darker turn as the former husband has his ex-wife's new lover killed. However, this is a new Nawal, one who is no longer prepared to simply accept what life throws at her. The ending is far too tragic to call the film a feminist fable, but at least the husband gets his comeuppance (*see* the Key Scene box). ★

Izzat is seated at the table with his ex-wife Nawal, who has invited him over for dinner. Given their bitter court battle he is surprised that Nawal would cook for him. She smiles and says that she will always cook for him. She hands him a plate and he starts eating. "What is it you like about that boy, the hairdresser?" he says with his mouth full. She tells him that she found in Shukri what she had never found in anyone else and she wishes she had met him long ago. Izzat notices that Nawal's plate is empty. He asks her why. Flustered, she starts to eat. He insists that she eat some of what he's having. She does. He resumes his meal. "Do you like it?" Nawal asks. "Yes, a little spicy, but delicious." She says that she remembers his love for spicy food. "You have a good memory. I'm sorry you've behaved better toward me than I have toward you. This," he gestures to the meal, "has won the battle." She assures him that it is he who has won. "You owned me at the start. You've killed me at the finish." He stares at her. "What do you mean?" he asks. "After you finally divorced me, I could hardly believe I was free, that I could live the life I wanted. But I was always a prisoner to my fear of you." He looks at her in surprise. "After Shukri was killed, I realized I didn't deserve to live. Neither do you." There is a long pause before Izzat asks, "Is there something in the food?" "Poison," Nawal replies. The movie ends with the same close-up of Nawal's eyes with which the film began.

Al-'Ar

Shame | 1982

The story of three brothers whose family is torn after they find out their respected late father was a drug dealer

Director Ali Abd al-Khaliq

Screenplay Mahmud Abu Zeid

Story Mahmud Abu Zeid

Dialogue Mahmud Abu Zeid

Produced by Adwa' al-Sinima (Movie Lights)

Music Hassan Abu al-Su'ud

Director of photography Said al-Shimi

Editor Hussein Afifi

Starring Nur al-Sharif, Hussein Fahmi, Mahmud Abd al-Aziz, Nura, Ilham Chahine, Amina Rizq, Abd al-Badie al-Arabi, Salah Nazmi, Hafiz Amin, Muhyi al-Din Abd al-Muhsin, Tarek al-Dessouki, Mas'ud Mitwalli, Mohamed Abu Hashish, Mutaweh Eweiss

Running time 123 minutes

First screening 11 October 1982

Color

THIS MOVIE IS PRACTICALLY a primer on how to write a script that combines art with commercial success. Mahmud Abu Zeid has spoken about how he crafted the screenplay, assigning each of the protagonists a thematic role to play and plotting out their course through the film, scene by scene. The story needed a tight grip, dealing as it does with four main protagonists whose attitudes and behavior are challenged and conflicted, and subject to change over the course of the two-hour running time.

After Hagg Abd al-Tawwab, a pious spice merchant, is killed in a car crash, it is discovered his riches were the result of an unexpected plant product: hashish. His children now have to decide whether to maintain the family business or dissolve it.

RIGHT Kamal (Nur al-Sharif, *left*), Shukri (Hussein Fahmy, *right*), Adil (Mahmud Abd al-Aziz, *center*)

أضواء السينما
تقدم
محمود عبد العزيز
نور الشريف
حسين فهمى
نورا
بالاشتراك مع:
أمينه رزق
إلهام شاهين
عبد البديع العربي
صلاح نظمى
العار
اخراج
على عبد الخالق
قصة وسيناريو وحوار
محمود أبو زيد
مدير التصوير
سعيد شيمى
منتج منفذ
ابراهيم المشنب
الموسيقى التصويرية
حسن أبو السعود
مونتاج
حسين عفيفى
الإشراف الفنى والإدارى
مأمون عطا
محمد أبو العز
توزيع الداخلى: أضواء السينما ٣ ميدان عرابى / القاهرة
التوزيع الخارجى: فالكون للسينما "رياض العقاد" ٣٣٦ شارع الهرم / جيزة
الفيديو كاسيت: بنش فيلم "ايجبت" ٣١ شارع احمد عرابى / الجيزة

One son, Kamal (Nur al-Sharif), had already been initiated and joined his father in dealing drugs; another son, Shukri (Hussein Fahmi), is a public prosecutor, while Adil (Mahmud Abd al-Aziz) is a doctor who treats drug addicts. There is also a daughter, Layla (Ilham Chahine). Naturally Kamal and Shukri come into conflict over the business, with Adil acting as mediator, but nothing is entirely black and white. Moral stances are questioned and hypocrisies unmasked—their father had completed the Hagg not just once but six times and would not touch alcohol. Sin, it seems, is in the eye of the beholder. Eventually, compromise is reached: they will sell their father's drug stash to a rival and get out of the business—but keep the money. Shukri convinces himself that this is okay because they did not actually deal any drugs themselves. Even so, he feels sufficient shame that he quits his job. He doesn't need it anyway; his share of the drug money will make him rich. But his mother does not ease his conscience any when she points out, "Shame is in the lack of morality, not the lack of money." It was a message that won the approval of audiences, who flocked to see the film and made it a huge box-office success. ★

KEY SCENE

This is the film's climax. Shukri joins his brothers, Adil and Kamal, at the salt flats, where they will recover their dead father's cache of drugs and then sell them. Kamal goes into the water first and disconnects the electrical charge that serves as a security measure. By now, the dealer who is to buy the drugs from the brothers has shown up. Kamal and Adil board a small boat to row out and retrieve the drugs. As Kamal lifts the first of the metal containers from the water, he is shocked to find that the salt has dissolved its bottom and the drugs have leaked out. The dealer asks, "Wasn't the stuff packed in plastic?" Kamal says no and throws himself into the water. He dives, surfaces, and dives again, frantically searching but coming up empty-handed. He wails in despair. The drugs are gone, the dealer tells him. It is too much for Shukri, who shoots himself. Adil breaks down in hysterics. Kamal screams over and over again to Adil to get in the water and help him search, but Adil has completely lost it and just starts singing the song "Al-mallaha" ("The Salt Flats").

Sawwaq al-utubis

The Bus Driver | 1982

A hardworking bus driver struggles to meet his family's financial obligations

AUDIENCES AND CRITICS alike consistently rate *Sawwaq al-utubis* as one of the best movies ever to come out of Egypt. It served as the face of Egyptian cinema abroad, representing the country at numerous international film festivals. Its success can be attributed to several factors, foremost of which is a good story and screenplay—*Sawwaq al-utubis* is the crowning achievement of screenwriter Bashir al-Dik's career. Hassan (Nur al-Sharif), a veteran of the October War, is a bus driver by day and a taxi driver by night. His father owns a workshop on which he owes back taxes, so Hassan looks to his sisters in Port Said and Damietta, but they are unable or unwilling to help. Throughout the rest of the film, he struggles to find the money, encountering only bureaucracy, corruption, and greed. The country Hassan fought for has gone to the dogs.

Director Atef El-Tayeb

Screenplay Bashir al-Dik

Story Mohamed Khan

Dialogue Bashir al-Dik

Produced by Haderma

Music Kamal Bekir

Director of photography Said al-Shimi

Editor Nadia Shukri

Set design Farouk Khurshid

Starring Nur al-Sharif, Mervat Amin, Imad Hamdi, Nabila al-Sayyid, Wahid Seif, Hamdi al-Wazir, Abdu al-Wazir, Mahmud Abdullah, Sha'ban Hussein, Mohamed Kamil, Safa' al-Sab', Hassan Husni, Zahrat al-Ula, Ali al-Ghandur, Aziza Hilmi, Mohamed Shawqi

Running time 108 minutes

First screening 11 July 1982

Color

LEFT Hassan (Nur al-Sharif, *right*), (Sha'ban Hussein, *left*), (Samir Wahid, *middle*; leaning on the car)

Festivals Nur al-Sharif was awarded Best Actor at the 1982 New Delhi Film Festival, and Atef El-Tayeb won Best First-Time Director at the Carthage Arab and African Film Festival in Tunisia. In addition, the film was awarded the Silver Sword at the Damascus Film Festival, and Nur al-Sharif was awarded Best Actor at the Film Association Festival.

Hassan is an unusual character to carry a film, a blue-collar transport worker, unassuming and meek, but steadily pushed beyond his limits. Over the course of the movie his anger grows until it finally erupts in the last scene (*see* the Key Scene box). Nur al-Sharif is simply superb, and although he would go on to become a giant of Egyptian cinema, this performance remains one of his most memorable. His was a character with which audiences could easily empathize: he is no great hero, just an ordinary man trying to do what is right, enduring endless disappointments and setbacks. There is no villain, just a country failing its people.

Said al-Shimi's cinematography puts the audience inside the action. The camera squeezes onto the overcrowded bus, tracking the backs of passengers as they barge and jostle for standing space. On occasion, the camera ends up seated at the back, settling in for the ride. The soundtrack is similarly hardworking, full of appropriate choices, such as Sayyid Darwish's classic "Til'it ya mahla nurha" ("The Sun is Up and Shining"), which plays at the start of the bus driver's day to evoke that rise-and-shine feeling. It does not last long. ★

KEY SCENE

The film's final scene mirrors one from early on, when a cry from a woman who has had something stolen by a pickpocket causes Hassan to stop the bus, only to shrug and continue under pressure from passengers who just want to get to where they are going. Now, once again, a woman cries that she has been robbed and calls on everyone to find the pickpocket. Hassan stops the bus. The pickpocket tries to get off but Hassan closes the doors. The thief then jumps out of a window and runs off down the road. Hassan gives chase. The pickpocket pulls a knife and slashes at Hassan but he manages to disarm him. Hassan smashes the young man against the barrier dividing the lanes and punches him, and again, and again, and again. "You sons of bitches!" he hisses, as the pickpocket becomes the stand-in for every social climber, freeloader, black marketeer, opportunist, unhelpful bureaucrat, and self-centered individual Hassan has met.

Al-Harrif

The Champion | 1984

Scenes from the life of a lowly, middle-aged shoemaker whose only freedom comes from playing street football—and betting on the outcome

"THERE ARE PEOPLE who play football in the street, sing in the street, and take pictures in the street. People trade insults, hit each other, kill each other in the street. There are those who sleep in the street, sell their virtue in the street. In the streets much that is wrong has become right. But what a scandalous sight, if we once forget ourselves and kiss each other in the street." So reads the prose-poem prologue that begins Mohamed Khan's *al-Harrif*. The next sound we hear is heavy breathing, but it belongs not to an amorous kissing couple but to an out-of-shape man running up the tram tracks beneath Cairo's 6 October Flyover. This is Fares "al-Harrif," another of Khan's anti-heroes (he wrote the story on which *Sawwaq al-utubis* was based). Played by Adil Imam, Fares is a man who has reached middle age seemingly without learning anything much along the way.

Released internationally as *Streetplayer*

Director Mohamed Khan

Screenplay Bashir al-Dik

Story Mohamed Khan and Bashir al-Dik

Dialogue Bashir al-Dik

Produced by Aflam al-Suhba

Music Hani Shenouda

Director of photography Said al-Shimi

Editor Nadia Shukri

Starring Adil Imam, Fardus Abd al-Hamid, Abdullah Farghalli, Zizi Mustafa, Nagah al-Mugi, Hamdi al-Wazir, Adawi Ghayth, Farouk Yusuf, Hanim Mohamed, Abdullah Mahmud, Sayyid Khattab, Sami al-Salamoni, Sabri Abd al-Mun'im

Running time 110 minutes

First screening 6 August 1984

Color

LEFT Fares (Adil Imam, *left*), Rizq (Abdullah Farghalli, *right*)

أفلام الصحبة تقدم
عادل امام
فردوس عبد الحميد
عبدالله فرغلى
زيزى مصطفى
نجاح الموجى
فاروق يوسف
صبرى عبد المنعم
حمدى الوزير
اكتشف بعد فوات الأوان ...
ان الحياة مثل الكورة ... اجوال !!
STREETPLAYER
a film by mohamed khan
الحرّيف
فيلم ا. محمد خان
قصة: محمد خان وبشير الديك تصوير: سعيد شيمي
سيناريو وحوار: بشير الديك مونتاج: ناديه شكرى
PRODUCED BY SOHBA FILM
PRODUCTIONS.P.O.BOX 678
CAIRO, EGYPT
التوزيع الداخلى: جيبكو لتوزيع الأفلام "تاكفور أنطونيان وشركاه" ٢ شارع شريف القاهرة.
التوزيع الخارجى: الشركة المتحدة للأستديوهات "إيجيبت"
٢٤ شارع وادى النيل - المهندسين - الجيزة

He is a working-class, downtrodden Egyptian, full of contradictions: companionable but quick to anger; loyal to his wife but pursuing an affair. He is by trade a shoemaker but his passion is football and—although broke—betting on football. There is no story as such—Fares is far too old for anything to come of his silky ball skills and it is not the kind of film to provide a feel-good ending in which a bet pays off big time. Instead, the film (made from another superb screenplay by Bashir al-Dik) presents scenes from Fares's life and his interactions with a wide-ranging cast of equally flawed but sympathetic characters.

Much of the film was shot on location in downtown Cairo. Cinematographer Said al-Shimi keeps things gritty, moving his camera along shadowy narrow streets and alleys, maintaining a sense of claustrophobia despite the outdoor settings. When we visit Fares's home, it is a cramped room on the roof, with a view of other ramshackle rooftops. The only freedom comes during the games of street football, when Fares's still considerable talent is wildly celebrated by the watching kids. The film ends, as it began, with the sound of its protagonist's heavy breathing. How much longer, the audience wonders, can he keep on? ★

Festivals Berlin, where it ran in the Mediterranean Film section; Moscow; Valencia. The movie was awarded the Movie Fund grant, and the Film Association's Best Picture and Best Director awards.

KEY SCENE

Fares starts up the long staircase leading to the rooftop where his father is scraping the poorest of livings weaving baskets from palm fronds. His father reproves him for not coming to visit more often and asks why. Is it because he no longer remembers his father? Or because his father is no longer good enough for him? Fares jokes around and tells his father he has grown old. "You're the one who's getting on," replies the older man. Then he asks Fares where his son is. "Why don't you bring him to visit his grandfather?" Fares brings news that his mother—his father's ex-wife—has died. The father's spirits sink for a moment but then he shrugs it off, saying that everyone must die sometime. His current wife, Nargis, arrives, welcoming Fares. "Do you still dance?" asks Fares. Nargis is old and very obviously does not dance and she bursts out laughing. "I heard your dancing was something to see," Fares tells her. His father tells him that that was long ago, when people were happier. Nargis leaves to go cook, while Fares' father complains of poverty and hardship. "Take back your wife," he tells Fares, "so your son can grow up healthy with two parents." Fares promises and makes to leave. "When I die," his father says, "bury me in the village by your mother's side."

Al-Bari'

The Innocent Man | 1986

A simple military conscript blindly follows orders at a brutal camp for political prisoners until the arrival of an old friend opens his eyes

Director Atef El-Tayeb

Screenplay Wahid Hamid

Story Wahid Hamid

Dialogue Wahid Hamid

Produced by Video 2000 Films

Music Ammar al-Shiri'i

Director of photography Said al-Shimi

Editor Nadia Shukri

Set design Rushdi Hamid

Starring Mahmud Abd al-Aziz, Ahmad Zaki, Gamil Ratib, Salah Qabil, Ilham Chahine, Mamduh Abd al-Alim, Ahmad Ratib, Abdu al-Wazir, Aliya Abd al-Mun'im, Shawqi Samih, Badr Nofal, Hassan Husni, Samir Wahid, Abdullah Hefny, Mahmud al-Iraqi, Ahmad Abu Abiya, Gharib Mahmud

Running time 110 minutes

First screening 11 August 1986

Color

LIEUTENANT SHARKAS IS the warden of a political prison, which is remotely sited out in the desert, away from prying eyes. To his family he is a kind and loving husband and father, a good-natured man who abhors violence—to the extent he even refuses to play cops and robbers with his children. At work, however, well, that's a different matter: he is nothing less than a monster and sadist, routinely torturing the prisoners in his care. It goes without saying, this is not a subject normally dealt with in Egyptian cinema.

The story kicks in when Ahmad Sab' al-Leil Radwan al-Fouli, a simple farmer from a small village, is assigned to the prison for his military service. Not the most intelligent of individuals, al-Fouli just does as he is told, and when his superiors tell him that the political

RIGHT Ahmad (Ahmad Zaki, *left*), Tawfiq (Mahmud Abd al-Aziz, *right*)

افلام ڤيديو ٢٠٠٠
صفوت غطاس وشركاه
تقدم
محمود عبد العزيز
احمد زكى
الهام شاهين
ممدوح عبد العليم
صلاح قابيل جميل راتب
ناهد سمير
حسن حسنى
احمد راتب
عليه عبد المنعم
حسنى عبد الجليل
سمير وحيد
شوقى شامخ
بدر نوفل
البرئ
قصة وسيناريو وحوار
وحيد حامد
سعيد شيمى
عمار الشريعى
نادية شكرى
رشدى حامد
محمد زين
انتاج سميره احمد صفوت غطاس
التوزيع لمصر وجميع أنحاء العالم شركة مصر للتوزيع ودور العرض السينمائى
توزيع الڤيديو هليوبوليس ڤيديو فيلم
اخراج
عاطف الطيب
ترخيص رقم ٨٥/

Festivals Pyongyang, where it won the Silver Award. Best Egyptian Picture at the Cairo International Film Festival. Ahmad Zaki won Best Actor at the Film Association Festival; both he and Ammar al-Shiri'i were granted awards of merit by the International Critics' Guild Committee. The film was also screened at the Mediterranean Film Festival in Valencia, Spain.

prisoners held here are "enemies of the homeland," al-Fouli does not hesitate to kill a prisoner who attempts to escape. He even willingly cooperates in the torture of prisoners. However, when an educated friend from his village is brought to the camp, al-Fouli begins to question what is going on and his own role in the brutality. Eventually he suffers a breakdown—*see* the Key Scene box.

Ahmad Zaki is fantastic, employing clumsy body language and slow speech to convey al-Fouli's simplemindedness. It is clear he is as much victim as victimizer. The ending was so shocking at the time that the Egyptian censors banned the film, then allowed it but cut short the final scene, ending with al-Fouli's anguished yell. ★

KEY SCENE

Al-Fouli stands in a watchtower high above the prison yard, playing softly on a *nayy* (a crude reed flute). The instrument is symbolic of his country roots, his innocence, and his melancholy. He has witnessed his former teacher killed in front of him and he could do nothing to save him. He has come to understand that the prisoners are not enemies of the country, only men who disagree with the oppression of the regime. He hears the klaxon announcing the arrival of a new transport wagon with its cargo of prisoners ready for beating and perhaps even death. He sees the waiting reception of guards with snarling dogs and whips. The anger erupts inside him: he lets out a howl, aims his rifle, and commences to fire. He manages to take out most of the guards before he is shot and killed.

Al-Gu'

Hunger | 1986

An alley strongman becomes a tyrant terrorizing the poor until his sister-in-law organizes a popular revolt

***AL-GU'* IS A TIMELESS** parable based on some of the episodes contained within Naguib Mahfouz's epic novel *The Harafish*. Specifically, it is the story of Farag al-Gibali, a weak-willed man who, by a twist of fate, becomes the strongman of the alley. His intentions start off honorably enough, but he quickly becomes corrupted by greed and colludes with the profiteering merchants who store up grain in their warehouses in order to inflate prices while the people of the alley go hungry. In contrast to Farag is his pious brother Gaber, who tries to persuade Farag of the error of his ways. When this fails, Gaber secretly steals from the warehouses and distributes the food to the needy. He is found out by Farag, who plans to execute him. He is saved by his wife, Zubayda, who stirs the people of the alley to revolt.

Director Ali Badrakhan

Screenplay Ali Badrakhan, Mustafa Muharram, and Tarek al-Mirghani

Story Naguib Mahfouz

Dialogue Ali Badrakhan, Mustafa Muharram, and Tarek al-Mirghani

Produced by Egypt Videocassette

Music Georges Kazazian

Director of photography Mahmud Abd al-Sami'

Editor Adil Munir

Set design Salah Mar'i

Starring Su'ad Husni, Mahmud Abd al-Aziz, Abd al-Aziz Makhyun, Yusra, Sana' Yunis, Samiha Tawfiq, Thuraya Hilmi, Sayyid Sadek, Hafiz Amin, Ahmad Abu Abiya, Said Tarabik, Hanan Suleiman, Abd al-Hayy Azab, Abd al-Ghani Nasser, Fathi Ibrahim, Sayyid Salim, Madiha Yusuf

Festivals Carthage Festival, Tunisia

Running time 110 minutes

First screening 1 September 1986

Color

LEFT Farag (Mahmud Abd al-Aziz, *right*), Malak (Yusra, *left*)

EVC
تقدم
الجوع
سعاد حسني
محمود عبد العزيز
يسرا
عبد العزيز مخيون
سناء يونس
ثريا حلمي
سميحة توفيق
علي بدرخان مصطفى محرم
صلاح مرعي جورج كازازيان
محمود عبد السميع عادل منير
علي بدرخان
ت: ١٩٤/٢١/٨٦
الشركة العالمية للتليفزيون والسينما
٥ شارع الجزيرة الوسطى - الزمالك
أفلام البلجون
١٧٥ شارع الهرم - الجيزة
ايجيبت فيديو كاسيت
١٢٥ شارع السودان - المهندسين
مطابع السينما العربية (٥٠٥ - جسور) ت/٧٥٤٧٣٥٠

The central message of the film is that even the poorest classes of society can effect meaningful change if they act with unity.

Mahfouz's source novel treats the alley very much as a self-contained universe into which the real world hardly ever intrudes—so much so that the reader imagines we might be back in the days of the Mamluks, until the jarring arrival of a police inspector indicates that we are, in fact, in more modern times. To replicate this effect in the movie, director Ali Badrakhan decided against using the existing "traditional alley" set at Cairo's Nahhas Studios because, at just four meters high, the buildings were too low for his purposes. He had a new alley built, with buildings more than twenty meters high, which took four months to complete at a cost of 170,000 Egyptian pounds. With more than a little help from some excellent performances, in particular, from Mahmud Abd al-Aziz as the slimy Farag, Abd al-Aziz Makhyun as Gaber, and Su'ad Husni as Zubayda, Badrakhan's gambit paid off handsomely, resulting in a crowd-pleasing film with an appealing central message that performed well at the box office. ★

The people of the alley carry Gaber aloft on their shoulders in triumph, having just liberated him from the clutches of his brother Farag al-Gibali, whom they have just stoned to death. The people want to appoint Gaber as their new *futuwwa* (strongman). They deposit him beside the mosque and clamor for a speech. When he speaks it is to disappoint them: he declines to be their new *futuwwa*. He has no physical strength, he says, and is too sick. He recommends that they pick someone else. A debate follows, from which there is a general agreement that the people of the alley cannot trust anyone with absolute power, not even Gaber himself. "I agree," says Gaber. He tells them that if they all come together as one working hand, no one will be able to oppress them from this day on. The message finds appreciative ears and the people start to make plans.

Al-Tawq wa-l-iswira

Necklace and Bracelet | 1986

A sobering saga of three generations of women in a poor family in Upper Egypt

Director Khairy Beshara

Screenplay Yahya Azmi and Khairy Beshara

Story Yahya Taher Abdullah

Dialogue Abd al-Rahman al-Abnudi

Produced by al-Sharika al-'Alamiya li-l-Tilifisyun wa-l-Sinima (World Television and Cinema Company)

Music Intisar Abd al-Fattah

Director of photography Tarek al-Tilmissani

Editor Adil Munir

Set design Mahmud Muhsin

Starring Izzat al-Alayli, Sherihan, Fardus Abd al-Hamid, Ahmad Bedeir, Ahmad Abd al-Aziz, Mohamed Munir, Abdullah Mahmud, Dinar Anwar, Hanan Yusuf, Mohamed Dardiri, Fathiya Tantawi, Hassan al-Adl

Festivals Valencia, where it won the bronze palm jointly. It was awarded Best Picture, Best Director, and Best Actress (Sherihan) at the Film Association Festival.

Running time 114 minutes

First screening 7 June 1986

Color

IN *AL-TAWQ WA-L-ISWIRA*, director Khairy Beshara revisits the first half of the twentieth century as it was in the Luxor village of Karnak. Although the history is not greatly distant, the rural setting makes the events of the movie seem remote in both time and place. The village is poor; it has few links to the outside world and it is an environment governed by deep-rooted tradition and even superstition, where people still believe in djinns and demonic possession. Charlatan

ABOVE Kaheela (Sherihan, lying down), Ahmad Khalil (Izzat al-Alayli)

الشركة العالمية للتليفزيون والسينما تقدم
عزت العلايلى
شريهان
فردوس عبد الحميد
الطوق والاسوره
أحمد عبد العزيز
محمد منير
أحمد بدير
عبد الله محمود
عن قصة:
يحيى الطاهر عبد الله
إخراج:
خيرى بشارة
سيناريو: يحيى عزمى
حوار: عبد الرحمن الأبنودى
مدير التصوير: طارق التلمسانى
مونتاج: عادل منير
موسيقى تصويرية: انتصار عبد الفتاح
ديكور: محمود محسن
المنتج المنفذ: حسام على
انتاج وتوزيع سينما وتليفزيون وفيديو لمصر والعالم: العالمية للتليفزيون والسينما ٤١ الجزيرة الوسطى . الزمالك ت ٣٤٠٢٠٨٩ - ٣٠٤٢١٣٢ - ٣٤٠٢١١٧ تلكس: 20190 KALLA.UN

sorcerers and mystics offer "supernatural solutions" to a husband's impotence, a charade in which the men collude to avoid the scandal of the truth, while the "dishonor" a woman brings on her family through extramarital sex can only be righted by her death.

The story centers on Hazina, the mother, and Fahima, the daughter, who struggle to get by, as the man of the house, Hazina's husband, is an invalid. As their circumstances worsen, Fahima is forced to marry a man who turns out to be not only useless but also impotent. Nevertheless, she gives birth to a daughter and then dies. The girl, Farhana, is brought up by her grandmother, who sees her as a daughter—until Farhana becomes pregnant out of wedlock. A cousin, Sa'd, murders the girl to remove the stain from the family, but the person who gives the order is Hazina.

The movie was shocking to audiences, not because of the content (honor killing is a recurrent topic in Egyptian films), but because of the minimal dialogue. Much of the action was wordless, requiring greater effort from audiences to engage with the movie, not to mention testing the abilities of the actors. In this respect Sherihan proves herself an actress of the first order. She plays not only Fahima, but also her daughter, Farhana, and so convincingly that one could swear there were two different actresses. Fardus Abd al-Hamid is also excellent as the appropriately named Hazina (the word means "sorrowful"), who silently embodies the misery of all the women of Upper Egypt. ★

KEY SCENE

Mustafa is the uncle (Hazina's brother) who has been working abroad in Palestine and who has recently returned home to find his unmarried niece pregnant. He is talking with a teacher, Mohamed, who is attempting to convince Mustafa not to deal with the issue of the girl's lost virginity by slitting her throat, as tradition would demand. He reminds him that he has lived abroad and been exposed to more progressive cultures. "When a person leaves his country," Mustafa responds, "he thinks he's broken the collar of tradition that hangs around his neck. But the minute you're back with your family and in your old surroundings, you wake up. That's when you find yourself tied down with chains stronger than the ones that ever held you before. The collar around my neck is thicker than the one I used to wear: its roots are deeper than I could have imagined." He rejects Mohamed's words and leaves, refusing to speak with him further.

Gari al-wuhush

Wild Beasts | 1987

Against good advice, a rich businessman pays for a suspect operation that he hopes will enable him to father a child

THIS IS THE THIRD collaboration between director Ali Abd al-Khaliq and screenwriter Mahmud Abu Zeid, working with cinematographer Said al-Shimi and composer Hassan Abu al-Su'ud. Plainly, Abd al-Khaliq believed in not breaking up a successful creative team. The story they collaborated on this time around concerned Said, a wealthy but impotent businessman, looking to spend some of his riches to enable him to have children. With the assistance of a doctor friend, but against the advice of his lawyer, he undergoes a radical gland-transplant

ABOVE *Left to right* Said (Nur al-Sharif), Abd al-Qawi Shadid (Mahmud Abd al-Aziz), Doctor Nabih (Hussein Fahmy), Abd al-Hakim (Hussein al-Shirbini)

Director Ali Abd al-Khaliq

Screenplay Mahmud Abu Zeid

Story Mahmud Abu Zeid

Dialogue Mahmud Abu Zeid

Produced by Hussein al-Sabah

Music Hassan Abu al-Su'ud

Director of photography Said al-Shimi

Editor Hussein Afifi

Starring Mahmud Abd al-Aziz, Nur al-Sharif, Hussein Fahmi, Nura, Huda Ramzi, Hussein al-Shirbini, Lamya al-Giddawi, Saida Gamal, Fu'ad Khalil, Na'ima al-Sughayar, Hafiz Amin, Ra'fat Ragi, Salim Mustafa, Abdullah Hanafi, Abdullah Musharraf, Adli al-Sharqawi, Sayyid Mustafa

Festivals Mahmud Abd al-Aziz won the Best Actor award at the Film Association Festival.

Running time 119 minutes

First screening 9 November 1987

Color

operation. Once done, he divorces his wife, who is now too old to be pregnant. However, as a result of his medical procedure Said becomes paralyzed.

Abd al-Khaliq's directorial job was made much easier by the sparkling script of Abu Zeid, a writer with a talent for penning lines that leapt from the screen to become catchphrases you would hear on the street. Which is only appropriate, because it is the street where many of his fine phrases came from in the first place: Abu Zeid was in the habit of visiting the locales that his characters might frequent. For *Gari al-wuhush* he spent time in the gold district in Khan al-Khalili, where he found the term "yaft," meaning pure metal, and to the area of the furnituremakers, where he picked up jargon like "azk" (to winnow cotton) and "daqq" (to spool it). He employed some of this specialized vocabulary to comic effect: when Abd al-Qawi's wife tells him that a gold bracelet was swapped for a brass copy by the undertaker's daughter, he picks up a thick stick and says, "We'll just bury them without a shroud, then." When the wife corrects herself—"I meant the barber's wife" —Abd al-Qawi says, "Oh, then I'll cut her life short." There is similar fun in Abu al-Dahab's conversation with Abd al-Qawi about the latter's flirtations with women. "You're a real rake and no mistake." Abd al-Qawi remonstrates, "Not so, sir! It's only talk and nothing else. You see, one must charge the batteries of one's heart if one is to light up the prison of matrimony." Mahmud Abd al-Aziz as Abd al-Qawi delivers these lines beautifully. ★

KEY SCENE

Abu al-Dahab is complaining to his friend, Abd al-Hakim the lawyer, about the fact he cannot have children. "I've been denied things too," says al-Hakim. "It is hard to deal with but we must be thankful for what we have. God has divided up His bounty among His creatures, and you've received your share too, Abu al-Dahab." Abu al-Dahab is skeptical. "If God's blessings are twenty-four carats, each of us will find that they have the full twenty-four," says al-Hakim. Abu al-Dahab then asks what divine wisdom dictates that the bounty not be distributed equally. "If God granted everyone too much bounty, they would all become corrupt." Abu al-Dahab asks, "Does that mean we shouldn't work hard and be successful?" "No, of course not," al-Hakim reassures him. "But without cutting out the flesh of your fellow human beings." Abu al-Dahab says, "Well, if we're speaking of meat, there are those who sell their kidneys and other body parts." Al-Hakim tells him that such a sale is null and void, since our bodies belong to God and He does not permit anyone to sell any part of them. "I want to have a child at any cost," says Abu al-Dahab. "And I've got money."

حسين الصباح
يقدم
نور الشريف
نــــــورا
حسين فهمى
محمود عبد العزيز
هدى رمزى
حسين الشربينى
الوجه الجديد
لمياء الجداوى
جرى الوحوش
قصة وسيناريو وحوار :
محمود أبو زيد
إخراج :
على عبد الخالق
بالاشتراك مع
سعيده جلال
نعيمه الصغير
فؤاد خليل
عادل الشرقاوى
مونتاج : المهندس حسين عفيفى
مدير التصوير :
سعيد شيمى
المنتج الفنى :
فؤاد الألفى
موسيقى تصويرية : حسن أبو السعود
التوزيع الداخلى : الشركة المصرية اللبنانية للتجارة والسينما
توزيع الفيديو بمصر : الدقى فيديو فيلم
التوزيع الخارجى : الشركة اللبنانية للتجارة والاستثمار السينمائى

أكرم حجار يقدم
نور الشريف
كمال الشناوى
ليلى علوى
صلاح قابيل / عبد الله فرغلى / محمد الدفراوى / شريف منير
مع ضيفي الشرف
سميره محسن / حسن حسنى
والوجه الجديد
بسام رجب
ضربة معلم
إخراج
عاطف الطيب
تأليف بشير الديك
مدير التصوير محسن نصر
إنتاج أكرم حجار
مونتاج سلوى بكير
المنتج المنفذ سيد اسماعيل
موسيقى تصويرية محمد هلال
التوزيع الداخلى تاميد للإنتاج والتوزيع
الفيديو كاسيت حورس للفيديو والسينما
التوزيع الخارجى أفلام البلجون
ت ٨٧/٩٩

Darbat mi'allim

Masterstroke | 1987

A police officer arrests the son of a wealthy businessman despite his desperate financial situation and his family's wishes

ATEF EL-TAYEB is an actors' director who relies on his actors' ability to inhabit their characters. It was almost inevitable then that the director would work with the supremely talented actor Nur al-Sharif. In this joint venture, the pair are helped by a finely crafted script that invests time in setting out the social and political background to the characters and in establishing the circumstances that have created a corrupt breeding ground for crime. Another plus is the excellent cinematography. Despite rapid location changes in certain sequences, the shots are calm and unhurried, giving the viewer time to become acquainted with each location and familiarize themselves with its atmosphere despite limited screen time. The chase scenes, in particular, are handled brilliantly, in particular Rif'at's chase through an Upper Egyptian village. The camera following the chase appears to be a human point of view as opposed to a recording: there are

Director Atef El-Tayeb

Screenplay Bashir al-Dik

Story Bashir al-Dik

Dialogue Bashir al-Dik

Produced by Akram Haggar

Music Mohamed Hilal

Director of photography Muhsin Nasr

Editor Salwa Bekir

Starring Nur al-Sharif, Kamal al-Shinnawi, Salah Qabil, Layla Ilwi, Sharif Munir, Mohamed al-Dafrawi, Samira Muhsin, Abdullah Farghalli, Badr Nofal, Hassan Husni, Sayyid Sadek, Ahmad Sadek, Bassam Ragab, Aliya Abd al-Mun'im, Magdi Subhi

Festivals Kamal al-Shinnawi was awarded the Jury Special Prize at the Film Association Festival for 1988. Atef El-Tayeb won Best Director.

Running time 108 minutes

First screening 28 September 1987

Color

LEFT Walid (Sharif Munir, *center*), Shaker Abd al-Rahim (Kamal al-Shinnawi, *left*), Rif'at (Nur al-Sharif, *right*)

no mechanical intersections nor flights of fancy in the camera work, which is neither mechanical nor forced, nor are the angles and cuts random or shaky. All that remains is a smooth and unforced atmosphere that makes the cinematographer not only a full member of the creative team, but a presence that arguably towers even above actors and director.

El-Tayeb made full use of Kamal al-Shinnawi's natural talent in the portrayal of an extremely emotional and very powerful character. Controlling and financially powerful, in a position of authority, he also has many illicit business ventures, which alienates audiences. He is also a father seeking to save his son in any way possible and fully cognizant of the mistakes he has made raising him, which wins audience sympathy. His cunning in planning crimes is admirable in a contrary and twisted kind of way. Walid Shaker, played by Sharif Munir, killed his mother's lover, who is also his friend. Shaker, played by Kamal al-Shinnawy, is a successful businessman, living in Kwuait. A case is made against Walid, so Walid's father, a man with connections in high places, attempts through bribery and the relationships he has with influential individuals to exonerate his son, to the extent that he manages to get Officer Bakry, the policeman on the case, played by Salah Qabil, fired. Shaker puts in his place Officer Rif'at, played by Nur al-Sharif, whom he bribed. Rif'at is in dire straits and needs the money, so he agrees to protect Shaker's son, although the audience is in for a surprise twist with regard to this plot line. ★

KEY SCENE

This starts when Officer Rif'at comes into his office after securely locking Walid the murderer in a holding cell, to find quite a few people waiting for him. They include Shaker, Walid's father, who has kidnapped Rif'at's pregnant wife to force Rif'at to release his son and falsify a report stating his innocence in exchange for his wife and a promised bribe of 200,000 pounds. Rif'at sits at his desk and asks one of those present who he is. "Mansur Bey," says Shaker. "He's here to help you write out the report with Shaker's lawyer." Rif'at plays along and asks for the bribe money, then starts writing the report with the help of Mansur, who, Rif'at finds out, is a counselor. When Mansur dictates to Rif'at, "The weapon found at the scene is the murder weapon," Rif'at writes it down as "is not the murder weapon." Everyone bristles, and would attack him if not for Shaker calming them down. He finishes the report, which indicts Walid, Shaker, and all those with him for bribery.

Zawjat ragul muhim

The Wife of an Important Man | 1988

A devoted wife is slowly crushed by her police officer husband's narcissism and cruelty

THE SUCCESS OF this movie is almost entirely due to its dialogue. The achievement of screenwriter Ra'uf Tawfiq is right up there alongside the director and actors. The story follows the relationship of Hisham (Ahmad Zaki) and his romantically inclined wife, Mona (Mervat Amin), as he rises from low-ranking officer in a small village to colonel in a branch of State Security in Cairo. Along the way, Hisham's ego becomes ever more inflated and his behavior ever more cruel, while Mona becomes ever more despairing. Two main incidents propel the downward trajectory: the first, a miscarriage

Director Mohamed Khan

Screenplay Ra'uf Tawfiq

Story Ra'uf Tawfiq

Dialogue Ra'uf Tawfiq

Produced by al-Sharika al-'Alamiya li-l-Tilifisyun wa-l-Sinima (World Television and Cinema Company)

Music Georges Kazazian

Director of photography Muhsin Ahmad

Editor Nadia Shukri

Set design Anas Abu Seif

Starring Mervat Amin, Ahmad Zaki, Ali al-Ghandur, Nahid Samir, Zizi Mustafa, Khairy Beshara, Hafiz Amin, Hassan Husni, Nazim Sha'rawi

Running time 104 minutes

First screening 11 January 1988

Color

LEFT Hisham (Ahmad Zaki, *left*), Mona (Mervat Amin, *right*)

Festivals Carlo Vivari, where Ahmad Zaki won Best Actor; Damascus, where Ahmad Zaki won Best Actor jointly. Moscow, where Zaki won an award of merit. In 1987-88, the film toured a number of world cities, including Montreal, Valencia, Istanbul, and Nantes.

that ends the couple's dream of children, and the second, Hisham's enforced retirement in the wake of the 1977 riots, as a result of which his world falls apart.

The characters' journey is charted in their dialogue: it is not just the lines they speak, it is how they speak. Early on, when Hisham speaks about his background it is in speech that is free of vanity. He is happy to have it known he comes from a large family hailing from an unsophisticated town, Sohag, where his parents are humble farmers. When he first meets Mona he tells her how it has been his lifelong dream to be a policeman: when he was a small boy, his father even bought him a little policeman's uniform. When he finally managed to get into the Police Academy he would wear his uniform even off-duty, basking in the admiring looks of passers-by. Here the seeds are sown for Hisham's obsession with how others view him; at first it is simple pride but later his craving for admiration, respect, and even fear becomes like a drug. When she first meets Hisham, Mona is a dreamy young woman, living in a world conjured by the songs of Abd al-Halim Hafiz. Hisham is her knight in shining armor. She basks in the admiring glances he receives. However, it is through her eyes that we see the corrupting influence of Hisham's neediness and his addiction to power, hence the film's title.

Ahmad Zaki is brilliant as Hisham, delivering a performance that it may not be an exaggeration to call unsurpassable. His joy in the abuses of power his uniform permits is truly disturbing, as is his treatment of his patient and long-suffering wife, captured in another stand-out performance by Mervat Amin. ★

KEY SCENE

Hisham walks into his apartment to find his wife Mona listening to a recording of a radio program featuring Abd al-Halim Hafiz. He stalks over to the cassette player and rips out the tape, destroying it completely. Mona just stares; while she is obviously upset, by now she is resigned to this kind of appalling behavior. And then Hisham sits next to her and begins rubbing her shoulders, as if nothing has happened. "Help me," he says. "You have to stand by me. The world has turned against me and I'm losing everything. I feel so alone." He tells her he has to get his job back but it has been some time now and there is no indication that this is going to happen. He bursts into tears. She listens patiently but she can no longer feel any sympathy for him, now that he has extinguished her love.

الشركة العالمية للتليفزيون والسينما
أحمد زكى ميرفت أمين
زيزى مصطفى على الغندور حسن حسنى نظيم شعراوى أحمد مختار
فيلم لـ ..
محمد خان
زوجة رجل مهم
قصة وسيناريو وحوار رءوف توفيق
تصوير محسن احمد
مونتاج نادية شكرى
موسيقى جورج كازازيان
منتج منفذ فتحى يسرى

أفلام مصر العربية تقدم
فريد شوقي
نور الشريف
مديحة كامل
أصدقاء الشيطان
إخراج
احمد ياسين
سيد زيان
محمود الجندي
صابرين
فريدة سيف النصر
مصطفى متولي
أبو بكر عزت
فؤاد احمد
إنتاج
واصف فايز
ابراهيم الموجي
مدير التصوير
سمير فرج
مونتاج
سلوى بكير
التوزيع الداخلي
أفلام مصر العربية
الشركة اللبنانية للاستثمار السينمائي "صباح اخوان"
العالمية للسينما والتليفزيون ITC

Asdiqa' al-shaytan

Friends with the Devil | 1988

A neighborhood strongman requests eternal life from a sorcerer and believes himself safe from death

IN THE YEAR he was awarded the Nobel Prize for Literature, yet another alley story by Naguib Mahfouz was transferred to the big screen. Everything in the film is freighted with symbolism. The alley stands for Egypt, made clear in lines like "The alley is full of wealth! It's just unfairly distributed." Galal is a stand-in for President Nasser, who sought to impose socialism by force. He wants to live and rule as long as possible, to be the "eternal leader," which is what Nasser used to be called. To achieve power in the alley, Galal faces many obstacles, including a botched assassination attempt during an outdoor gathering, just as Nasser was the subject of a failed assassination attempt while giving a speech in Mansheyya Square,

Director Ahmad Yassin

Screenplay Ibrahim al-Mugi

Story Naguib Mahfouz

Dialogue Ibrahim al-Mugi

Produced by Aflam Misr al-'Arabiya (Egypt Arab Films)

Music Mohamed Sultan

Director of photography Samir Farag

Editor Salwa Bekir

Set design Maher Abd al-Nour

Starring Farid Shawqi, Nur al-Sharif, Madiha Kamil, Sabrin, Mahmud al-Gindi, Sayyid Zayyan, Abu Bakr Izzat, Mustafa Mitwalli, Fu'ad Ahmad, Ahmad Aql, Farida Seif al-Nasr, Abd al-Salam Mohamed, Ulfat Sukkar, Na'ima al-Sughayar, Abd al-Ghani Nasser, Mohamed Tarabik

Festivals Special Acting Award for Farid Shawqi at the Ennaba Mediterranean Film Festival, Algeria

Running time 130 minutes

First screening 16 May 1988

Color

LEFT Galal (Nur al-Sharif, *left*), al-Jinn (Fu'ad Ahmad, *right*)

Alexandria. Galal is killed by poisoning, which conspiracy theorists claim is how Nasser died, not from a heart attack.

Farid Shawqi is captivating in his role, convincing as a cuckolded widower with a single son, the constant taunting at his wife's reputation pushing him into alcoholism. Shawqi plays the role of *mi'allim* Abdu for laughs, as a comic drunk who escapes his harsh reality by retreating into an imaginary world where he is special and strong. Nur al-Sharif as Galal, *mi'allim* Abdu's son, outdoes himself as a devout young lover turned strongman with aspirations to immortality, standing in the face of a death that eventually catches him unawares. ★

KEY SCENE

One night Galal visits the home of the soothsayer. He knocks and the door opens of its own accord. Galal walks in to find a darkened house heavy with incense. He stands and waits, and the door slams shut. Shawir the soothsayer appears in his red *gallabiya* and asks for his visitor's name. Galal tells him, adding that he is the strongman of Husseiniya, Darrasa, and Kafr al-Zaghari. Shawir snaps at him: "Name, nothing more. Don't embellish!" Galal repeats his name only, whereupon Shawir demands his mother's name. Galal angrily refuses, as any traditional Egyptian man would. He tries to hit Shawir with his staff, only he cannot make contact and only hits the furniture. Shawir repeats the question over and over. Eventually, Galal gives in and tells the soothsayer that his mother's name is Zahira. He tells Shawir of his fear that everything he has built for the people of his alley will one day be destroyed: "I've created a system where there is no place for ignorance, poverty, and disease. I don't want to lose my strength." Shawir asks him, "Whyever would you?" Because time weakens the strong and kills the weak, says Galal. "How can you change that?" asks Shawir. "By not dying," says Galal. "Noah lived for nine hundred years, but even he died in the end," says Shawir. Galal asks Shawir if he can make him immortal. "I can," says Shawir, "by helping you become possessed by a djinn." The price for this service, he says, is an entire apartment building in the alley. "Those buildings are owned by the people of the alley," says Galal. "They are not mine to give." Nevertheless, says Shawir, that's the price. Galal eventually accepts. Shawir explains what he must do: he must go alone and lock himself in an abandoned, pitch-dark place until the demon appears. Once he is joined with the demon, he will never die.

Qalb al-layl

The Heart of the Night | 1989

A man kills his wife's friend after he ridicules his incoherent legal thesis, and is sent to jail a broken man

DEFINITELY NOT ONE of Naguib Mahfouz's strongest works, his novella *Qalb al-layl* nevertheless resulted in a very entertaining movie. It is a book of ideas in which ideological trends and philosophies abound, each of which offers us a path to a better life. But how is a person to choose? Such dilemmas have driven men to madness.

The central character of both book and film is Ga'far al-Rawi, played by Nur al-Sharif. After his parents die, he is brought up by a wealthy grandfather, al-Rawi, played by Farid Shawqi. His grandfather wants to control Ga'far's life, and plans that he should study at al-Azhar, then continue his studies abroad, before marrying a woman of al-Rawi's choosing. However, the strong-willed Ga'far falls in love with a Bedouin woman, played by Hala Sidqi, and so al-Rawi banishes him. Eventually Ga'far comes around and marries a high-class woman. The film follows the controlling behavior of a grandfather toward his family.

Director Atef El-Tayeb
Screenplay Muhsin Zayid
Story Naguib Mahfouz
Dialogue Muhsin Zayid
Produced by Mu'assasat Shuruq li-l-Intag al-Fanni
Music Moody al-Imam
Director of photography Abd al-Mun'im Bahnasi
Editor Nadia Shukri
Set design Rushdi Hamid
Starring Farid Shawqi, Nur al-Sharif, Hala Sidqi, Mahmud al-Gindi, Muhsina Tawfiq, Salah Rashwan, Karima al-Sharif, Safinaz al-Gindi, Atiya Eweiss, Nabil al-Dessouki, Sayyid Sadek, Maha Abd al-Rahman
Festivals Nur al-Sharif won best actor jointly at the Film Association Festival.
Running time 130 minutes
First screening 2 October 1989
Color

LEFT Ga'far (Nur al-Sharif, *left*), al-Rawi (Farid Shawqi, *right*)

Director Atef El-Tayeb depicts al-Rawi as being quite literally above other people in many of his scenes. So as to avoid the charge of apotheosizing al-Rawi or using him as a stand-in for the Deity, El-Tayeb places al-Rawi among the guests at the Thursday party at his mansion, surrounded by them, as Mohamed Shakrur entertains them with his song. Since partying is considered a secular, not to say profane, activity in Egyptian society, this would automatically do the job for Egyptian viewers. Farid Shawqi conveys the hints that Mahfouz makes in his novel with his delivery of well-crafted words and phrases laden with reverence and dignity. Nur al-Sharif plays his role with variety, as can be seen from the script, and shows his skill as a young graduate of al-Azhar and lover of art.

The dialogue is careful to sidestep the issue of manifesting any kind of deity onscreen for obvious reasons, not least among them the box office. Muhsin Zayid's dialogue between al-Rawi and the other characters, for example, Ga'far and his friend Shakrur, emphasizes that he is no deity, but a devoted servant faithfully following a religious path. Atef El-Tayeb took great pains to bring Mahfouz's work to life—a tall order, as the work is built on abstractions, demanding that the director concretize abstract concepts which El-Tayeb and Zayid, for the most part, filled admirably. ★

KEY SCENE

This takes place in Huda Hanim's cultural salon. Huda's husband, Ga'far al-Rawi, has shut himself away for more than a year, refusing to emerge because of some great work he is engaged in. Some of those present ascribe his odd behavior to the shock of his grandfather's death and Ga'far's exclusion from the will. But Huda insists that Ga'far has never been in need of any inheritance. At this point, a butler comes in to announce that Ga'far has unexpectedly arrived from the countryside. Huda rushes to greet him. "Everyone's here," she says. Ignoring her, Ga'far flings down a manuscript before the assembled company. He tells them to forget everything they have ever known because he has a startling new revelation. "History will record," he says, "that you were the first to learn of this. I shall place it in your hands for safekeeping: read it, and try to understand it. Spread the word to the people so we may solve the problems of humanity." He then excuses himself and goes upstairs to bed.

مؤسسة
الشروق للإنتاج
تقدم
قصة أديب مصر العالمى
نجيب محفوظ
بطولة
فريد شوقى
نور الشريف
هاله صدقى
محمود الجندى
صلاح رشوان كريمة الشريف
صافيناز الجندى عطيه عويس
نبيل الدسوقى سيد صادق
مهجه عبد الرحمن
بالاشتراك مع الفنانة القديرة
محسنة توفيق
الراقصة
عايده نور
قلب الليل
إخراج
عاطف الطيب
سيناريو وحوار
محسن زايد
إنتاج
مطيع زايد
مدير التصوير عبد المنعم بهنسى
موسيقى مودى الإمام
مهندس الديكور رشدى حامد
مونتاج نادية شكرى
مختار زايد
ت.ر ٨٩/٤٠
التوزيع الداخلى والخارجى : شركة مصر للتوزيع ودور العرض السينمائى
توزيع الفيديو : الدقى فيديو فيلم
مطابع مصر العربية ت ٥٣٨٤٨٢

Ayyam al-ghadab

Days of Rage | 1989

A man returns from abroad to discover his fiancée has married someone else and the couple conspire to have him thrown into a mental hospital

Director Munir Radi
Screenplay Bashir al-Dik
Story Bashir al-Dik
Dialogue Bashir al-Dik
Produced by Radi Color
Music Mustafa Nagi
Director of photography Maher Radi
Editor Ahmad Mitwalli
Set design Salah Mar'i
Starring Nur al-Sharif, Yusra, Ilham Chahine, Nagah al-Mugi, Said Abd al-Ghani, Amal Ibrahim, Mohamed Khairy, Salah Nazmi, Ahmad Abd al-Hadi, Mohamed Lutfi, Mohamed Abu Dawud, Hamdi Yusuf, Ala' Waliyy al-Din, Mohamed al-Sawy, Mukhlis al-Beheiri, Marwa al-Khatib
Running time 115 minutes
First screening 4 September 1989
Color

ONE WOULD BE forgiven for thinking that *Days of Rage* is the work of a veteran director, but viewers might be shocked to learn that this is the debut feature of Munir Radi. Not long graduated from the Cinema Institute, he decided not only to direct but also to produce this film himself, working from a superbly crafted film script by the always reliable Bashir al-Dik. The cinematographer was Munir's brother Maher Radi.

It is a surprisingly mature work, achieving that fine balance between artistic ambition and commercial success—in fact, it topped the box office for several weeks in late 1989. The story is a strong one and you can see why it found an audience: Ibrahim returns home from working overseas and immediately goes to see his fiancée, to whom he has been wiring all his earnings. He is dumbfounded to find

RIGHT Kawthar (Yusra, *left*), Ibrahim (Nur al-Sharif, *center*), Diya' (Said Abd al-Ghani, *right-center*), Mustafa (Nagah al-Mugi, *left-center*), (Mohamed Abu Dawud, *right*)

راضى قطر
للانتاج والتوزيع السينمائى
تقدم
نور الشريف
يسرا
الهام شاهين
سعيد عبد الغنى
نجاح الموجى
محمد خيرى
صلاح نظمى
أمل ابراهيم
فيفى يوسف
حمدى يوسف
بالاشتراك مع
محمد أبو داوود
سعيد الصالح
محمد الصاوى
ايام الغضب
اخراج
منير راضى
قصة وسيناريو وحوار
بشير الديك
مدير التصوير
ماهر راضى
ديكور
صلاح مرعى عادل المغربى
منتج منفذ
فاروق عبد الخالق
مدير الانتاج
ملاك توفيق
مونتاج
أحمد متولى
موسيقى تصويرية
مصطفى ناجى
رقم الترخيص ٨٩/١٢
التوزيع الخارجى: الشركة العربية للتجارة والاستثمار السينمائى (محمد على الصباح) توزيع الفيديو كاسيت
التوزيع الداخلى: افلام النصر - (محمد حسن رمزى) ش عرابى القاهرة الدقى فيديو فيلم

Festivals Damascus, where Ilham Chahine and Nagah al-Mugi won Best Supporting Female and Male Actor, respectively. Nur al-Sharif was awarded Best Actor jointly at the Film Association Festival.

her already married and pregnant—while living in the apartment he has paid for. He goes crazy and attacks the new husband, as a result of which the conniving couple have Ibrahim committed. In the mental hospital he encounters all manner of injustice before escaping and taking his revenge.

The film was partly shot on location at the historic Abbasiya Mental Hospital. The asylum setting allowed the filmmakers to paint a critical picture of Egypt's then-ruling regime by having the patients voice the criticisms. The cinematography is excellent throughout, full of well-crafted and inventive framing and camera angles. There is a sophisticated use of light and shadow, too. Aside from al-Dik's script, another huge plus for the Radi brothers is the involvement in the project of Nur al-Sharif, who brings his consummate professionalism to the key role of the hapless Ibrahim. Ilham Chahine, as Ibrahim's fiancée (and cousin), also gives a fine performance in what is a small but important role. ★

KEY SCENE

Ibrahim has recently returned to Egypt. He stands before the door of the apartment that his overseas earnings have bought for himself and his wife-to-be, Safa'. It is the first time he has seen it and the first he has seen of his fiancée in a long time. It is a surprise visit. He rings the bell. It is opened by Safa'. She staggers back in shock. Ibrahim breezes in happily. "You mustn't have gotten my telegram! I sent one to tell you I was coming!" Still in the flush of delight, he looks at Safa' and now it is Ibrahim who staggers back in shock as she is visibly heavily pregnant. "Sorry," he stammers, "I must have the wrong address." He steps outside, checks the address, and goes back in. He starts yelling at Safa', only to be interrupted by the appearance of a man, who attempts to push him out of the apartment. Ibrahim is utterly incredulous. As this is going on he looks into another room and catches sight of his wife's parents, his uncle and aunt. He asks them what's going on. His uncle cannot answer. "I'm her husband," says the man, "and this apartment is in my name." He throws Ibrahim out and slams the door. Ibrahim pounds on the door and shouts that the apartment is his. He breaks in, grabs a knife, and tries to stab Safa''s husband. Neighbors who have come to see what all the noise is about help to subdue Ibrahim and he is handed over to the police.

Al-Kitkat

Kitkat | 1991

A blind, nonconformist sheikh rises above the frustrations and deprivations of life through sheer force of personality and humor

BASED ON THE NOVEL *The Heron* by Ibrahim Aslan, *al-Kitkat* (named for a Cairo neighborhood) is unlike any other Egyptian movie. For a start, the main character is a blind sheikh who is aging and a bit of a deadbeat, and he has an idiosyncratic way of speaking—and this was the era before the popularity of working-class characters. But Sheikh Husni was a huge hit with audiences, who adored his ribald sense of humor, and recycled his jokes and aphorisms on the street. When Sheikh Husni tells his fellow hash smokers the reason he went blind—from watching a woman strip naked on the beach and enter the sea—one of the group asks, "Did you ever find out who she was?" "Of course I did," replies Husni. "Who?" asks the friend. "Your mother!" says Husni, roaring with laughter. Much comedy derives

Director Dawud Abd al-Sayyid

Screenplay Dawud Abd al-Sayyid

Story Ibrahim Aslan

Dialogue Dawud Abd al-Sayyid

Produced by al-Sharika al-'Alamiya li-l-Tilifisyun wa-l-Sinima (World Television and Cinema Company)

Music Rageh Dawud

Director of photography Muhsin Ahmad

Editor Adil Munir

Set design Anas Abu Seif

Starring Mahmud Abd al-Aziz, Sharif Munir, Nagah al-Mugi, Aida Riyad, Amina Rizq, Gihane Nasr, Ahmad Kamal, Amal Ibrahim, Mohamed Gibril, Galila Mahmud, Ali Hasanein

Running time 132 minutes

First screening 9 September 1991

Color

LEFT Husni (Mahmud Abd al-Aziz, *left*), Yusuf (Sharif Munir, *right*)

الشركة العالمية للتليفزيون والسينما
حسين القلا
محمود عبد العزيز
فى
الكيت كات
عن رواية مالك الحزين لإبراهيم أصلان
إخراج داوود عبد السيد
التوزيع الداخلى والڤيديو كاسيت داخل ج. م. ع شركة افلام النصر « محمد حسن رمزى وشركاه » ٣٣ شارع عرابى _ القاهرة ت : ٧٤٤١٩١

from his friendship with Sheikh Ubaid, who is also blind but from whom Husni hides his own blindness—his intelligence, he believes, gives him better vision than the sighted. Husni sees in Sheikh Ubaid a golden opportunity to prove he is no less competent than a sighted person. At one point he grabs a motorcycle and offers to give Ubaid a lift, saying, "We're all brothers in this world. If a sighted person like myself can't give a sightless person like yourself a lift, well then, what's the world coming to?"

Much of the success of Husni is due to the comic abilities of the actor playing him, Mahmud Abd al-Aziz. Abd al-Aziz was a friend of the real-life, blind, hash-smoking Sayyid Mekkawi, one of Egypt's musical giants, and it is likely he drew on him for his portrayal of Husni. Like Husni, many of the film's other characters are also misfits and outcasts, and there is a real joy to be taken in some of the performances. This is just as well, because there really is not much of a plot to drive the film—it succeeds by being supremely entertaining and heartwarming. Modern classical string composer Rageh Dawud supplies a lovely melancholic score that depends on the oud as its main solo instrument. In the context of the movie, this is a brilliant choice: the stringed instrument evokes both a deeply personal voice and the authentic Egyptian milieu of the film. ★

Festivals Damascus, where it won the Gold Award, and also Best Actor for Mahmud Abd al-Aziz. Dawud Abu al-Sayyid won Best Director at the Biennale des Cinémas Arabes in Paris. It won Best Picture, Best Actor, Best Director, and Best Screenplay at the Cinema Society Festival. It won the Gold Award, Best Screenplay, and Best Set Design at the National Film Festival, as well as Best Picture at the Cairo International Film Festival, and Best Screenplay at the Institut du Monde Arabe festival in Paris.

KEY SCENE

Sheikh Husni sits on the banks of the Nile in a plant nursery, strumming an *oud* and humming to himself. He hears footsteps and recognizes the approach of Abu Yusuf. "You used to stomp your feet so much as a kid," says Husni, "but now you're older you barely touch the ground at all because you want to fly." He then asks him what he thinks of what happened—"what happened" being that recently Husni inadvertently divulged all the scandals of the neighborhood via an open microphone. "Well, you pretty much ruined everyone," says Abu Yusuf. "I'm blind," says Husni, "so it doesn't count." They laugh together at the memory of al-Haram, who heard the broadcast and came rushing down from his girlfriend's apartment, with lumps of hashish scattering from the pockets of his *gallabiya*. Husni places a hand on Yusuf's face. "You've grown up, my boy. Your face has taken shape." They giggle together at the memory of Husni driving their friend Suleiman's motorbike. "You know," Husni says to Yusuf quietly, "sometimes I wake up and I can't breathe." He continues: "I want to get on a motorbike and fly." He sings a song with Yusuf accompanied on the *oud*, and when Yusuf offers him a lift on his motorbike, he gladly accepts. They ride off together.

Inzar bi-l-ta'a

Obedience Law | 1993

A young lawyer files a lawsuit when his girlfriend becomes engaged to another man

Director Atef El-Tayeb

Screenplay Khalid al-Banna

Story Khalid al-Banna

Dialogue Khalid al-Banna

Produced by Aflam Misr al-Gadida

Music Mohamed Hilal

Directors of photography Mohamed Taher and Hisham Wadid Sirry

Editor Ahmad Mitwalli

Starring Layla Ilwi, Mahmud Hemeida, Mamduh Wafi, Ashraf Abd al-Baqi, Ahmad Adam, Sayyid Azmi, Nadia Izzat, Mohamed al-Sawy

Festivals Layla Ilwi was awarded Best Actress by the Film Association.

Running time 106 minutes

First screening 20 December 1993

Color

THIS REALISTIC SOCIAL drama continues in the tradition of the new socially conscious cinema that sought to present authentic Egyptian characters to shine light on a hitherto unrecognized social or legal issue, at least by the general public. Atef El-Tayeb skillfully presents a painful reality with all the attendant symbolism, using social background and aesthetics to make his point and draw us in, respectively. His style draws his actors into his naturalistic and unforced world, where the acting is not palpable and his points are not preachy.

Equally harmonious is the performance of the actors, particularly Mahmud Hemeida and Layla Ilwi, supremely realistic and convincing, with a vibrant inner life of social and behavioral dimensions. Ilwi's accurate performance in one of her best roles is part her usual typecast character of the pretty university girl in love: she plays Amina, who falls for a neighbor boy and engages in 'everything but' with him, only to have him cause a scandal when she decides to marry someone else. Mahmud Hemeida excels with mature versatility as the romantic lover who enjoys sex because he loves his girlfriend and not out of carnal lust, suffering from the prevalent social ailment of not finding an apartment for marriage, who turns into a jealous lout who will stop at nothing to keep his girlfriend from marrying another, using his profession as a lawyer to coerce her into submitting to his will although he knows she is as crushed by financial pressures as he is. The film's famous courtroom scene is graced by Mahmud Hemeida, who is utterly convincing as a lawyer, helped by the script, which provides him with brilliant legal lines and conclusive arguments, showing him as not only a lawyer, but a good one. When he is done, he leaves Amina in abject misery at the betrayal of someone she once loved, someone who did not hesitate to turn on her when they became estranged. The camera

شركة أفلام مصر الجديدة تقدم من إنتاج أوزوريس فيلم
ليلى علوى محمود حميدة
انذار بالطاعة
ممدوح وافى أشرف عبد الباقى أحمد آدم
إخراج عاطف الطيب
نادية عزت السيد عزمى
محمد الصاوى لمياء الأمير
ميار هانم محمد
خالد البنا أحمد متولى
محمد هلال
محمد طاهر هشام وديد سرى
إنتاج عمران على
التوزيع الداخلى ، شركة أفلام مصر الجديدة • التوزيع الخارجى ، شركة أوسكار للتسجيلات الفنية • توزيع الفيديو ، شركة النجوم
٣٦ شارع شريف / القاهرة ٣٣ شارع رمسيس ٦١ شارع الوحدة - إمبابة

RIGHT Ibrahim (Mahmud Hemeida, *right*), Amina (Layla Ilwi, *left*)

angles realistically express the events of the film: for example, when the senior lawyer, Ibrahim's boss, goes into his office, there is a long shot of him, exaggerating the length of the corridor through which he has to walk to reach Ibrahim: the lawyer walks softly toward the room, evoking a kind of suspense for their encounter. ★

KEY SCENE

The father is sitting beside the Nile with his daughter as she tells him of her dalliance with Ibrahim. When she is done, he speaks very bitterly. "If I killed you," he says, "people would call me strong, and praise me to the skies." What he has heard from her, he says, of her sleeping with her boyfriend and going out with him, is driving him half insane: "If a madman heard it, he'd go sane from the shock! If a sane man heard it, he'd lose his mind from the insult to his honor." Such a lack of respect for him, he says, it is as if his daughter considers him dead, or nonexistent, dragging him through the mud, destroying his dignity, staining his reputation, and crowning him with shame for the rest of his life. Amina stares fearfully at him. The glass he handed her slips from her fingers. But to her surprise her father reigns in his anger and takes pity on his daughter's fear. He embraces her reassuringly, and tells her that he could never hurt her and has always loved her, indeed he loves her the best out of all his children. When Amina hears this, the embrace and the words wound her more than any knife. She feels keenly how badly she has sinned against her poor father, offering a cautionary tale, apparently, for every girl who does as she has. In floods of tears, she blubs that she is unworthy of such great love from such a merciful father.

Tuyur al-zalam

Birds of Darkness | 1995

Two mismatched but equally corrupt lawyers conspire to get rich at society's expense

THREE YEARS PREVIOUSLY the collaboration between director Sharif Arafa, screenwriter Wahid Hamid, and actor Adil Imam resulted in the enormous hit movie *al-Irhab wa-l-Kebab*. This movie revisits similar themes: notably using comedy to address injustices in the Egyptian system, while taking swipes at overt piousness and the abuses of religion. *Tuyur al-zalam* is, however, quite a bit darker. In the earlier film Adil Imam was a bumbling everyman just trying to switch his children's schools. In this film he is Fathi Nawfal, a crooked lawyer with a liking for alcohol and loose women. The story centers on his representation of Samira (Yusra), a woman up on prostitution charges. His opponent in court is Ali al-Zanati (Riyad al-Kholi), a lawyer who works for the Muslim Brotherhood. Both men are equally venal

Director Sharif Arafa
Screenplay Wahid Hamid
Story Wahid Hamid
Dialogue Wahid Hamid
Produced by Wahid Hamid
Music Moody al-Imam
Director of photography Muhsin Nasr
Editor Adil Munir
Set design Rushdi Hamed
Starring Adil Imam, Yusra, Gamil Ratib, Riyad al-Kholi, Ahmad Ratib, Izzat Abu Auf, Nazim Sha'rawi, Lutfi Abd al-Hamid, Said Tarabik, Kawthar Ramzi, Hamdi Yusuf, Husni Abd al-Galil, Mustafa Hashim
Running time 116 minutes
First screening 14 August 1995
Color

LEFT Fathi (Adil Imam, *left*), Ali al-Zanadi (Riyad al-Kholi, *right*)

Festivals Bronze Award at the Festival for Mediterranean Film in Valencia, Spain, and Best Picture and Best Director at the same festival. It won Best African Film at the Milan Film Festival, and Wahid Hamid Best Screenplay at the Cinema Society Festival. Riyad al-Kholi won Best Supporting Actor and Gamil Aziz Best Sound Engineer from the Cinema Arts Society. In addition, the Egyptian Catholic Center awarded it Best Picture.

and self-serving in their own ways, and the film contains serious undertones linking the corrupt politics and religious extremism that the filmmakers believed was damaging the country.

It is a good story, well acted, with some serious points to make. It is also very well crafted. Arafa and his director of photography, Muhsin Nasr, cleverly use lighting to set the tone in many scenes. For example, when Ali visits Fathi's office in order to try to convince him to work with the Muslim Brotherhood, the lighting is dim and mysterious, evoking the atmosphere of—quite literally—a shady backroom deal. In another scene, when Ali looks at the *oud* he loves to play, his face is half in light, half in shadow, suggesting the conflicting emotions inside. Special mention should also be given to Moody al-Imam's original score. Imam is an innovator in the field of composing for film. More often than not, violent scenes in Egyptian cinema are underscored with cacophonous percussion and romantic scenes by soft strings; however, in the scene in which the Muslim Brotherhood kills a team of policemen, Moody has a soft, elegiac melody playing, as the scene intercuts with shots of Fathi and Samira sitting at a Nile café. The scene is all the more powerful for it. ★

KEY SCENE

We are in prison, where Fathi is being held in custody pending investigation. He is let out into the yard for some exercise. He hears someone call his name and looks around to see Ali. He is shocked, and lets out a bark of laughter. He tells Ali they seem inseparable, even by jail. "Always in the same boat," says Ali. They begin tossing a ball between them. "I'm being investigated too," says Ali. He asks Fathi what his charges are. "I'm not accused of anything! I'm innocent of any charges." Ali says that he too is blameless. Ali asks Fathi if he is afraid. Not in the least, he says. "I'm getting out of here." Ali says, "I'm getting out too," to which Fathi responds, "Me before you." They look at the ball, which has been dropped, and then at each other, in an unspoken challenge as to who will get there first. They both start running; they reach it at the same time, and give it a powerful kick. It flies toward a pane of glass behind which we can see a view of the city, and the glass shatters.

أفلام وحيد حامد تقدم
عادل إمام يسرا
طيور الظلام
إخراج
شريف عرفة
تأليف
وحيد حامد

أفلام جرجس فوزى
تقدم
عفاريت
الأسفلت
إخراج
أسامة فوزى
إنتاج
هانى جرجس
تأليف
مصطفى ذكرى
محمود حميدة سلوى خطاب جميل راتب
حسن حسنى عبدالله محمود عايدة عبد العزيز
أمل أبراهيم لطفى لبيب علاء عوض محمد شرف الممثل القدير محمد توفيق
لأول مرة منال عفيفى سماح البابلى ماجد الكدوانى مع كمال سليمان المغنى الشعبى شعبان عبد الرحيم
منتج فنى: مجدى عبد المسيح تصوير: طارق التلمسانى مونتاج: أحمد متولى ديكور: صلاح مرعى موسيقى: راجح داود
التوزيع الداخلى شركة أتحاد الفنانين
التوزيع الخارجى شركة أتحاد الفنانين
المشرف العام محمد حسن رمزى
الفيديو كاسيت تاميدو فيديو فيلم
مدحت الشريف

'Afarit al-asfalt

Demons of the Asphalt | 1980

A vital and exuberant slice of street life in the company of an extended family of microbus drivers

A LOVE AFFAIR with the local, as opposed to the global, and a desire to plumb the depths of Egypt's underbelly, led debut director Usama Fawzi to bring Mustafa Zikri's story to the big screen. The subject matter is a very specific sector of society: the drivers of Egypt's ubiquitous microbuses. What the real-life drivers made of the movie I don't know, but they can't have been happy. As portrayed by Fawzi, the "demons of the asphalt" are a bunch of vulgarly behaved, sex-crazed louts, with Stone Age attitudes toward women. What little plot there is focuses on the extended family of bachelor bus driver Sayyid (Mahmud Hemeida). His best friend Ringo (Abdullah Mahmud) is a hash addict who is secretly engaged to Sayyid's sexually frustrated

ABOVE Insharah (Salwa Khattab, *right*), Sayyid (Mahmud Hemeida, *left*)

Released internationally as *The Asphalt Kings*

Director Usama Fawzi

Screenplay Mustafa Zikri

Story Mustafa Zikri

Dialogue Mustafa Zikri

Produced by Guirguis Fawzi Films

Music Rageh Dawud

Director of photography Tarek al-Tilmissani

Editor Ahmad Mitwalli

Set design Salah Mar'i

Starring Mahmud Hemeida, Gamil Ratib, Salwa Khattab, Hassan Husni, Abdullah Mahmud, Aida Abd al-Aziz, Lutfi Labib, Mohamed Tawfiq, Manal Afifi, Amal Ibrahim, Mohamed Sharaf, Samah al-Babli, Magid al-Kidwani, Shayma' Kamal Suleiman, Sha'ban Abd al-Rahim, Alaa Awad

Festivals Special Jury Prize at the first Locarno Festival in Switzerland. Special Jury Prize at the Carthage Festival. The film was also awarded Best First Film and Best Actor at the Egyptian National Film Festival.

Running time 101 minutes

First screening 8 July 1996

Color

sister, but Sayyid will not countenance his sister marrying another bus driver and wants her to marry into a better social class.

The dialogue strives for authenticity: Sayyid is coarse and uneducated in the way he expresses himself, with the vocabulary of a thug. In a generally excellent cast, Hassan Husni is particularly funny as the local barber, who cannot resist telling his clients long-winded stories lifted from *The Thousand and One Nights*.

Fawzi has no great point to make. Instead he offers the audience a short, humorous ride in the company of these colorful characters, during which we can steal a peek and eavesdrop on their messy, lusty, and occasionally violent lives. It concludes with an eyebrow-raising sequence (*see* the Key Scene box) that raises more questions than it answers, but which also suggests that life goes on, without any neat endings. ★

KEY SCENE

A funeral dinner has brought together family and neighbors. One of those present is the barber, who regales those assembled with a tale. Sultan Harun al-Rashid, says the barber, after a quarrel with his trusted friend and companion, Ibrahim al-Mawsili, dismisses the latter from his magnificent palace. One day he hears his former friend sitting under the palace walls cursing his ill fortune after being banned from the palace. The sultan pledges to pardon him on condition that al-Mawsili brings him eighty poets, each accompanied by his own slave girl. Al-Mawsili was to do likewise. Each slave girl was then to put her foot out of the palace window and each poet would have to identify his slave by kissing her foot. Anyone who failed to identify correctly would be given a choice between having his tongue cut out or his head cut off. The sultan would get the slave girl. Al-Mawsili agrees to this and conspires with his slave girl to perfume her foot with rose water so that he can identify her. However, the slave girl would rather have the sultan, so she tells the other girls to perfume their feet with rose water too. All the poets, al-Mawsili among them, fail to identify the girls. While all the poets choose to lose their tongues, al-Mawsili opts for decapitation. The barber's story ends and the scene cuts to all the men standing side by side with their lovers; each of the men kisses his partner's foot and enters her bedroom. In this way we learn that the barber's wife, whom we have so far seen to be Sayyid's girlfriend, is actually the secret lover of the neighborhood idiot—who, we are informed, is well endowed. It makes for a surprising, comical, and highly unusual end to a memorable film.

'Imarat Ya'qubyan

The Yacoubian Building | 2006

A social drama which follows the inhabitants of a downtown Cairo building, each of whom embodies a different slice of Egyptian society

BASED ON THE best-selling novel by Alaa Al Aswany, *'Imarat Ya'qubyan* is the best-performing Egyptian film internationally to date. It no doubt helped that it had the biggest ever budget at that time of any Egyptian production, but it is also a terrific piece of filmmaking, with a top-class cast, and a fine screenplay by veteran Wahid Hamid. The film follows the diverse inhabitants of the Yacoubian Building in downtown Cairo. There is the faded aristocrat Zaki (Adil Imam), Buthayna (Hind Sabri), the beautiful, poor girl he falls for, Hagg Azzam (Nur al-Sharif), a rich businessman, Taha al-Shazli (Mohamed Imam), the bright but disadvantaged son of the building's janitor, Hatim Rashid (Khalid al-Sawy), the gay editor of a French-language newspaper, and many others. In its mix of rich and poor, conservative

Director Marwan Hamid

Screenplay Alaa Al Aswany

Story Wahid Hamid

Produced by Good News

Music Khalid Hammad

Director of photography Samih Selim

Editor Khalid Marie

Set design Fu'ad al-Awamry

Starring Adil Imam, Nur al-Sharif, Yusra, Hind Sabri, Is'ad Yunis, Ahmad Ratib, Ahmad Bedeir, Sumaya al-Khashab, Khalid Salih, Khalid al-Sawy, Bassem Samra, Mohamed Imam, Tamer Abd al-Mun'im, Abbas Abu al-Hassan, Yusuf Dawud, Mohamed al-Dafrawi, Said Tarabik, Said al-Salih, Salwa Uthman, Layla Sami, Gihan Amari, Ahmad al-Sa'dani, Tal'at Zakariya

Running time 162 minutes

First screening 11 February 2006

Color

LEFT Mohamed Azzam (Nur al-Sharif, *left*), Kamal (Khalid Salih, *right*)

Festivals Berlin; Tribeca New York. Hamed won Best Director. Cannes Film Festival; London; Locarno; India; Japan; Festival of the Institut du Monde Arabe in Paris. The stars of the work, Adil Imam, Nur al-Sharif, and Khalid al-Sawy, won Best Actor awards, and the film earned its director, Marwan Hamid, the Grand Prize. The movie was shown at the closing ceremony of the Beirut Festival, at the Rome Festival, and at the Academy Awards.

and liberal, old and young, the building is a metaphor for life in Egypt. Zaki lives in the past in faded luxury, Buthayna endures sexual harassment, Taha is rejected by the police and joins a radical Islamic group, while Hatim's homosexuality is a metaphor in itself—a wealthy, half-European, foreign-educated intellectual who literally mounts a simple Egyptian soldier.

The ensemble cast mesh wonderfully. There is some stereotyping, notably in the character of Hatim, but just the fact that a gay man is portrayed in an Egyptian film and not in a derisory fashion is a breakthrough in itself. With so many characters, there are a lot of stories to be told, but they are all tidily marshaled and we never lose track of what's happening. It is also very beautiful to look at, with lovely sweeping crane shots and gorgeous lighting, particularly in the scenes of Downtown streets in the early morning hours. For a film touching on so many contemporary issues, it has a wonderful old-school feel to it. ★

KEY SCENE

Staggering drunkenly down the street, Zaki al-Dessouki is ramblingly comparing post-Revolution Egypt unfavorably to how it used to be. With him is Buthayna, whom he leans on for support as he talks. "You asked me once," he says, "why I didn't settle in Paris. Egypt was better than Paris during the monarchy, you see. We were at the forefront of the fashion world. The streets were sparkling. People were well-mannered; the people who lived in this building"—referring to the Yacoubian Building, where he is the longest-standing resident—"were refined and well-behaved. The country has gone to the dogs. The roofs of the buildings are garbage dumps: times have changed." Modern-day Egypt, Zaki informs Buthayna, is a travesty.

good news group
presents
عمارة يعقوبيان
MEMPHIS
Yacoubian Building
Written by Waheed Hamed
Directed by Marwan Hamed
www.goodnews4films.com

Index of English Titles

Index of Arabic Titles

Index of Directors